Poets and the Visual Arts in Renaissance England

T0324416

POETS AND THE VISUAL ARTS IN RENAISSANCE ENGLAND

Norman K. Farmer, Jr.

UNIVERSITY OF TEXAS PRESS, AUSTIN

First edition, 1984

Requests for permission to reproduce material from this
work should be sent to:
  Permissions
  University of Texas Press
  Box 7819
  Austin, Texas 78712

LIBRARY OF CONGRESS CATALOGING IN PUBLICATION
DATA
Farmer, Norman K. (Norman Kittrell), 1934–
    Poets and the visual arts in renaissance England.
    1. English poetry—17th century—History and criticism.
2. Art and literature—England. 3. Ut pictura poesis (Aesthet-
ics).   I. Title.
PR545.A78F37   1984   821'.3'09357   83-14771

ISBN: 978-0-292-74440-0

First paperback printing, 2012

For Cora, Lydia, Colin, and Edward

Contents

Preface

The creative interaction between visual representation and verbal expression has long harbored a mystery no less for artists and poets than for thinkers of a more speculative, critical cast. Plato in *The Republic* suggested that the imitative poet might be placed beside the painter, since the tasks undertaken by each were concerned with an inferior part of the soul and thus had no place in a well-ordered state (bk. 10). Aristotle was only slightly more generous, conceding that epic poetry resembled the other arts in its representation of life. In the *Poetics* he likened the use of color and form by artists to the use of the human voice by poets and compared plot in tragedy to outline in pictorial representation (bk. 1.2). It fell to Horace to explore more speculatively the creative relationships between visual and verbal art. In his *Ars Poetica* he likened poems to pictures in a phrase that has become almost as popular as it has proven ambiguous: *ut pictura poesis*, "as with a painting, so with a poem" (11. 347–390). There he concluded that one strikes the fancy more the nearer the viewer stands, while the other makes its most efficacious appeal the farther it is from the beholder's eye. Quoting Simonides, who called painting inarticulate poetry and poetry articulate painting, Plutarch in *On the Fame of the Athenians* extended the interart comparison and endowed it with new authority (l. 347). Accordingly, when the body of ancient critical thought began to be sorted out during the early modern period it became a commonplace of criticism that poems and paintings indeed had much in common and that the practice of either visual or verbal art quite naturally owed much to the other. Matthew Coignet's *Politique Discourses on Trueth and Lying* offers a representative view: "And as touching Painters, they have beene greatly misliked of, for representing such fictions & Poetical deceits. For as Simonides saide: Painting is a dumme Poesie, and a Poesie is a speaking painting: & the actions which the Painters set out with visible colours and figures the Poets recken with wordes, as though they had in deede beene perfourmed."[1] Between the ancients and the critics of the Renaissance there lay, of course, a significant body of thought devoted to the mysteries of visual epistemolgy.[2] What is most pertinent to the discussion in the following pages, however, is that the creative interaction between poetry and the visual arts has retained its hold on the imagination of critics and poets and artists alike, and has in our own time become the subject of a virtual discipline variously referred to as the comparative arts, the parallelism between literature and the arts, the mutual illumination of the arts, and so on.

The emergence of this discipline has not been without setbacks and pitfalls. Indeed, conservative forces within the fields of literary study on the one hand and art studies on the other continue to resist the encroachment of a comparatist point of view. But such resistance is minimal when one considers the potential for self-destruction that is inherent in the study of literature and the other arts, a potential that has been shrewdly identified by Rene Wellek and, most recently, Ulrich Weisstein.[3] The vain pursuit of an illusive *Geistesgeschichte* by means of every possible parallel and analogy between the arts, no matter how farfetched, was the dominant product of Oswald Spengler's *The Decline of the West* (1918), probably the most representative work in this vein. The ultimate absurdity, perhaps, may be glimpsed in the efforts of one critic during the 1930s to interpret eight lines from Pope's *Moral Essays* as "a body of equidistant parallels like the string courses and cornices of a Palladian building."[4] To discover serious and sustainable points of contact between the visual and verbal arts has thus been the challenge to comparatists in recent years. Consequently, much thought has gone into the definition of specific interart problems and of critical procedures appropriate to the discussion of those problems. Weisstein, for example, has recently proposed that, following the wise counsel of Rene Wellek, critics begin "by looking at tangible works of art," and that "in all interdisciplinary and inter-medial enterprises [they] would do well, at all times, to proceed discreetly from the small to the large and from the particular to the general. Their choice of topic ought to be gauged . . . to the subject matter at hand." He quotes with approval the remark by Jean Seznec that "the time of brilliant generalizations seems to be passing; the studies on art and literature, while they still depend on aesthetics, are tending more and more towards precise, fully documented investigations, for which monographs are the proper framework. Literary criticism can only gain from such studies, limited in their object, and rigorous in their form."[5] Weisstein identifies eight areas that call for such study: " 1. Works of art which depict and interpret a story, rather than merely illustrating a text; 2. Literary works describing specific works of art (*ekphrases*, and *Bild-*, as distinguished from *Ding-*, *gedichte*); 3. Literary works constituting or literally re-creating works of art (*technopaignia*, including pattern poems and much of the so-called Concrete Poetry); 4. Literary works emulating pictorial styles; 5. Literary works concerned with art and artists or presupposing specialized art-historical knowledge; 6. Literary works using artistic techniques (montage, collage, the grotesque); 7. Synoptic genres (emblem); 8. Literary works sharing a theme, or themes, with works of art."[6]

Several of these avenues, with certain variations of course, have been followed in critical discussions of works by Spenser, Shakespeare, and Milton. The poetry of Andrew Marvell has also received comparatist attention.[7] The chapters that follow thus take up specific interart features in works by Philip Sidney, John Donne, Ben Jonson, Thomas Carew, Lord Herbert of Cherbury, Richard Crashaw, Robert Herrick, Richard Lovelace, and Edmund Waller that have not hitherto been examined in this fashion. Sidney's *New Arcadia*, for example, emerges as a work that describes specific works of art, that emulates pictorial styles, that is concerned with specialized art-historical knowledge, and that shares themes with works of art. Works by John Donne presuppose a great deal of specialized art-historical knowledge, the poet's verbal performance quite often revealing pictorial habits of mind. Ben Jonson, on the other hand, exhibits much distrust of visual representation, a motif in a number of his poems; and more important still is his apparent willingness to challenge even Anthony Van Dyck in a poem praising Venetia Digby and competing with a painting by Van Dyck of that lady. Thomas Carew's "A Rapture" and Lord Herbert's "To his Mistress for her true Picture" emerge from interart comparison as verbal performances highly dependent upon a knowledge of an appreciation for visual art on various themes. Richard Crashaw, it turns out, possessed a double talent: he painted in addition to writing poetry. And an investigation of his poetry within the intriguing phenomenon of *Doppelbegabung* shows him to have been extraordinarily sensitive to the physical configurations and colors of things. Richard Lovelace and Edmund Waller owed a great deal

to the flowering of English art under the influence of Van Dyck; in fact, Waller's famous "Instructions to a Painter" emerges from comparison with contemporary works of art as a far more serious piece than hitherto assumed. It not only presupposes art-historical knowledge, but it pursues in verbal terms particular goals avidly pursued in visual terms by painters. Robert Herrick's *Hesperides* has never previously been considered as an expression of the Horatian maxim *ut pictura poesis*, but when it is subjected to comparison with contemporary theory and practice of visual art the poems assume a new expressiveness.

A word on the final chapter about Lady Drury's oratory is appropriate. This curious little chamber is a composite work of visual art, a collection of painted panels whose subjects were taken from emblem books (Weisstein's "synoptic genre"). This chamber is evidently unique, there having been no general practice in England of decorating rooms in this fashion. The program for this particular room, if there ever was one, cannot now be known, but the fundamental questions raised by these paintings all pertain to the possible network of styles to which they belong: where did the idea of such pictures come from? why do they look the way they do? what is their kinship with other comparable works? In the absence of similar painted rooms, the answers seem to lie in books rather than in the practice of any particular group or school of painters. The connections between this room and the emblem books of the period become clear only when specific correspondences can be established. The similarities between the images on the paneled walls and those on printed pages must be permitted to speak for themselves, although a critical rather than simply interpretive concept on interart relationships is at stake here. This concept is expressed in a poem that is practically contemporaneous with the painted chamber. Spenser's allegorical houses in *The Faerie Queene* (the House of Pride, the House of Holiness, Mamon's cave, Busyrane's Hall of Tapestries, and the like) permit that poet to express the significance of certain psychological or moral conditions in terms that seem as closely related to notions of space as to those of unfolding time.[8] In each case, Spenser's reader is invited not merely to enter an enclosure vicariously with the protagonist, but to view the details visible therein through the eyes of the protagonist. The effect is a curious double perspective, for while we share the perception of things with the viewer, we retain an objective, critical understanding of those things that is denied to the character within the fiction. Spenser's emblematic enclosures thus exhibit generic affinities with the painted chamber at Hawstead in the sense that finite boundaries distinguish beteen real and symbolic space and promote the conversion of thought from a preoccupation with things as they are in quotidian experience to things as they are in more abstract, ideal, even metaphysical terms. The rhetorical source of such effects is known simply as allegory. But literary allegory requires a narrative vehicle, something quite lacking in the seemingly random emblems of the Hawstead room. Nevertheless, to enter that chamber and to meditate upon the significances of those panel paintings in a devotional (that is to say, in a self-reflective) manner is a real-life analogue to the literary experience conveyed rhetorically by allegory. The reader of allegory becomes a direct participant in this painted chamber. To shift back and forth between these two modes of perception does not require intellectual agility so much as an acceptance of the fact that in such instances of mutual illumination art and literature seek comparable goals.

The allegorical point that makes possible such a transition from a reading experience to a direct experience will become evident in the opening chapter of this book where one of the subjects is the literary expression of such enclosure in *The Countess of Pembroke's Arcadia*. Like Kalander's picture gallery, the oratory at Hawstead is a visual summation of ideas; where the Arcadian gallery exhibits images expressing the significance of Ovidian texts, the painted chamber of Hawstead exhibits expressions of truth embedded in a broad range of moral texts and images. In both cases, the architectural surroundings have framed a particular kind of inner experience by creating boundaries within which the transcendent meanings of art may be received. The oratory, then, exhibits a habit of mind that supports the literary construction of the opening episodes in Sidney's *Arcadia* no less than the episodes that involve Spenser's allegorical "houses."

Our capacity for reading such images has been greatly enhanced by such studies as E. H. Gombrich's *Art and Illusion* (1960), Erwin Panofsky's *Studies in Iconology* (1939), and Edgar Wind's *Pagan Mysteries in the Renaissance* (1958). Gombrich in particular argues that the beholder enjoys a considerable share in the creation and maintenance of the visual illusion offered by the artist, and he provides support for the view that pictorial art is often engaged in efforts to overcome its limits as a medium and to gravitate toward the verbal. To a painting or a statue the viewer brings artistic conventions, gestures, and stories. According to signals formulated by the artist on the basis of such familiar schemas, the viewer projects meanings. "And what we call 'reading' an image may perhaps be better described as testing it for its potentialities, trying out what fits. The activation of these phantoms has been most frequently tested in the many psychological experiments in which an image is flashed on the screen for a brief moment only. There are many accounts of the wide range of different things

which subjects report to have 'seen', that is to say, of the images they were induced to project onto the screen by the clues presented to them just long enough to induce a hypothesis but not long enough to check it." Further, "once a projection, a reading, finds anchorage in the image in front of us, it becomes much more difficult to detach it." Gombrich adds, "We are so trained in assigning to each its potential living space that we have no difficulty whatever in adjusting our reading to a configuration in which each figure is surrounded by its own particular aura." Ambiguity, he concludes, "is clearly the key to the whole problem of image reading." And "if proof were needed of the kinship between the language of art and the language of words," it would be found in drawings and paintings that offer us such instances of ambiguity. In this respect, art shares a projective potential with literature. Even in the latter we find "a limit to the information language can convey without introducing such devices as quotation marks that differentiate between what logicians call 'language' and 'metalanguage'. There is a limit to what pictures can represent without differentiating between what belongs to the picture and what belongs to the intended reality."[9]

Such observations on the nature of projection and the threshold signals that trigger projective response to artistically defined objects (nonfunctional as opposed to functional or merely natural objects) lend support to the assumption in the following pages that the very appearance of Renaissance texts generated particular kinds of response from Renaissance readers. Frontispieces (such as that in Herrick's *Hesperides*) were decorative, but we may rightly suspect that they were symbolic as well. They often denoted for the reader the difference between the act of reading (and its imaginative consequences) and the act of seeing, for it is a fact that when we look at pictured images we project into an imagined space while our attention to the written word demands a focus upon the printed or inscribed surface.[10] The inevitable tension between looking *at* and looking *into* is a phenomenon difficult enough to isolate in the complicated task of both reading and seeing (a task comparable, perhaps, to Gombrich's example of reading "rabbit-or-duck" as opposed to "rabbit-and-duck"[11]). The following chapters, however, suggest that one of the delights of late Renaissance English imaginative writing emerged from just this tension. Poets, it appears, did indeed depend upon the visual arts, and their readers in turn brought to the works of poets visual concepts and conventions of beholding that established a powerful creative interaction between the verbal and visual arts. It is to specific instances of such interaction that the following chapters are devoted.

Acknowledgments

The staffs of the Warburg Institute, the British Library, the Folger Shakespeare Library, the Huntington Library, the Columbia University Library, the Houghton Library, and the Humanities Research Center Library of the University of Texas at Austin have been most generous with their professional expertise. I am grateful for their skill and care. Patricia M. Butler, former curator of Ipswich Museums, has been especially helpful on matters pertaining to Lady Drury's oratory, and her attitude of cordial cooperation was assumed by her successor, A. G. Hatton. My colleague Douglass Parker graciously provided translations of the mots from Lady Drury's oratory. Material in chapter 6 has been adapted from my chapter in *"Trust to Good Verses": Herrick Tercentenary Essays*, edited by J. Max Patrick and Roger B. Rollin. A grant from the University Research Institute of the University of Texas made it possible for the book to be drafted in relative freedom from classroom responsibilities. A further grant, generously facilitated by William S. Livingston, vice-president and dean of Graduate Studies at the University of Texas at Austin, made it possible for this book to be published. For reading earlier drafts and for suggestions that have made this book more readable than it might otherwise have been I am grateful to A. C. Hamilton, S. K. Heninger, Jeffry B. Spencer, J. Max Patrick, and Roger Rollin. The faults that remain in the book are most assuredly no fault of theirs. My debt to Cora, Lydia, Colin, and Edward far surpasses the limits of conventional thanks. The best I can offer of a tangible nature is the dedication of this book to them. The real message is beyond mere words.

Poets and the Visual Arts in Renaissance England

1. Visual Art in the *New Arcadia*

By all accounts, Sir Philip Sidney's revision of *The Countess of Pembroke's Arcadia* produced a far more visually expressive piece of writing than the original had been. In addition to altering in quite radical ways the development of characters and the thematic emphasis of his story, Sidney recast much of his narrative and a great deal of his description in an apparent effort to appeal more vividly to his reader's sense of specific pictorial genres: landscape, paintings on mythological themes, portraits, statuary, jewelry, emblems, and impresas. Various commentators have suggested that this different emphasis in the *New Arcadia* may have been stimulated to a degree by the imagery in such Greek romances as *Clitophon and Leucippe* and *An Aetheopian History*. Others have suggested that he would have found comparable pictorial features in more contemporary romances such as Sannazaro's *Arcadia* or Montemayor's *Diana*. These suggestions have been, and remain, persuasive.[1]

The case can also be made, though, that Sidney found creative encouragement in the visual arts. Evidence to be discussed shortly indicates that in addition to his other accomplishments he possessed the knowledge, the interest, and, above all, the curiosity that in a later age would be characteristic of the virtuoso or connoisseur. The question naturally arises, then, whether there is value as well as validity in a reading of the *New Arcadia* that places special emphasis upon its incorporation of the visual arts. Though his own medium was the word, what Sidney wrote in the revised version of his romance is expressive, as the *Old Arcadia* had not been, in a strikingly visual way; on this point there is no debate. Similarly, no one conversant with Sidney or more generally the literature of the Renaissance would argue that his skillful use of the visual was due to a fascination with the possibilities of literary or pictorial realism. Nowhere in his works is there any evidence of relish for mere literal fidelity to external detail in the world of experience. Rather, Sidney expresses deep concern for the value of those riches conceived by poets in their artful treatment of nature: "Nature never set forth the earth in so rich tapestry as divers poets have done. . . . Her world is brazen, the poets only deliver a golden."[2] His achievement in the *New Arcadia* suggests, then, that its particularly visual character was due, instead of to literary concerns alone, to a fascination with the ways perception is recorded in the human mind, with the way the eyes select details from the random array of nature and focus on them to the exclusion of other details, and the way the artist—through such devices as shadowing and perspective illusion—can manipulate imagination, producing thereby an ideal rather than a mere replication of the so-called real. Presently, in connection with further remarks Sidney made on poetry in his *Defence*, we will consider the compatibility between his theories of poetry and the views on art expressed by some of his contemporaries. If the case is to be made for literary pictorialism in his art, it is reasonable to expect some validation in the critical literature on both the visual and verbal arts. For the moment, though, a more immediate question is, what did Sidney know about art? And what reasonable grounds are there for even offering to discuss visual art in the *New Arcadia*?

Verbal Limning and the Criterion of Expressiveness

The earliest (and most authoritative) critical remarks about *The Countess of Pembroke's Arcadia* come from Sidney's close friend Fulke Greville. In his letter to Walsingham about the intention of William Ponsonby to publish Sidney's romance, he declared that he had in his possession "a correction of that old one don 4 or 5 years since."[3] This, he told Walsingham, "is fitter to be printed then that first." And it was from Greville's own copy that the *New Arcadia* came to be published.

It was out of such firsthand knowledge of Sidney's revision of the romance that Greville later declared in his *Life of Sir Philip Sidney* the author's purpose to have been far more than providing a simple diversion for his sister and her friends. After praising Sidney for conceiving such "a large field [for] an active able spirit . . . to walk in," Greville remarked that "in all these creatures of his making, his intent and scope was, to turn the barren Philosophy precepts into pregnant Images of life." Sidney, he says, was "an excellent image maker." In those images he sought "lively to represent the growth, state, and declination of Princes, change of Government, and lawes, vicissitudes of sedition, faction, succession, confederacies, plantations, with all other errors, or alterations in publique affaires." "His purpose" in the *Arcadia* "was to limn out such exact pictures, of every posture in the minde, that any man being forced, in the straines of this life, to pass through any straights, or latitudes of good, or ill fortune, might (as in a glasse) see how to set a good countenance upon all the discountenances of adversitie, and a stay upon the exorbitant smilings of chance."[4]

These comments convey a singularly visual appreciation for the *New Arcadia*. Indeed, Greville might as well have been describing the work of a painter. And the compatibility of his terms to both visual and verbal art is an appropriate reminder that "imitation," "invention," and "expression" were often used to describe the appeals of both arts.[5] Sidney's appeal to the "active able spirit" of the thoughtful reader, then, is comparable to the appeals of the graphic artist to the thoughtful viewer. Further, the author's "pregnant Images of life" may be seen by the inner eye of the reader no less specifically than images painted in oils may be viewed by one standing before a picture. These images in the *Arcadia* thus address the reader visually through the medium of words. And they are grounded in the author's capacity to express the human condition while simultaneously calling readers' attention to the kind of experience they are having with the fictive representation.

Though Greville does not directly say so, it is clear that he believed Sidney to possess that capacity for penetrating vision explained by Horace's "Si vis me flere, dolendum est primum ipsi tibi" (If you want to move me to tears, you must first feel grief yourself). To experience feeling, and then to gain an objective purchase on the quality of that feeling through artistic representation—this seems to be the point of Greville's praise no less than the point of episodes in the *Arcadia* to be discussed below. That Greville is not expressing his high regard for Sidney's achievement as a limner in words in the terms of an idle metaphor becomes even more evident when we consider his remarks alongside those by Paolo Lomazzo on the expressive quality of the speaking picture as an instrument of both poetry and painting.

The "motions," Lomazzo explains in *A Tract Containing the Artes of Curious Paintinge* (translated in 1598 into English by Richard Haydock), are "the severall passions and gestures which mans bodie is able to perform." Proper expression in painting is a visible effort to show "the inward affections of the minde." By means of such "outward and bodily Demonstration," he says, "mens inward motions and affections may be said as well (or rather better) signified; as by their speech: which is wrought by the proper operations of the bodie." The perfect knowledge of this motion is "accounted the most difficult part of the arte, and reputed as a divine gift: insomuch as herein alone consisteth the comparison between *Painting* and *Poetrie*."[6] Motion or expressiveness is conveyed by the apt combination of written speech and visible signification, or through the capacity of one of these mediums to suggest the effects of the other. It was undoubtedly Greville's perception of true expressiveness in the *Arcadia* that led him to draw his conclusions about Sidney's combined visual and verbal success.

To the suggestions made by Greville that Sidney consciously expressed himself in ways that echoed the statement attributed by Plutarch to Simonides about the speaking pictures of poetry, we are able to add evidence from Sidney's own experience which suggests that the author of the *Arcadia* enjoyed and exercised an informed awareness of visual art. Perhaps the most dramatic is his search for and discovery of an artist qualified to paint a portrait he wished to give to Hubert Languet. In a letter written to Languet from Venice on February 26, 1574, Sidney says he has at last chosen none other than Paolo Veronese, whose work on the portrait has begun "today."[7] The choice, he implies, has not been easy. For he has been unable till now to decide between Veronese and Jacopo Tintoretto. That Sidney should consider commissioning either of these artists is itself evidence of keen discernment. That he should have chosen Veronese, however, proves his discernment, especially since history has confirmed that artist's superiority as a portraitist.

In the absence of further comment on this matter by Sidney, we are left to infer from remarks made by others the criteria that must have led to his decision. Languet judged the portrait (now lost) to be a fine likeness, though he believed the painter had presented Sidney a bit too sad and pensive, if not too youthful.[8] But Daniel Rogers, who was Languet's house guest when the portrait arrived, composed a Latin poem on the likeness which permits us a rare glimpse into the qualities of expressiveness then believed appropriate for a portrait.[9]

According to Nicholas Hilliard, the most prominent limner of the English Renaissance, Sidney was knowledgeable about the theoretical and practical concerns of painters. In *The Arte of Limning*, Hilliard relates that Sidney once questioned him

> whether it weare possible in one scantling, as in the lenght of six inches of a littel or short man, and also of a mighty bige and taulle man in the same scantling, and that one might weel and apparently see which was the taule man, and which the littel, the picture being just of one lenght. I showed him that it was easely decerned if it weare cuningly drawne with true obseruations, for ower

eye is cuninge, and is learned without rulle by long vsse, as littel lads speake their vulger tonge without gramour rulls. But I gaue him rules and suficient reasons to noet and obserue, as that the littel man[s head is] comonly as great as the tawle man[s], then of nececity the rest of the body must be the lesse in that same scantling, a littel man comonly hath also comonly short legs and thieghes in comparison to the bulke of body or head, but though the head be as great as the tall mans, yet shall his forme and face and countena[n]ce be fare otherwise, easey enough to diserne. The talle man hath comonly low showlders, long shankes, thieghs, armes, hands, and feet, wherwith ouer eye is so comonly aquainted that without rule to vs knowne it knoweth it straight, but if an ile painter come which will make a childs head as littel for his body as a tall mans (a childe is but fower times the length of his face, and a man tene tymes and more), or his eye as littel for his face as a mans, or his nose as great, I will not take vpon me to knowe his tall man from a dwarfe. There is notwithstandinge much faire worke wherin such grosse error is, and much disproportion and false perspective, but [by] neatnes and well coulloring the worke oft times soe graceth the matter that common eys neuer note it, but men do beleeue it to be exquesit and perfect becausse of the neatnes. But knowe it you for a truth that the cheefest mastery and skill consisteth in the true proportion and line, and a tall mans picture exactly drawne but in the lenght of six inches shall shewe to be a taller mans picture than a littel mans picture drawne at the lenght of fowre and twenty inches, or in his owne full height, if his true shape be obserued, and so of horsses and other beasts and cattel the like. Lamatzo confirmeth this by naming some men to be six heads, some of tenne, some of twelue; other authors the like.[10]

Additional evidence of Sidney's commerce with art on the Continent appears in a letter he sent to the earl of Leicester from Frankfort on March 18, 1573. There Sidney informs his uncle that "this bearer having showed me the works he doth carry into England . . . hath promised me to let no man see that which he carrieth until he have showed them unto your Lordship."[11] Leicester was adding in these years to his vast if unsystematic collection of original art and miscellaneous artifacts, a collection larger than those of Archbishop Parker and Lord Lumley (both of which we may suppose Sidney also to have viewed).[12] It seems reasonable, therefore, that the reference in Sidney's letter would be to pictures, though we unfortunately have no further information that Sidney might have approved works purchased abroad by the earl for his collections.

Finally, if the identification of a picture in the National Portrait Gallery ultimately proves correct, Sidney on one occasion had a portrait done in the manner of the impresa.[13] But whether this painting represents Philip Sidney or his brother Robert, it is a matter of record that he made far more use of his impresas in the *New Arcadia* than in the *Old*.[14] It is also a matter of

record that he added significantly to his knowledge about this curious genre during his travels in 1573 and 1574, the period of the Veronese portrait and the possible dispatch of pictures to Leicester. We have in this connection another letter to Languet, written in December 1573. There Sidney proudly refers to his recent purchase of Girolamo Ruscelli's *Le Imprese Illustri*, reissued in Venice only the year before.

From Rogers' poem on the Veronese portrait we sense a cultivated and informed attitude toward art and the pleasure of discovering that the artist accomplished far more than the representation of a likeness: "Quis frontem gestu, radiis animavit ocellos? Inditus est labris cuiss ab arte lepos?" (Who enlivened your forehead with expression, your eyes with radiant beams? Whose art has given your lips that keen expression?) We have every reason to believe that Rogers' delight with the expressive quality of the picture was no different in value from the expectations of the sitter who selected an artist who could supply such expressiveness. And what Rogers praises in the portrait is the very quality of expressiveness that Sidney himself cultivated through both speech and signification in his Arcadian fiction, the quality that Greville later acknowledged in his remarks about the "excellent image maker" whose goal was to "limn out . . . exact pictures." Though the poem by Rogers is no more distinguished, perhaps, than Hilliard's prose, it reveals the sort of dialogue that passed between cultivated persons when they talked of pictures, dialogue that should not be ignored when we look beneath the surface of Renaissance literature. Rogers' praise, in fact, echoes remarks that occur in the writings of numerous Renaissance critics of art.

Francesco Bocchi, for example, remarks that painters and sculptors "should express in their figures not only the *costumi* of better men, or of heroes, but [should express] superhuman and divine ideas, in order to lift up the soul [of the beholder] to devotion and to inflame it with the love of God." And Benedetto Varchi, demonstrating the dependence of visual and verbal art upon one another, declared that "as the poets [sometimes] describe the exterior, so the painters show, as far as they can, the interior, that is, the emotions."[15] For Bocchi and Varchi, as for Sidney and Greville, expressiveness should be both impressive and instructive. One should not simply wonder when pictures "speak" and poems invite readers to "see." To add profit to delight, one must heed the words of the pictures and the images of the poem: *ut pictura poesis: ut poema pictura*. A picture properly spoke when it surpassed mere representation; a poem surpassed the limits of language when it invited the reader to imagine a concrete visual experience as though it were already shaped by the hand of the artist. The conscious pictorial quality of the *New Arcadia*, in addition to Sidney's heavy dependence upon *istorie*, landscapes, and portraits, is undoubtedly a consequence of this concept. Support for this conclusion may be found in the conversation between Sidney and Hilliard.

The artist's account of that conversation indicates that the young poet had more than a polite interest in proportional representation, to say nothing of the means by which an artist might convey successfully the illusion of reality.[16] Sidney's practice in the *New Arcadia*, his discussion of the writer's responsibility in the *Defence*, and Fulke Greville's remarks in the *Life*, however, demonstrate that the illusions of art should not deceive the viewer (as Zeuxis deceived the birds with his pictured grapes), but should promote and sustain the viewer's sense of a genuine *second* nature. Such, indeed, is the effect generated by the opening episodes in the revised *Arcadia*.

Arcadia Made Visible through Words

In the "Fourth Eclogues" of the *Old Arcadia*, two shepherds named Strephon and Claius complain of their failure to win the love of Urania. Though she is thought by many to be but the daughter of a shepherd, we learn that she is "in deede of farre greater birthe." Strephon and Claius themselves are, of course, gentlemen in disguise. To woo her, they have "bothe employ[ed] theyre best speede." At last, rejected by Urania, they merely "tarry in Arcadia" in the increasingly faint hope of hearing but a word from her.[17] The episode in the *Old Arcadia* is almost an afterthought, its potential for extended significance greatly diminished by the place of relative unimportance given it in the development of the narrative.

The *New Arcadia*, however, opens with Strephon and Claius (true shepherds now, and no longer burdened by disguise) who stand upon the shore from which Urania departed and ponder their loss. The tone is now altogether new. And the symbolic potential of the episode is significantly enhanced through careful pictorial realization, even though the passage is comparable in broad respects to the opening episode in Montemayor's *Diana* and retains a similar emphasis on the faculty of memory. "Yonder," says Strephon—and the reader responds by mentally following the line of his extended arm—"Urania lighted." And "there she sat." "Here she laid her hand over thine eyes, when she saw the tears springing in them." And "yonder, yonder, did she put her foot into the boat, at that instant as it were dividing her heavenly beauty between the earth and the sea" (p. 62).

Here Sidney inverts the action commonly described in the myth of Venus' birth and so vividly expressed, first by Poliziano in his *Stanze* and then by Botticelli in his painting which hangs at the Uffizi. In the present episode, we are to understand, Venus departs rather than arrives, leaving behind her a vague sense of dejection at the loss of so divine and inspiring a presence. But Sidney's repeated references to gesture in this passage encourage the reader to consider specific details. With the eye of imagination, for example, the reader follows the gaze of the shepherds, and soon is at one with them in the act of seeing. So subtly, though, is the appeal on the imagination that this initial chapter rewards close attention.

In the opening paragraph alone the method is unfolded through metaphors that combine the reading of the printed word with the vicarious sensation of seeing what the characters in the fiction are able to see. The reader is told, for example, that Strephon, before speaking to Claius, set "first down in his darkened countenance a doleful copy of what he would speak." Urania, the reader then learns, has "printed the farewell of all beauty" upon the ground with her very footsteps. Finally Sidney writes, with unmistakable reference to the place-system of memory in which an image contains all those things one wishes to remember, that "remembrance came ever cloathed unto [them] in the form of this place."

The passage is visually expressive in a variety of ways. In the broadest sense, it is a speaking picture whose purpose is to establish in the reader a willingness to imagine not only the details of the author's fictive world but to comprehend the significances folded within those details. Sidney's visual sense of place and his verbal control over the reader's perception of "place" (in both the mnemonic and descriptive sense of that word) anchor the reader's thought in specific percepts and guide the eye as a means of guiding the mind, thus effecting the transition of Sidney's reader from the world of mere fact to the world of his fiction where carefully selected details are given specific significance.

It is through the eyes of these same two shepherds that the reader first sees Musidorus, "a thing which floated, drawing nearer and nearer to the bank, but rather by the favourable working of the sea than by any self-industry." The fact that their "sight increased their compassion" adds an expressive dimension to the writer's invention. It is through their eyes, too, that we next see Pyrocles carried back out to sea on the broken mast, "having nothing upon him but his shirt which, being wrought with blue silk and gold, had a kind of resemblance to the sea" (p. 66). And it is their perception that results in the magnificent "picture," the set piece of the sea and the burned-out ship: "some way into the sea they might discern . . . a stain on the water's colour, and by times some sparks and smoke mounting thereout." These invitations to a kind of straightforward perception, however, soon yield to the more aesthetically complex phenomenon of visual perspective. From discrete objects the eye now frames or places visual limits upon scenes that are evoked within the inner field of vision through a carefully designed sequence of visual experiences.

The first stage in the sequence occurs when Musidorus (now calling himself Palladius) travels with the shepherds inland from the inhospitable coast and across the barren coastal plain (bk. 1, chap. 2). Joining his eye with theirs, he crosses through Laconia (wearied with "wasted soil") into a more inviting land "with delightful prospects."

> There were hills which garnished their proud heights with stately trees; humble valleys whose base estate seemed comforted with refreshing of silver rivers; meadows enamelled with all sorts of eye-pleasing flowers; thickets, which, being lined with the most pleasant shade, were witnessed so to by the cheerful deposition of many well-tuned birds; each pasture stored with sheep feeding with sober security, while the pretty lambs with a bleating oratory craved the dams' comfort; here a shepherd's boy piping as though he should never be old; there a young shepherdess knitting, and withal singing, and it seemed that her voice comforted her hands to work and her hands kept time to her voice's music. As for the houses of the country—for many houses came under their eye—they were all scattered, no two being one by the other, and yet not so far off as that it barred mutual succour: a show, as it were, of an accompanable solitariness, and of a civil wildness. (Pp. 69–70)

Defined according to boundaries and topographical regions perceived by the moving eye of the traveler, Arcadia readily assumes concrete spatial identity in the mind of the reader.

This identity, however, is quite unlike that conveyed by the traditional Hellenistic *ekphrasis*. Achilles Tatius, for example, opens *Clitophon and Leucippe* with an invitation to the reader to inspect an elaborate wall painting. Similarly the *Tabula Cebetis* opens with an extended *ekphrasis* in which the reader is told that everything seen has been painted prior to the inception of the dialogue. Sidney's manipulation of his own reader's inner eye, his control over the sequence in which more or less random percepts assume order in the beholder's mind, as when painters design and frame nature according to their art, creates a vital sense of pictorial landscape.

From such evidence Sidney would appear to be as indebted to the practice of Renaissance pictorialism as to the literary *ekphrases* he would have known from classical texts and from contemporary imitations. In those earlier texts the recreation of visual art has a static, iconic quality. Readers are simply asked to imagine that they are scanning a wall painting or lingering before a statue. They will not be invited by the author to imagine in any detail artful gradations of focusing and framing.[18] They will not, in other words, be offered terms that recall the painterly practice of depth perspective, nor will they be made particularly conscious of the discriminations made by the practiced eye as it sorts out the most balanced alignments (in both breadth and depth) among objects—the very subject of Sidney's reported conversation with Hilliard. What counts for Sidney is his reader's

vicarious sense of a carefully discriminated space.[19] To achieve that sense of space he describes a succession of increasingly smaller enclosures through which he guides his reader into Arcadia much as the viewer of a painting might imaginatively enter its depicted space through the picture plane.

Perhaps the most impressive instance of structured verbal "beholding" in the *New Arcadia* occurs when Kalander leads Palladius from his house through a garden landscape to his summer cottage.

> Kalander one afternoon led him abroad to a well-arayed ground he had behind his house, which he thought to show him before his going as the place himself more than in any other delighted. The backside of the house was neither field, garden, nor orchard, or rather it was both field, garden, and orchard; for as soon as the descending of the stairs had delivered them down, they came into a place cunningly set with trees of the most taste-pleasing fruits; but scarcely had they taken that into their consideration but that they were suddenly stept into a delicate green; of each side of the green a thicket, and behind the thickets again new beds of flowers, which being under the trees, the trees were to them a pavilion, and they to the trees a mosaical floor, so that it seemed that Art therein would needs be delightful by counterfeiting his enemy Error and making order in confusion.
>
> In the midst of all the place was a fair pond whose shaking crystal was a perfect mirror to all the other beauties, so that it bare show of two gardens; one in deed, the other in shadows. And in one of the thickets was a fine fountain made thus: a naked Venus of white marble, wherein the graver had used such cunning, that the natural blue veins of the marble were framed in fit places to set forth the beautiful veins of her body. At her breast she had her babe Aeneas, who seemed, having begun to suck, to leave that to look upon her fair eyes which smiled at the babe's folly, meanwhile the breast running.
>
> Hard by was a house of pleasure built for a summer retiring-place; whither Kalander leading him, he found a square room full of delightful pictures made by the most excellent workmen of Greece. There was Diana when Actaeon saw her bathing, in whose cheeks the painter had set such a colour as was mixed between shame and disdaine; and one of her foolish nymphs, who weeping, and withal louring, one might see the workman meant to set forth tears of anger. In another table was Atalanta, the posture of whose limbs was so lively expressed, that if the eyes were the only judges as they be the only seers, one would have sworn the very picture had runne. Besides many more, as of Helena, Omphale, Iole: but in none of them all beauty seemed to speak as much as in a large table which contained a comely old man, with a lady of middle-age but of excellent beauty; and more excellent would have been deemed, but that there stood between them a young maid whose wonderfulness took away all beauty from her but that which it might seem she gave her back again

by her very shadow. And such difference (being knowne that it did in deed counterfeit a person living) was there between her and all the other (though goddesses) that it seemed the skill of the painter bestowed on the other new beauty, but that the beauty of her bestowed new skill of the painter. (Pp. 73–74)

The reader's sense of location may at first seem somewhat indistinct. Rhetorically, the effect of this initial ambiguity is to prepare us to shift our attention from the nonspecific to the specific. The area behind Kalander's house, for example, is "neither field, garden, nor orchard, or rather it was both field, garden, and orchard." Leaving this ambiguously defined space, Kalander and his guest descend a flight of steps and reach a place that is slightly more definite; it is "cunningly set with trees." The appearance of this place being momentarily "taken . . . into their consideration" (much as the present succession of spaces is presumably being taken into consideration of the reader), Kalander and his guest now progress into "a delicate green," an enclosure where horizontal *and* vertical axes are more prominent. Trees tower over their heads creating the illusion of a pavilion within which the flowers readily assume the appearance of "a mosaical floor." The visual effect of the image is one of progressive enclosure, and the subjects (Kalander and Palladius) now stand before the reader's eye within the boundaries of a specific frame.

From enclosure (or framing) the eye soon shifts to the perception of reflected images. A pond mirrors the garden, "one in deed, the other in shadows." We are informed that this mirroring pond bears an emblematic message, for, as the narrator has told us, within the artful enclosure, art counterfeits "his enemy error . . . making order in confusion." Here art reflects reality in order that its beholder may be better equipped to understand truth. The basic image is doubtless derived from Clitophon's grove in the first chapter of Achilles Tatius' romance. There we read of "a fountain whose waters received into the square basin, the work of art, served the flowers for their mirror, and gave a double appearance to the grove, by adding the reflection to the reality."[20] But if Sidney did not exactly borrow from Greek romances or their Renaissance imitations, where did he obtain his visual vocabulary?

One of the major developments in Renaissance art was precisely this notion of ideal landscape, and there would seem to be direct connections between this development and Sidney's romance. Toward the middle of the seventeenth century, Edward Norgate could say, "It doth not appear that the antients made any other Accompt or use of it but as a servant to their other peeces, to illustrate or sett of[f] their Historical painting by filling up the empty Cornes, or void places of Figures and story, with some fragment of landscape." By Norgate's time landscape had won a secure place in the systemization of styles and was regarded as a genre in its own

right.[21] But in Sidney's England landscape was still more of a novel achievement, and theoretical interest in its applications and practice appears in various places including Lomazzo's *Tract* and an anonymous manuscript called *A Short Treatise of Perspective*. In the latter we read that landscape "expresseth places of larger prospects, as whole contries where the eye seemeth not to be hindered by any objects . . . ether of nature or arte, but to passe as farre as the force thereof can pierce. . . . And therfor all thinges seme by littell and little to diminishe and vanishe away both in color and shape."[22]

Sidney's own query to Hilliard pertains to the very same phenomenon of visual illusion. And it is his apparent effort to recall by means of the word the illusionist appeals of Renaissance visual art that so distinguishes his romance from others.[23] In the *New Arcadia* the eye of the reader follows a planned course much as it would in response to the illusion of perspectival planes in a painting where landscape frames and defines the pictorial subject. Sidney's verbal practice is analogous, for example, to the visual practice in Pieter Brueghel the Elder's *Magdalena Poenitens* engraved by Hieronymus Cock (fig. 1). There topography and trees are arranged to carry the eye along visually complex circuits before it is at last settled upon the subject. For Brueghel no less than for Sidney, landscape has its inherent delights. But both would agree with Henry Peacham, who in *The Art of Drawing with the Pen and Limning with Water Colours* (London, 1606) stated that landscape is seldom "drawn by itself, but in respect & for the sake of something else. Wherefore it falleth out among those thing[s] which we call *parerga*, which are additions or adjuncts rather of ornaments" (pp. 28–29). Many further examples in art could be substituted for Brueghel's, which has particular value in the present connection because it was widely disseminated through an engraving. Giovanni Bellini's *The Feast of the Gods* (National Gallery, Washington, D.C.) demonstrates in similar fashion how the woods—an apt subject themselves for later painters— enclose the setting for the revelers. Giorgione's *Adoration of the Shepherds* (fig. 2) offers the prospect of a grotto that frames the Holy Family, but with the further refinement that the configuration of the trees on either side of the landscape in the top left-hand corner of the painting gives a finite frame to the open sky which shows beyond. Finally, in a well-known engraving after a lost Titian, *The Death of St. Peter Martyr*, the violent action reverberates through the vigorous lines of the trees which reach out into the open space to the left of the picture as well as above the struggling figures below.

These examples of the visual use of landscape and setting to frame and distinguish a subject, as well as to invite particular expressive response from the beholder, parallel Sidney's own verbal control over the imaginative inner eye of his reader. His is not mere description—it is the evocation of a special kind of scene whose formal

Figure 1. Hieronymous Cock, after Pieter Brueghel the Elder, *Magdalena Poenitens.* Copyright Museum Plantin-Moretus, Antwerp.

arrangements favorably invoke Plutarch's paraphrase from Simonides. Whatever one might believe about the validity of that ancient formulation about speaking pictures and mute poems, it is evident that Sidney has tried his own hand at verbal limning. His goal is not merely a facile assimilation of a visual genre into a literary form; rather, it is a serious effort at expressiveness—the point made by his remarks on each of the paintings in Kalander's gallery. He would surely have been in total agreement with Lomazzo, who on the question of expressiveness declares that "herein alone consisteth the comparison between *Painting* and *Poetrie*." Such verbal control over the movements and the focusing of the reader's imaginative eye continues in Sidney's treatment of the fountain said to be surmounted by a statue of Venus.

Like Bartolomeo Ammanti's *Ceres* (Bargello, Florence), this literary statue is a set piece, an artistic curiosity placed alongside objects in nature for the purpose of asserting forms that are often hidden beneath nature's surface.[24] A piece of sculpture in this setting offers concepts of physical space quite distinct from the scenograph of the garden, for sculpture shares its physical coordinates with the viewer directly, not through the two-dimensional illusion of a third dimension. For this reason sculpture is more intimate than a picture and begs acceptance primarily in terms of volume and touch. The three-dimensional character of the Venus statue in the *New Arcadia* thus suggests two distinct but related meanings. One message is that pure forms often lie beneath the threshold of ordinary perception—a message

that encourages us to look deeply into the story we are reading. The other message is more visceral. Because statues share space with the viewer and offer multiple views of a single object in contrast to the single view permitted by a picture, the statue is a pivotal object in the visual transition from garden landscape to Kalander's "house of pleasure," where we are soon led into a "square room full of delightful pictures."

Even before we focus our attention upon these paintings, however, the spatial character of the room containing them should have conveyed a message of its own about the relation of art to nature. A cube, square in every respect, the room signals the ultimate control of nature by art.[25] It is an emblem that enjoys close kinship with the cube depicted on the engraved title page of Robert Recorde's *The Castle of Knowledge* (London, 1556) (fig. 3). There, surmounted by Knowledge, the image of the cube "speaks" of stability and order; it is the moral obverse of the globe so commonly associated with instable Fortune and depicted on the opposite side of the page. Sidney's cube invites comparison, too, with an emblem from Alciati (fig. 4) where Hermes (the god of art) sits upon a cube while Fortuna wavers precariously: "ut sphaerae Fortuna, cube sic insidet Hermes." Kalander's gallery, then, is the picture or image of art itself—in an emblematic sense. In a more representational sense it contains on its walls artful expressions of human passion, a major theme throughout the *Arcadia*. But in contrast to Arcadia at large, passions here are contained and controlled by art; as the two princes soon discover as they are assimilated into the

Figure 2. Giorgione, *The Adoration of the Shepherds.* Courtesy of the National Gallery of Art, Washington, Samuel H. Kress Collection.

Arcadian world, passions there are the province of Nature.

The character of the galley is both scenographic and symbolic. So is the contrast we have observed in our progress with Palladius from rugged coastline across the mountains and into Arcadia and from wooded glen to house to square room. With him we have journeyed from nature into art. But although we view with him the paintings in Kalander's gallery, it is clearly the author's intention to comment upon aesthetic experience in a way that distinguishes our perception from Palladius'. What occurs in this episode is thus the culmination of our vicarious journey through topographical, botanical, and architectural forms. Real travel ceases at the picture plane; thereafter movement into the world of picture is virtual, imaginary. Here the reader parts with Palladius,

who projects so fully into the picture that he becomes progressively ensnared by the Arcadian illusion. The reader meanwhile is invited to remain an objective viewer of the Arcadian scene, not a participant in its virtual world.

Standing before the painting of Diana, Palladius notes how the painter has used sensible color and form to convey the intangible moral values the goddess traditionally expresses. The color in her cheeks is "mixed between shame and disdain." The mystery of visual illusion is even more pronounced in the painting of Atalanta. There one would swear "the very picture had run," so expressively has the scene been represented. The *trompe-l'oeil* in these paintings is comparable to the sequence of visual scenes that has brought us to this room. Like the pond mirroring the garden, these paintings echo the very image-making skill the writer has himself employed. Thus far we have no reason to reject the illusion or to deny the skill of an artist capable of suggesting so subtle a metamorphosis within a static medium. With Palladius we continue to scan the paintings, noting their subject matter. But within a few words, the eye of the reader is moving so rapidly that the narrator who guides the reader's perceptions of this event drastically foreshortens the description to a mere generalized list of names: "Besides many more, as of Helena, Omphale, Iole." Abruptly, Palladius turns away from paintings on mythological themes (whose illusion of lifelikeness reinforces their allegorical suggestiveness) to a painting in a different genre—a portrait. Here he ceases to read objectively the painter's language of visible forms as his response shifts to immediate identification with the subject. No longer reading pictured images, he becomes totally absorbed by an image.

No longer interested in the painter's *art*, he projects himself uncritically into an identification with the painter's *subject*. As Sidney's narrator guides the reader through this episode a crucial distinction emerges. If readers yield unthinkingly to verbal skills alone, and if they identify uncritically with characters and settings, they may be apt to lose themselves in the Arcadian maze no less than do the visiting princes. On the other hand, if they can read the author's speaking pictures without becoming emotionally involved in them, they can profit from, rather than indulge in, the effects of verbal expressiveness.

Arcadia made visible in words is thus a planned sequence of images, what Sidney calls in *A Defence of Poetry* "pictures what should be, and not stories what haue beene." These remarks in the critical treatise support his practice in the revised version of the romance. For what we have observed indicates that he made detailed use of verbal pictures to couple "the generall notion with the particular example." Such, he affirms, is the "perfect picture," one that "yieldeth to the powers of the mind an image of that whereof the philosopher bestoweth but a wordish description, which doth neither strike, pierce, nor possess the sight of the soul so much as that other doth" (p. 85). The chief instrument of the soul, however, is thought and not merely feeling. There is thus a major difference between pictures that possess one in this manner and pictures that usurp the intelligence. Such, it would seem, is the meaning of Philoclea's portrait which "speaks" through Palladius to Pyrocles: "Cousin (said he [Pyrocles]) then began the fatal overthrow of all my liberty, when walking among the pictures in Kalander's house, you your selfe delivered unto me what you had understood of Philoclea. . . . [T]here were mine eyes infected, and at your mouth did I drink my poison" (p. 140). Here the picture of Philoclea speaks only within the boundaries of the fiction. But the episode as a whole speaks to the reader in the man-

ner Sidney has described in the words above. Surely it is this emphasis on the visual in the *New Arcadia* that prompted Fulke Greville to comment conspicuously on the pictorial quality of expressiveness in his friend's epic romance.

A Defence of Poetry: The Theory of Visual Thinking

The obvious care with which Sidney shapes his reader's visual experience in the opening chapters of the *New Arcadia* is the practical side of a theoretical position he took in the *Defence of Poetry*. A dominant theme in this critical treatise is that sensible precepts are a key to verbal communication. In this respect, Sidney's views are astonishingly comparable to those advocated by proponents of Gestalt psychology. "Purely verbal thinking," Rudolf Arnheim has said, "is the prototype of thoughtless thinking, the automatic recourse to connections retrieved from storage. It is useful but sterile. What makes language so valuable for thinking, then, cannot be thinking in words. It must be the help that

Figure 3. Title page, Robert Recorde, *The Castle of Knowledge* (1556). Courtesy of The Newberry Library, Chicago.

318   ANDREAE ALCIATI
Ars naturam adiuuans.
EMBLEMA XCVIII.

Vт *ſphæra Fortuna, cubo ſic inſidet Hermes:*
Artibus hic variis, caſibus illa præeſt.
Aduerſus vim fortunæ eſt ars facta: ſed artis
Cum fortuna mala eſt, ſæpe requirit opem.
Diſce bonas artes igitur ſtudioſa iuuentus,

Figure 4. Emblema XCVIII, from Andreae Alciati, *Emblemata* (Paris, 1611). Courtesy of Humanities Research Center, The University of Texas at Austin.

words lend to thinking while it operates in a more appropriate medium, such as visual imagery. The visual medium is so enormously superior because it offers structural equivalents to all characteristics of objects, events, relations." Furthermore, "the principal virtue of the visual medium is that of representing shapes in two-dimensional and three-dimensional space, as compared with the one-dimensional sequence of verbal language. This poly-dimensional space not only yields good thought models of physical objects or events; it also represents isomorphically the dimensions needed for theoretical reasoning." [26] The compatibility of such modern theory with the views expressed in *A Defence of Poetry* suggests that Sidney's practice in the *New Arcadia* may be less alien than a modern reader may initially think.

While Sidney affirms poetry to be "an art of imitation, . . . a representing, counterfeiting, or figuring forth," he adds that "to speak metaphorically" poetry is also "a speaking picture" (p. 80). Nature, he says, "never set forth the earth in so rich tapestry as divers poets" (p. 78), making it plain that there is a special

intimacy between invention and imitation—true imitation is never mere representation, either for the poet who invents dialogue or the painter who invents a scene. No doubt his emphasis on the primacy of the visual is indebted to the Neoplatonic view that sight is the noblest of the physical senses.[27] The poet, he says, disdains to be tied to mere "imitation of Nature" (p. 78), and in this he is to be distinguished from the mere rhetorician or logician who employs "what in Nature will soonest proue and perswade" (p. 78), for he constructs a "second nature" (p. 79) that resides within the boundaries of his "speaking picture" (p. 80). (This second nature is obviously the goal of those opening chapters in the *New Arcadia.*) Sidney's reliance on the visual assumes as well that the colors of rhetoric are the verbal equivalent of the painter's colors and that coloration in both mediums falls within the criterion of expressiveness. It is from this premise that he elaborates in the *Defence* upon the comparison of the poet and the painter.

Inferior poets, he says, are "wrapped within the folde of [their] proposed subject" and cannot follow the course of their own invention. These are the poets who "deale with matters Philosophicall . . . , or naturall . . . , or Astronomical . . . , or historical" (p. 80). They are like "the meaner sort of painters, who counterfeit onely such faces as are set before them" (p. 80). But the "right poets" are comparable to "the more excellent" painters who, "having no law but wit, bestow that in colours upon you which is fittest for the eye to see: as the constant though lamenting look of Lucretia, when she punished in herself anothers fault, wherein he painteth not Lucretia whom he never saw, but painteth the outward beauty of such a virtue" (p. 81). Rarely is the idea of expressiveness stated so plainly.

Poet and painter alike, then, are obliged to express the passions, subjects that require "no law but wit." Those who fail in this endeavor can lay no claim to greatness. Paolo Lomazzo says it well: "The spirit and life of the arte" lie in the artist's capacity to express "the inward affection of the minde, by an outward and bodily demonstration." And in his opinion one may "attaine vnto this so excellent a faculty [only] by industrious study, in the knowledge of these motions, and the causes whence they proceede: for from hence a man may easilie attain to a certaine vnderstanding, which afterwards putting in practice, with patience, together with the other pointed, he may vndoubtedly prooue a iuditious inuentor." Such an inventor, moreover, "shall attain vnto better perfection then the other, who is naturally indued with the dexteritie, without industry and patience." The values expressed here are identical with those Greville applied to the *Arcadia.* And in addition to the compatibility with modern theories of visual thinking, it is revealing that the Renaissance critic of literature should state his views in terms that parallel those used by the Renaissance theorist of art.[28]

To be sure, the poet has an advantage with words, which in the Neoplatonic sense enables him to produce what Sidney calls "a perfect picture"—an image that is ideal. He yields "to the powers of the mind an image of that whereof the philosopher bestoweth but a wordish description which doth neither strike, pierce, nor possess the sight of the soul" (p. 85). The reason for this is that, unlike the philosopher and historian, the poet "coupleth the general notion with the particular example." Here Sidney relies upon Fracastoro's *Naugerivs* (1555): "While the others consider the particular, the poet considers the universal. So the others are like the painter who represents the features and other members of the body as they really are in the object; but the poet is like the painter who does not wish to represent this or that particular man as he is with many defects, but who, having contemplated the universal and supremely beautiful idea of his creator, makes things as they ought to be."[29] And both Sidney and Fracastoro depend ultimately on Aristotle, for whom imitation was not a copy of nature as it is but an image of nature as it should be (*Poet*, 11.1–3).

Nevertheless, the advantage of language is also its disadvantage. If verbal art is to promote greater awareness of values that are no less real because they are intangible, it must accept its limitations and employ the images of visible things. To one who had never seen an elephant or rhinoceros, who, asks Sidney, "should tell him most exquisitely all their shapes, colour, bigness, and particular marks?" (p. 85).[30] And who should give to another person an adequate verbal description "of a gorgeous palace, an architector, with declaring the full beauties?" None of this could be accomplished through repetition—"by rote" of all that might be seen. Such verbal description "should never satisfy his inward conceit with being witness to itself of a true lively knowledge; but the same man, as soon as he might see those beasts well painted, or the house well in model, should straightways grow, without need of any description, to a judicial comprehending of them." This is why the philosopher "with his learned definitions" cannot adequately communicate ideas which "lie dark before the imaginative and judging power," for his concepts are "not illuminated or figured forth by the speaking picture of poesy" (p. 86).

Sidney's remarks on the relations of poetry to painting indicate a sustained intention to stress the positive relations between visual perception and verbal inducements to *imagine*. Poet and painter alike are responsible for "figuring forth good things," which Sidney terms *eikastike*, and for avoiding *phantastike*, that is, things which infect "the fancie with unworthy objects" (p. 104). The responsibility of the poet finds apt comparison with that of the painter who "should give to the eye either some excellent perspective, or some fine picture, fit for building or fortification, or containing in it

Figure 5. Bernard Salomon, engraver, "Daphne and Apollo," from Gabriele Simeoni, *La Vita et Metamorfoseo d'Ovidio* (1557). Courtesy of Humanities Research Center, The University of Texas at Austin.

some notable example (as Abraham sacrificing his son Isaack, Iudith killing Holofernes, David fighting with Goliah)" (p. 104).

The *Defence*, then, assumes a place alongside the sparsely recorded episodes in Sidney's life that point toward discriminating views on art and an effort to incorporate visual appeals in verbal forms. For the modern who would read the *New Arcadia* with renewed pleasure, the *Defence* offers the most appropriate point of theoretical departure. As Fulke Greville suggested, Sidney's revisions of the epic romance must surely have been motivated by the desire to practice the verbal art in ways compatible with the schemas and modes of presentation refined by visual art.

The Statue of Venus and the Parade of Portraits: "Pregnant images of life"

The statue of Venus is prominent among the works of art that Sidney deploys about Arcadia. It contributes not only to the reader's sense of space, but by its location it permits an imaginative transition from the visual experience of the garden to the square room and its numerous paintings. In purely iconographic terms, the subject is the very personification of those passions that prove so confusing and even destructive among the Arcadians and their neighbors. And in this regard no reader can fail to notice that this Venus is the very opposite of the celestial Venus Urania whom Strephon and Claius declare has left Arcadia forever. As a speaking picture, the statue expresses the endeavor of Sidney's art to incorporate the complexities of emotional life.

Figure 6. Titian, *Danae and the Shower of Gold.* Courtesy of
Museo del Prado, Madrid.

Made of white marble, it has been carved with such
cunning "that the natural blue veins of the marble were
framed in fit places to set forth the beautiful veins of her
body." The statue is all but alive. And the writer's *descriptio* conjurs up an aesthetically intriguing image
which may properly be said to so "strike, pierce, [and]
possess the sight of the soul" that virtually any reader
will pause and reflect. Why should these veins of dif-
ferently colored stone lie thus within a seemingly random block of marble? More astonishingly, how might
the sculptor have divined (for surely the physical eye
could not possibly have seen) so exquisite a form within
the uncut marble? The concept is worthy of a Michelangelo, who fervently believed that statues were hidden in
marble and that the sculptor's task was to free them
from their surrounding crust of stone. Only the vision-
ary artist, one who is capable of transcendence, could
discover such an infolded image by locating the iso-
morph of a pure idea in solid matter.[31] Thus the Venus
statue excites wonder. And the reader's response to that

wonder is a major ingredient in a willing acceptance of
the author's power to create a "second nature" that is
beyond *mere* nature. The pregnant images of life that
Greville discerned in the romance are thus figured (or
allegorized, if one prefers) in this remarkable statue
whose cunning should impress us no less than it does
Palladius. The significance of the statue, however, is not
a perception made within the fiction by Palladius himself but instead is invoked for the reader.

Like the anonymous sculptor, Sidney too appears to
borrow "nothing of what is, hath been, or shall be."
Rather, he prefers to "range, onely reined with learned
discretion, into the divine consideration of what may be,
and should be" (p. 81). The paintings on Kalander's
walls are instruments of that quest. They contain in
their imitations of familiar mythological stories the allegorical kernels of events that occur in the romance. The
painting of Omphale, for example, forecasts in its representation of Hercules' metamorphosis into a feminine
role the similar transformation of Diaphantus (formerly

Pyrocles) into the Amazon Zelmane. First we are shown the picture, which we see through Musidorus' eyes; later the message conveyed by the picture is dramatized in Pyrocles' behavior. Further, Kalander's picture of Diana and Acteon forecasts Pyrocles' spying on Pamela and Philoclea in book 2, chapter 11, as they bathe in the river Ladon. As the narrator shapes his readers' comprehension of the Arcadian world, he—like the sculptor at his block of marble—uncovers the veins of continuity that are hidden within the random chaos of events. As the sculptor makes three-dimensional sense of a formless bulk, the narrator makes sense of time by revealing in the context of his speaking pictures events that have shape and continuity.

A second painting in Kalander's gallery allegorizes in similar fashion a sequence of events that occurs in the fifteenth through eighteenth chapters of book 1. The painting of Hippomenes' famous race with Atalanta (the outcome of which had been fixed by Venus herself) figures the episode of the jousts which the arrogant Phalantus stages to prove through the ritual of knightly combat the honor of Artesia, his mistress. He has challenged the knights of Arcadia and surrounding lands to run against him in the lists. And to impress the Arcadians with the seriousness of his challenge he mounts an elaborate procession distinguished by an impressive sequence of pictures.

Artesia, of course, rides prominently in the procession upon a triumphal car. But the principal feature of this muster is the group of footmen who march two by two, carrying between them "one picture after another of them that by Phalantus' well running had lost the prize in the race of beauty." Ceremoniously, they pause "at every pace . . . turning the pictures to each side so leisurely that with perfect judgment they might be discerned" (p. 57). These paintings, of which there are eleven in all, depict an assortment of ladies, each of whose champions have fallen to Phalantus. They are retrospective in that they symbolize past events, but they point as well toward the narrative future in that many of them visually assert traits of personality and character that will presently find expression.

The first, a portrait of Andromana, Queen of Iberia, exhibits an unflattering physiognomy. Her "exceeding red hair with small eyes" express a character whose deficiencies unfold through events narrated in the twentieth chapter of book 2. Here, however, the painter has captured through line and color the image of a crafty, although indiscriminate, character. That a man so caught up in a ceremonial role as Phalantus should once have run in the lists to prove Artesia's superiority to Andromana is implicitly a species of hollowness. And, indeed, we have learned from Basilius that Phalantus has styled himself according to his passion and in contradiction to his true nature.

The "counterfaite of the Princesse of Elis" is little more appealing. Her picture speaks, but it says nothing of "majestie, grace, favour, nor fairness" (p. 158). The character revealed by the portrait is of one who, in wishing to be beautiful, can claim only the wish. Not so Artaxia, Queen of Armenia. From her portrait it is evident that nature has bestowed "delightful colours" upon her and has proportioned her "without any fault" (p. 158). To this, however, Sidney adds a qualification: no fault "quickly to be discovered by the senses"—a warning that applies to virtually all sensible appearances in Arcadia. When he comments that Artaxia has a somewhat "mannish countenance, which overthrew that lovely sweetness," the judgment is one that a perceptive viewer would reach after studying the work of a skilled painter. The artist, then, speaks through visible forms what the poet will later narrate in book 2, where we learn how Artaxia has reduced her husband to incompetence and has assumed an irresponsible power.

Limning further, Sidney writes of the portrait of Erona. Her brown hair and delicate complexion are the only physical details he gives, but we learn that her face "was thought longer than the exact symmetrians perhaps would allow" and that love nevertheless "played his part so well, in every part, that it caught hold of the judgment before it could judge making it first love, and after acknowledge it faire" (p. 158). We are not told how the picture looked but instead respond to it as a viewer might. Sidney's picture is thus expressive in a double sense.

The portrait of Bacca is a shocking contrast. Her breasts are "over-familiarly laide open," and she has a "mad countenance about her mouth, between simpering and smiling" (p. 159). Her head is slightly bowed, but at the same time she casts an inviting look upward. The sheer physicality of detail shapes our judgment of her character, suggesting thereby how description is adequate mainly for gross rather than refined perceptions. Leucippe, on the other hand, is rather appealing, the characterization depending upon description of her eyes, which had "in them such a cheerfulness as nature seemed to smile in them" (p. 159). The queen of Laconia in turn is allowed only the briefest of all the descriptions: "she was a queen and therefore beautiful," the emphasis here being upon evocation of her role rather than particulars of lineament.

Sidney then shifts to the portrait of Queen Helen. This queen is said to have "jacinth hair, curled by nature, intercurled by arte [and] (like a fine brooke through golden sands) [she] had a rope of fair pearle which now hiding, now hidden by the haire, did as it were play at fast or loose each with other, mutually giving and receiving richness." As we might expect of a portrait presented in verbal terms which echo the wonder manifest in Kalander's statue of Venus, this portrait has presented a challenge to the painter: "In her face so much beauty and favour [were] expressed, as (if Helen had not been known) some would rather have judged it the painter's exercise to show what he could do than the counterfeiting of any living patterne." Consequently, the portrait *strikes* admiration: "it ravished with delight." And "no indifferent soul there was . . . that would not long to have such a playfellow" (p. 160).

In the remaining three pictures, Parthenia's large grey eyes and "exceedingly fair forehead" speak visibly of her noble nature. And again Sidney heightens his own narrative by means of the comments evoked from the bystanders by this portrait. The painting that follows, however, is the most curious of them all. It depicts the shepherdess Urania pulling a thorn from a lamb's foot, "her look so attentive upon it, as if that little foot could have been the circle of her thoughts" (p. 160). No other picture in the procession imitates the sitter in relation to another creature or presents a dramatic expression of the sitter's character through action. The quality of pathos in the painting speaks of a tenderness and capacity for sympathy that seem strangely out of place in Basilius' kingdom of passions. And there is also a mnemonic quality to the painting, for it recalls the longing after the ideal, celestial Venus that led Strephon and Claius to the sands of Cithera at the very beginning of the book. While seven of the eleven women portrayed in Phalantus' procession will reappear in subsequent episodes, Urania is not among them. Her portrait is retrospective and points backward in time to a past the Arcadians have little hope of regaining.

The last is the portrait of Zelmane, who we are told resembles Philoclea until closer inspection shows the likeness to be such "as an unperfect glass doth give, answerable enough in some features and colors, but erring in others." Not at all descriptive in the usual sense of portraiture, these remarks on the imitative quality of images recall again the principle of the infolded form exhibited by the statue of Venus. Like the sculptor who discovers the form defined by the colored veins in the block of marble, the storyteller hints at thematic relationships whose apt symbol is the mirror. The lady Zelmane (who will assume narrative importance in book 2) is said here to resemble Philoclea. Pyrocles, passionately infatuated with Philoclea from the time Musidorus told him of her portrait, has named himself Zelmane after his willful metamorphosis into a feminine role. In thus becoming female—and Zelmane—Pyrocles has in a sense become but an image of what he ardently desires. There is a certain irony, then, in his disparaging comments on the procession of portraits: "here be some pictures which might better become the tombes of their mistresses." Clearly his judgment of the pictures differs from the reader's. While his attitude is colored by jealousy and the hot-headed passion signified by his original name (Pyrocles), the reader has been conditioned by Sidney's continued use of sculpture and painting to see in these pictures and their mirrored themes what Greville called "every posture in the minde." To Pyrocles, no less than to Phalantus, the portraits are mere symbols of conquest, of status. To us they yield "to the powers of the mind an image of that whereof the philosopher bestoweth but a wordish description."

These "pregnant Images of life" which grow to eventual maturity in the consciousness of the reflective reader comment, too, upon the images of Pamela and Philoclea that loom in the minds of Musidorus and Pyrocles. Not only does Philoclea's pictured image recur eidetically from time to time, but with each recurrence it is increasingly psychologized. Soon Pyrocles himself confesses that each thing he sees in the painting seems "to figure out some parts of my passion." And the way he sees the real-life Philoclea is clearly influenced by his perception of the pictured image. When she appears in her nymph-like apparel in the thirteenth chapter of book 1, the verbal picture emphatically echoes the statue of Venus. She is "so near nakedness as one might well discerne part of her perfections, and yet so apparelled as did show she kept best store of her beauty to her self: . . . her body (O sweet body) covered with a light taffeta garment, so cut as the wrought smock came through it in many places, enough to have made your restraind imagination have thought what was under it." So closely, indeed, have the painted and the psychologized images come to approximate one another that the expertise of the reader would be sorely taxed if it were not for the principle of the speaking picture. Through visual thinking, Sidney makes it possible for us both to participate sympathetically in the fiction and to remove ourselves sufficiently from it in retrospect to comprehend the meanings he has given to this extraordinary second nature.

Figure 7. "Triumphe," from Francesco Colonna, *Hypnerotomachia Poliphili* (1499). Courtesy of Humanities Research Center, The University of Texas at Austin.

Figure 8. Engraving after Francesco Primaticcio, *Danae and the Shower of Gold*. Courtesy of Musée Condé de Chantilly, Photographie Giraudon.

Emblems, Impresas, and Visual Conceits

In the second and third books of his romance, Sidney continues to shape his reader's view of Arcadia according to such genres as landscape, mythological paintings, and portraiture. But he brings to these books an added emphasis on emblems and impresas, and the result is a greater frequency of visual conceits. Zelmane (in the second chapter of book 2) begs Musidorus to "bestow a map of his little world upon her that she might see whether it were troubled with such unhabitable climes of cold despairs and hot rages as hers was." Later in the same chapter Love is said to lay burdens upon its victims while at "another time [it] giveth wings," an allusion to the familiar emblem of Cupid whose right arm is winged and from whose left hangs a ponderous weight. And in

the thirteenth chapter of book 3 Dametas gives a painter an order for a device, "which was a plough with the oxen loosed from it, a sword, with a great number of arms and legs cut off, and lastly a great army of pen and inke-horns, and books." The meaning is "that he had left off the plowe, to do such bloody deeds with his sword as many inke-horns and books should be employed about the historifying of them." Collectively such speaking pictures urge a synoptic attitude upon the reader while individually the map, the emblem of Cupid, Dameta's impresa, and the like give the particular shape of detail to the world of Arcadia.

One of the strangest—and perhaps most psychologically disturbing—images appears in the fourteenth chapter of the second book. There Miso describes for Pamela and Dorus a painting of Love once shown to her by a strange old woman. In contrast to the conventional images of Cupid as the mischievous *putto* indiscriminately shooting arrows, or as the handsome young god of the Neoplatonists, Love is here depicted as a "foul fiend" reminiscent of medieval pictures of the Devil:

> he had a pair of horns like a bull, his feet cloven, as many eyes upon his body as my gray mare hath dapples, and for all the world so placed. This monster sat like a hangman upon a pair of gallows. In his right hand he was painted holding a crown of laurell, in his left hand a purse of money; and out of his mouth hung a lace of two fair pictures of a man and a woman, and such countenance he showed as if he would persuade folks by those allurements to come thither and be hanged.

Following the description is the poem "Poor Painters oft with silly Poets join, / To fill the world with strange but vain conceits." This poem, Miso says, accompanied the picture in explanatory fashion. But within a few lines of narrative Sidney contrives to have Mopsa, who is certainly the most inspired grotesque in the entire romance and who has been the subject of Kalander's mock-blazon "What length of verse can serve," offer a version of the Cupid and Psyche myth. Pamela will not permit her to finish the tale, but in its truncated form it allegorizes the condition of incompleteness that characterizes Love in the fictive Arcadia.

This sequence of picture, verse, and allegorical tale is too much like the three standard parts of the emblem to be entirely accidental. Indeed, this chapter in the *New Arcadia* is highly emblematic both in its objective presentation of Love and in its synoptic appeal to the reader. Zelmane (Pyrocles) is predictably offended at the things related by Miso and Mopsa, for she (he) suffers already from the disorders fostered by love and clings to the common stereotypes. Sidney's reader will instead see it as the perfect emblem whose three parts comprise a speaking picture of something which inferior poets and "the meaner sort of painters" can offer only in terms of fanciful and misleading illusions. Sidney's method may properly be said to offer the reader *eikastike* as opposed to *phantastike*.

Another curious episode has a similar bearing upon the false illusions of art, and like the former it is a complex speaking picture where the image presented in the text achieves independence of it and becomes, in the mind's eye, a commentary upon it. In the twenty-fifth chapter of the second book, Pyrocles (still as Zelmane) and Philoclea are set upon by a band of rebels. The young prince is able to fight them off with the aid of Dorus. Their struggle is observed closely by "a poor painter who stood by with a pike in his hands. This painter was to counterfeit the skirmish between the Centaurs and Lapithes, and had been very desirous to see some notable wounds, to be able the more lively to express them; and this morning . . . the foolish fellow

was even delighted to see the effect of blows. But this last, hapning neere him, so amazed him, that he stood stock still, while Dorus, with a turn of his sword, strake off both his hands. And so the painter returned well skilled in wounds, but with never a hand to perform his skill."

Here Sidney alludes to the common practice among painters of observing nature so closely as to collapse the commonsense differences separating it from art. This overzealous painter, though, pays a severe penalty for bringing art too close to the actual stuff of life—in his loss of perspective, he loses as well the means of practicing his art. The episode illustrates in emblematic fashion a theme that is constant throughout the *New Arcadia*. Extensive interest in naturalistic or illusionistic detail constitutes a neglect of what *might* be in favor of what merely *is*.

Sidney's goal is always to penetrate the veil of appearances, and the frequency of visual conceits keeps this ambition before the reader constantly. In the fourth chapter of book 2 Zelmane's passion for Philoclea is such that she no longer needs to "paint her face with passions; for passions shone through her face." In chapter 26 Zelmane's gestures are such that "as her words did paint out her mind, so they served as a shadow, to make the picture more lively and sensible." In the third book, chapter 4, Amphialus is said to be "amplified with arguments and examples, and painted with rhetorical colours"; his purpose is to bend "his outward and inward eyes, striving to make art strive with Nature, to whether of them two that fortification should be most beholding." In chapter 24 (again with reference to Amphialus) we read that "who would lively describe the manner of these speeches should paint out the lightsome colours of affection, shaded with the deepest shadows of sorrow, finding them between hope and fear, a kind of sweetness in tears." Throughout, it is the painter who teaches the reader how to behold.

It is, finally, three allusions to pictures illustrating Ovidian myths that summarize the writer's use of speaking pictures in the *New Arcadia*. In the first book, when Musidorus discovers Pyrocles decked out like an Amazon, his amazement appears in the way "Apollo is painted when he saw Daphne suddenly turned into a laurel" (chapter 12). In the second book when Basilius kneels before the Amazon he holds up his hands "as the old governess of Danae is painted when she suddenly saw the golden shower" (chapter 16). In the third book, when Amphialus discovers Philoclea in her chamber he notices a shadow across her face "as a good painter would bestow upon Venus, when under the trees she bewailed the murder of Adonis" (chap. 3). In each of these highly representative cases the reader's perception is channelled through images from visual art. We are not permitted to see through verbal *descriptio* either the amazement of Musidorus, the desire of Basilius, or the

Figure 9. Tintoretto, *Danae and the Shower of Gold.* Courtesy of Musée des Beaux-Arts, Lyon.

delicate shadow upon Philoclea's face. Instead, we are led to see art through *art* so that what the writer represents is expressed in terms of a second nature.

The woodcuts by Bernard Salomon illustrating Ovid's *Metamorphosis* can provide the appropriate visual analogue for Sidney's Apollo image (fig. 5). His hand raised in disbelief, the sun-god stares incredulously at Daphne, whose arms are already luxuriant branches and whose legs have take firm root. The Ovidian source of the image also characterizes Pyrocles' disguise as a peculiar metamorphosis.

The allusion to Danae could be a reference to one in which the nurse is seated on Danae's bed, holding out the corners of her apron to catch the golden coins raining from above (fig. 6). Done by Titian in 1554 for Philip II, it was sent to England along with a painting of Venus and Adonis. Sidney had a wide range of iconographic commonplaces to draw upon, and his selection of these details has implications beyond a single painting. He could, for example, have cited details from the woodcut of Danae in Francesco Colonna's *Hypnerotomachia Poliphili* (fig. 7). But there is no nurse in this well-known version. He could have envisioned a scene similar to that in the painting by Francesco Primaticcio for the Gallerie Francois I er (fig. 8), where the nurse holds a jug in the background while Danae herself holds out the apron for the falling gold. Instead, he

chose a version comparable to Titian's and Tintoretto's (fig. 9), which he might have seen firsthand.

These examples indicate that depictions of Danae fell into a relatively stable iconographic range. Those showing the nurse herself in an attitude of expectation, holding up either a sack, an apron, or a basin to the shower of golden coins, may generally be said to represent some cruder aspects of *Avaritia*, a spiritual as well as carnal sin. Now if Danae is the passive victim, a martyr to the irresistible power of gold, then the nurse, with her obvious display of physical greed for the gold, represents the *peccatum carnale*.[32] By associating Basilius with the nurse, Sidney comments pejoratively on the king's obsessiveness. Because we know the true male identity of Zelmane, we know Basilius to be victimized by his desires as surely as (in Titian's and Tintoretto's versions) Danae's nurse is morally victimized by hers. Without these iconographic distinctions, one is apt to regard this highly complex simile as just one more instance of literary pictorialism.

The shadow that falls so alluringly upon Philoclea's face begs comparison with any one of dozens of Renaissance paintings and engravings that show Venus mourning Adonis.[33] But Sidney's specific instructions that his reader is to see this scene "under the trees" suggests that he had in mind a painting by Tintoretto. Though this painting has been identified as *Venus and Endymion*, it nonetheless shows a boarspear prominently in the foreground.[34] Could Sidney have seen this picture (whose location is presently unknown) when he was deciding whether Tintoretto or Veronese should paint his portrait? He is so specific about Venus "under the trees" in this passage that the possibility looms large. So also does the visual echo of Nicholas Hilliard's comment that "great shadow is a good sign in a picture." That Sidney knew enough about art to regard this as a desirable quality in a painting is evident elsewhere in the *New Arcadia* (chapter 29 of the second book) where he writes that Erona's appearance is like that of a picture "which receives greater life by the darkness of the shadows, then by more glittering colours."

Conclusion

We are able to obtain a better purchase on the significance of the *New Arcadia* if we consider it in the context of visual art as well as Renaissance literary experiments with the romance. Sidney's second version clarifies his goals and suggests that he had developed a keen awareness of language and grammar of visual forms. He incorporates the concepts of landscape, portraiture, mythological painting, emblems, and impresas because by his time they had developed clear generic identification and could be used to convey, through a kind of expressive shorthand, notions that were of particular concern for the verbal artist. As certain visible schemas took on specific identity and significance for painters and their viewers, these schemas developed an added usefulness for writers.

Sidney's use of visual art in the *New Arcadia* is neither impressionistic nor intellectually loose. His identification of the pictorial genres that can shape a reader's perception of the story is always clear and specific; his descriptions of landscape and of individuals' appearances are never done merely for the sake of description, but are instead composed in a way that engages readers' imagination and promotes their understanding. Further, there is a conscious order in the progression from landscape to portraiture to emblem and impresa in the three existing books of the *New Arcadia*. The forms of visual art he invites his reader to bear in mind thus become increasingly abstract, openly symbolic, and intellectual as the romance unfolds. The author's use of visual art becomes one way of measuring the ever increasing psychological depth of his narrative, to say nothing of its increasingly complex demands upon the reader. Every informed reader will discount Sidney's insistence that his romance was a mere plaything. But as one marvels at Sidney's sophisticated use of visual art to comment upon and to deepen the meanings of his verbal art, it becomes all the more apparent that the *Arcadia* is so innovative as to be ahead of its time. Even the verbal riches of Spenser, which are of a quite different sort, hearken back to medieval realism and iconography more than they anticipate the subtleties of baroque illusion and the techniques by which it was generated.

In sum, Sidney's use of visual art in the *New Arcadia* is a concrete example of success in achieving synesthesia. For Sidney, painting and sculpture were a bridge between the concrete and the abstract, between the consciousness of the teller and that of one listening to a tale, and between the silent word on the page and the "active able spirit" of the thoughtful reader. Accordingly, they became a principal device for bringing narrative or description "into the deuine consideration of what may be, and should be."

2. Donne, Jonson, and the Priority of Picture

John Donne may not so readily come to mind as Philip Sidney in discussions of literary pictorialism. His poetry, like that of his fellow Metaphysicals, places such emphasis upon wit that tropes constantly displace or utterly transform figures of mere description. Moreover, the subjects of his elegies, his songs and sonnets, and even his verse letters generally preclude literary descriptions of works of graphic art. Iconic poetry that has a secure place in the *Arcadia* or in *The Faerie Queene* seems out of place in the tight little dramas of Donne's lyrics. Ben Jonson, too, is not customarily thought of as a literary pictorialist. While exception has been made for his contributions to the masque, his short poems have not encouraged interart comparison so much as rhetorical investigation. No more than the conscious wit of the Metaphysicals does the plain style of the neoclassicist seem compatible with the concerns of visual art.[1]

Nevertheless, the work of these two major poets exhibits attitudes toward verbal limning that deserve wider recognition. Neither is a pictorialist writer in the sense that Sidney and Spenser are. But Sidney and Spenser wrote in the genres that permitted—perhaps even required—pictorialism, while Donne and Jonson did not. Comparison of the two later writers on this point reveals, however, that they were aware of current conventions of seeing and their underlying rationale. Not surprisingly, though, they emerge on opposing sides of the issue, Donne as a proponent of picture and Jonson as a staunch opponent.

To view Donne's poetic career from the perspective of his mature work as a preacher and the dean of Saint Paul's shows just how basic to his thought was the concept of seeing in pictorial terms. Among the major topoi that contribute so vividly to the expressive quality of his sermons, "the eyes of the soul" reveals the great value Donne placed on the representation of understanding as an act of visual perception.[2] At this late stage in his career, the motif expresses a theological rather than painterly idea. But when we turn to his use of comparable images in the earlier poetic works, we perceive that even

there the expression of things seen was grounded in conventions associated with pictorial seeing, upon formal constituents of representation that would permit coherent (though often highly elliptical) verbalization. "The sight," he writes in the Easter Day sermon of 1628, "is so much the Noblest of all the senses, as that it is all the senses. As the reasonable soul of man, when it enters, becomes all the soul of man, and he hath no longer a vegetative, and a sensitive soul, but all that is one reasonable soul; so sayes S. Augustine . . . All the senses are called Seeing . . . ; And so of the rest of the senses, all is sight."[3]

This emphasis on the priority of sight quite naturally gravitates to the imagery of mirrors, for which Donne cites scriptural justification from Paul's First Epistle to the Corinthians, "We see through a glass, darkly." In the 1628 Easter sermon, for example, he poses the question: "But how doe we see in a glasse? Truly, that is not easily determined. The old Writers in the Optiques said, That when we see a thing in a glasse, we see not the thing itselfe, but a representation onely; All the later men say, we doe see the thing itselfe, but not by direct, but by reflected beames. It is a uselesse labour for the present, to reconcile them. This may well consist with both, That as that which we see in a glasse, assures us, that such a thing there is, (for we cannot see a dreame in a glasse, nor a fancy, or a Chimera) so this sight of God, which our Apostle sayes we have *in a glasse*, is enough to assure us, that a God there is" (8:222–223). To be sure, Donne's evocation of mirror imagery and his use of metaphors to express the nature of certain obstructions to spiritual vision are all sustained by his apparently extensive knowledge of commentaries pertaining to the *oculus corporeus* and the *oculus interior*. Paul's imagery, of course, had long been the subject of highly specialized discussions of optics. Donne, in turn, was sensitive to the implications these controversies held for imagery of reflection, imitation, and reflexiveness.

Also in the sermons Donne will occasionally develop the motifs of "seeing" and "image" in terms of pictures, as he did on the day of Saint Paul's Conversion in 1628/1629. Discussing our natural inclination to stray into "a superstitious worship of God," he cautions the need for diligence but declares, "I doe not intend, that we should decline all such things, as had been superstitiously abused, in a superstitious Church." Because "pictures have been adored, we doe not abhor a picture." Rather, "we are diligent to preach to the people the right use of these indifferent things" (8:331). Pictures continue to be on his mind some weeks later in a sermon preached to the king at court in April 1629. Discussing whether the image of God is in the body of man, he says: "So far is this Image of God in the body above that in the creatures, that as you see some Pictures, to which the very tables are Jewells; some Watches, to which the cases are Jewells, and therefore they have outward cases too; and so the Picture and the Watch is in that outward case, of what meaner stuffe soever that be: so is this Image in this body as in an outward case." "The Sphear then of this intelligence, the Gallery for this Picture, the Arch for this Statue, the Table, and frame and shrine for this Image of God, is inwardly and immediately the soule of man." "We should wonder to see a man, whose Chambers and Galleries were full of curious master-peeces, thrust in a Village Fair to look upon six-penny pictures, and three farthing prints. We have all the Image of God at home, and we all make babies, fancies of honour, in our ambitions. The master-peece is our own, in our own bosome; and we thrust in Countrey Fairs, that is we endure the distempers of any unseasonable weather . . . ; we endure the guiltinesse, and reproach of having deceived the trust, which a confident friend reposes in us, and solicit his wife or daughter: we endure the decay of fortune, of body, of soule, of honour, to possesse lower Pictures; pictures that are not originalls, nor made by that hand of God, nature; but Artificiall beauties" (9:79–81).

In this passage which is so impressive for its sustained use of the picture as metaphor, Donne asks his auditors to ponder the ontological difference between the picture or the statue and the devices used to frame them. Here as elsewhere in his sermons we discover "the process of focusing, multiplying, and coloring spiritual vision." Any trope, even mere description, can accomplish the preacher's aim, which is "to adjust and readjust proportions and scales of values." And yet "the representation of such changes of spiritual perspective in terms of optical processes, so frequent in Donne's sermons, is the most concrete expression of the design he has on his congregation. Although such tropes often deal with man's extremity, their appeal to a sense of perspective and proportion removes them at least one step from mere evocation of the horror of death. By their 'intellectual' nature they even help to balance scenes of horror.[4]

The man who was thus so concerned with the expressive value of pictorial and perceptual metaphors was no

less fascinated at an earlier age with the verbal recollection of visual schemas. Perhaps no passage in all of Donne's works is more visually evocative than the icastic image of the *Tabula Cebetis* presented in "Satyre III":

> On a huge hill,
> Cragged, and steep, Truth stands, and hee that will
> Reach her, about must, and about must goe;
> And what th' hills suddenness resists, winne so;
> Yet strive so, that before age, deaths twilight,
> Thy Soule rest, for none can worke in that night.[5]

These lines have long been recognized for their narrative expression of spiritual struggle. But the verbal force of this passage depends to a great degree upon the poet's evocation of an often repeated visual schema (fig. 10). Whether they knew Cebes' *Table* from sixpenny pictures, three-farthing prints, the frontispieces of books such as George Wither's *Emblems* (1635), or the paintings by more ambitious artists, many of Donne's contemporaries certainly recognized the source of the passage.[6]

In a similar way visual analogues echo throughout *The First Anniversarie.* There Donne not only acknowledges the Neoplatonic commonplace that "Sight is the noblest sense of any one" (l. 353), but the entire poem assumes the character of a portrait. Joseph Hall's introductory lines, "To the Praise of the Dead, and the Anatomy," make this assumption plain. The poem, he declares, can relate

> Thy worth so well to our last nephews eyne,
> That they shall wonder both at his, and thine:
> Admired match! Where striues in mutuall grace
> The cunning Pencill, and the comely face:
> A taske, which thy faire goodnes made too much
> For the bold pride of vulgar pens to tuch.[7]

Through a mystical conversion of the word, too often merely the tool of "vulgar pens," this poet will now employ his own "cunning pencill" to create a portrait worthy of being handed down through generations of the family. Those who were critical of Donne's hyperbolic treatment of Elizabeth Drury in the poem would appear simply to have ignored his emphasis on the transformation of logos to picture, a representational genre which, as Leon Battista Alberti had long before said in *Della Pittura*, was the means whereby "the face of someone long since dead may keep on living." Certainly, the "idea of a woman" which Donne later declared was the object of his poem would be compatible with Renaissance notions of portraiture, with which Donne was certainly familiar.

Of course the very subtitle, "An Anatomy of the World," would evoke specific pictorial topoi, many of which were made familiar by successive editions of the most famous Renaissance book on anatomy, Andreas

Figure 10. M. Merian, engraver, *Tabula Cebetis* (1638). Courtesy of Humanities Research Center, The University of Texas at Austin.

Vesalius' *Humani Corporis Fabrica, Libri Septem*, first published in Basel in 1543. By Donne's time, anatomy as a form of public demonstration had not only become a popular and widespread practice, but it had developed its own theatrical architecture and broad array of technical instruments. Indeed, it is but a short step from the circular design of the Anatomical Theater at Leiden (available in the early seventeenth century in a popular "three-farthing print") (fig. 11) to the design of the Ptolemaic cosmos itself (fig. 12). And while there may be only a coincidental relation between the seven circles of the theater and the seven planetary spheres of the Ptolemaic cosmos, it would hardly exceed the stretch of Donnean wit to permit such an image to stand in the manner of a synecdoche for the world view called into doubt by the "New Philosophy." The anatomy of the world is conducted within the shell of the old creation; the "round proportion" formerly enjoyed by the heavens has now degenerated into "so many Eccentrique parts" (ll. 251–257). While the world once had "his just proportion, / Were it a ring still, yet the stone is gone" (ll. 341–342). Certainly Donne's focus on Elizabeth Drury as the epitome of the world places her at the very center of his anatomy and figuratively at the center of the anatomical theater, which is analogous to the placement of the world in the Ptolemaic system.

Some fifteen years later Rembrandt would paint his famous *Anatomy of Dr. Nicolaas Tulp*, and would pick up from pictorial and literary sources many of the same ideas that Donne uses. Like a cadaver under the dissecting knife, the earth scarcely sustains the anatomist's best efforts:

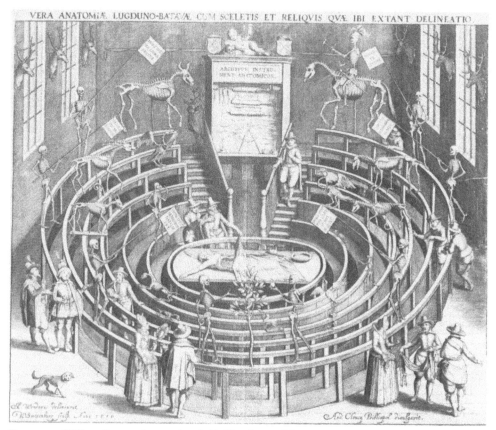

Figure 11. Willem Swanenburg, after J. C. Woudanus, *The Anatomical Theater at Leiden.* Courtesy of Prentenkabinet der Ryksuniversiteit, Leiden.

But as cutting vp a man that's dead,
The body will not last out to haue read
On euery part, and therefore men direct
Their speech to parts, that are of most effect.

[435–438]

The distinguished doctors gathered about the body in Rembrandt's painting are no less intent upon a correct understanding of the world than Donne, the poetic anatomist. But where they, as men of the new science, are interested in the microcosm of the human body as an end in itself, Donne seeks a poetic transformation of Elizabeth Drury from microcosm to macrocosm, a verbal metamorphosis from logos to symbolic image visually understood and perceived tangibly in the mind's eye. And there is a further connection between Rembrandt's painting and Donne's poem: both are indebted to Vesalius' book, which was among other things a refutation of Ptolemy's geocentric astronomy.[8] Here, though, Donne is the conservator of the old world view, while Rembrandt invents his scene in the Anatomical Theater in terms that affirm the value of the new science.

In whatever Donne writes there is a persistent appeal to sight, an appeal that is frequently stated in terms of established pictorial modes of beholding or in terms of familiar iconographical combinations. Even in the less ambitious and far less expressive prose piece *Ignatius his Conclave*, he exhibits characteristic care in establishing the scene. The satirist declares at the outset that he will relate what he has seen. "I was in an Extasie," he remarks, and "my body had liberty to wander through all places, and to survey and reckon all the roomes, and all the volumes of the heavens." Presently, "in the twinckling of an eye, I saw all the roomes in Hell open to my sight." And from the prospect of the heavens at large and of the particular rooms of Hell Donne guides his reader's inner eye "to more inward places . . . where there were not many, beside Lucifer himself." The opening passage, though by no means so carefully planned or as symbolically effective as the beginning of the *New Arcadia*, nevertheless serves a comparable function: to focus attention through a focusing of imaginary vision. Here, as in the Cebes' *Table* passage in "Satyre III," there is a precise visual analogue, a schema without the imaginative possession of which a reader will surely lose much of the writer's meaning.[9] In both instances, Donne depends upon the rhetorical figure *tractatio*, which J. C. Scaliger identified as a generic term for figures describing things as they are, putting their features before the eyes of the hearer and illuminating each detail. And in Donne's practice we may understand Quintilian's assessment of the figure: "Though you cannot see this with your bodily eyes you can see it with the mind's eye." Donne's use of pictorial concepts was thus grounded in a rhetorical notion which, in turn, promoted "Sight . . . [,] the noblest sense of any one."

There can be no doubt, then, that Donne placed a great value on the potential of picture:

> a hand, or eye
>
> By *Hilliard* drawn, is worth an history,
> By a worse painter made.

But long before writing sermons he knew the limitations of pictures as instruments for moral improvement:

> To teach by painting drunkards, doth not tast
> Now; Aretines pictures have made few chast,
> No more can Princes courts though there be few
> Better pictures of vice, teach me vertue

Nevertheless, Donne's poetry depended on visual models held jointly in his mind's eye and that of his reader. He frequently uses images of maps and pictures to enhance verbal expression, as in the verse epistle "To Mr. T. W." ("At once, from hence, my lines and I depart"):

> So, though I languish, prest with Melancholy,
> My verse, the strict Map of my misery,
> Shall live to see that, for whose want I dye.
> Therefore I envie them, and doe repent,
> That from unhappy mee, things happy 'are sent;
> Yet as a Picture, or Bare Sacrament,
>   Accept these lines . . .

Such evidence of a deep interest in picture is what we would expect from a man who was uncommonly preoccupied with having his own portrait painted, engraved, and sculpted—a man who also had a modest (but evidently a noteworthy) collection of art. From Donne's will we learn that he owned upwards of twenty pictures, a substantial number in view of his modest economic resources. At least two of them appear to have been by distinguished painters, one even by Titian ("the picture of the Blessed Virgin which hangs in the little dining chamber"). The collection is evidence that Donne "possessed a keen and accurate eye for visual detail which is as obvious in the vivid realism in his work as in the essentially dramatic quality of almost everything he wrote"[10] and that he participated in the seventeenth-century movement to embrace visual art.[11] He had his own image painted, sculpted, or engraved far more than any other poet of the age—from the melancholy self-

dramatization of the Lothian portrait to the swashbuckling energy of the frontispiece to the second edition of his poems (which William Marshall may have copied from a Hilliard miniature) to the lugubrious statue in his shroud (still at Saint Paul's)—which has led to the comment that these portraits present "the image of a man who is attempting to hold within his consciousness an almost unbearable range of interests."[12]

Do the roles in his portraits tell us anything about roles and identities in his poems? Whatever the answer, Donne often refers to pictures throughout his poetry. Among the "Songs and Sonnets" alone, these poems come readily to mind: "A Valediction of Weeping," "The Extasie," "Valediction of my Name, in the Window," "The Canonization," "The Dampe," and "Witchcraft by a Picture." In the first of these the lover's tears reflect the image of his lady's face which "coins them," and the worth of each falling tear is measured by that pictured image. In "The Extasie" the speaker declares:

> So to'entergraft our hands, as yet
>   Was all the meanes to make us one,

Figure 12. "The Cosmos," from Peter Apian, *Cosmographia* (1539). Courtesy of Humanities Research Center, The University of Texas at Austin.

And pictures in our eyes to get
    Was all our propagation.[13]

The "Valediction of my Name" returns to the theme of reflected images:

'Tis much that Glasse should bee
As all confessing, and through-shine as I,
    'Tis more, that it shewes thee to thee,
And cleare reflects thee to thine eye.

In "The Canonization" the climactic final stanza is addressed to those for whom

                love was peace, that now is rage;
Who did the whole worlds soule extract, and drove
    Into the glasses of your eyes,
    So made such mirrors, and such spies,
That they did all to you epitomize

And in "The Dampe" he employs the concept of a picture engraved in the heart:

When I am dead, and Doctors know not why,
    And my friends curiositie
Will have me cut up to survay each part,
When they shall finde your Picture in my heart,
    You think a sodaine dampe of love
    Will thorough all their senses move,
And worke on them as mee, and so preferre
Your murder, to the name of Massacre.

Here, as in the later "Anatomie," the wit of the poem depends upon the conventional postmortem scene, but with the added detail of a heart imprinted with the image of a lover. Donne uses the image of a picture imprinted in the heart in at least four additional poems.[14]

Such use of images that depend upon details perceived when the eye is closely trained on the work of painters, coiners, and engravers suggests Donne's "discriminating interest in the fine arts" rather than "his egoism and devouring interest in his own personality."[15] We do not know if Donne wrote "The Expostulation," but four lines in that poem are thoroughly compatible with his interest in the painter's art:

I could beginne againe to court and praise,
    And in that pleasure lengthen the short days
Of my lifes lease; like Painters that do take
    Delight, not in made worke, but whiles they make.

Testimony to his interest in the fine arts is evident in the elegy "On Going to Bed," where he compares women's apparel to "pictures or books gay coverings," and in the remarkable couplet from "Break of Day":

Light hath no tongue, but is all eye;
If it would speake as well as spie

and these lines from "Tutelage," which could have been addressed to a reader who had never learned from artists how truly to see:

Foole, thou didst not understand
The mistique language of the eye nor hand.

Once the principle of such creative responses to pictures is established, we find that several poems take on new meaning. The epigram "Phyrne," for example, turns out to be much more than just a cut at prostitutes.

Thy flattering picture, Phryne, is like thee,
    Onely in this, that you both painted be.

The success of any epigram depends on the poet's ability to condense multiple meanings into a simple statement, the game of epigrams being won or lost according to the ability to perceive those meanings simultaneously. Here the meanings are dependent upon a story and particular concepts of art.

The first line refers to the vignette given by Athenaeus in *The Deipnosophists* of the courtesan Phryne and the painter Apelles:

At the great assembly of the Eleusinia and at the festival of Poseidon, in full sight of the whole Greek world, she removed only her cloak and let down her long hair before stepping into the water. She was the model for Apelles when he painted his Aphrodite Rising from the Sea.[16]

Even without recognizing this specific allusion one can perceive the double sense Donne gives to "painted." (As Castiglione and others frequently observed, cosmetic artifice was a mark of "the most wanton and dishonest women in the world.") But the allusion to the artist Apelles involves meanings less obvious now than in the seventeenth century. In the ancient world he was known for his remarkable use of colors. Pliny said that "four colors only were used by the illustrious painters Apelles, Aetion, Melanthius, and Nichomachus to execute their immortal works . . . although their pictures each sold for the wealth of a whole town."[17] And it was on this authority that Propertius praised Apelles as a colorist in one of his elegies:

Would Idas and Apollo meet in combat
    for a Marpessa decked out like a whore,
Hippodamia even win by boldness
    the prince who whirled her to a distant shore?
Their features shone as clearly as the colors
    shine in a picture from Apelles' hand.[18]

Color, then is the *unstated* pictorial quality in Donne's opening line. And its significance in the epigram relates closely to Renaissance art-theory where color was regarded as the rhetorical equivalent to a writer's *elocutio*. As a collector of art and as a trained rhetorician, Donne would have been familiar with the principles of color in Lodovico Dolce's *Dialogues* whether or not he knew the work. "Coloring is so important and compelling," says Dolce, that "when the painter produces a good imitation of the tones and softness of flesh and the rightful characteristics of any object there may be, he makes his paintings seem alive, to the point where breath is the only thing missing in them." As the colors of rhetoric facilitated persuasive appeal, so did the *colorire* employed by the painter increase verisimilitude in art. "The main problem of coloring," Dolce adds, "resides . . . in the imitation of flesh, and involves diversifying the tones and achieving softness. Next one needs to know how to imitate the color of draperies, silk, gold and every kind of material so well that hardness or softness seems to be communicated to the greater or lesser degree which suits the quality of the material." But the goal of such illusionistic appeal is not illusion for its own sake; rather, it is to evoke emotional response from the beholder:

> What is needed is that the figures should stir the spectators' souls—disturbing them in some cases, cheering them in others, in others again inciting them to either compassion or disdain, depending on the character of the subject matter. Failing this, the painter should not claim to have accomplished anything. For this is what gives the flavor to all his virtues. Exactly the same thing happens with the poet, the historian, and the public speaker. . . . Nor can the painter stir emotion unless he already experiences in his own being, while executing the figures, whose passions . . . he wishes to imprint on the mind of another. And this is why Horace, who has been quoted so many times observes:
>
>> If you want me to cry, then there's a need
>> That sorrow on your part should precede.[19]

In Donne's epigram, then, both Phryne and the famous artist who painted her as *Aphrodite Rising from the Sea* have used color to "stir the spectators' souls." In both cases the vehicle of persuasion is "painting" whose object has been an emotional response. But here the comparison ends. Because the artist's goal was verisimilitude, *his* painting is to be distinguished from *hers*, which could only be described as an enticement.

Here lies the central core of the epigram. The poem pertains directly to the threshold lying between art (what Apelles did) and lived experience (Phryne's way of life). And at this core is a typically Donnean paradox. For as Dolce claimed (following Horace), an artist cannot stir emotion unless he experiences it first. Therefore, Apelles modelled the goddess of love and beauty upon his sexual response to the beauty of a courtesan. Donne's witty incorporation of the Apelles story, of Renaissance notions about the expressive characteristic of color, of social criticism, and of art theory not only fulfills the genre's demand for highly condensed but rigidly local meaning but demonstrates the range of his awarenesses as well.

In "Witchcraft by a Picture" portraiture lends a visual dimension to the emotions of love. The lover, whose image first burns in the eye of his beloved, discovers he is also drowned in each successive tear that rolls down her cheeks—a Petrarchist image of dissolution and replication. The concept occurs again in "A Valediction: of Weeping." There his mistress' tears "coin" the lover's face, the coins in turn become "emblemes" of his wretched condition, and then these coins are metamorphosed into globes manufactured by faceless workers. "My face in thine eye, thine in mine appears," Donne writes in "The Good-Morrow."

Donne appears in these poems to have been no less fascinated than Leonardo da Vinci had been with the mirror. "The air," Leonardo writes,

> is filled with endless images of the objects distributed in it; and all are represented in all, and all in one, and all in each, whence it happens that if two mirrors are placed in such a manner as to face each other exactly, the first will be reflected in the second and the second in the first. The first being reflected in the second takes to it the image of itself with all the images represented in it, among which is the image of the second mirror, and so, image within image, they go on to infinity in such a manner that each mirror has within it a mirror, each smaller than the last one inside the other. Thus, by this example, it is clearly proved that every object sends its image to every spot whence the object itself can be seen; and the converse: that the same object may receive in itself all the images of the objects that are in front of it. Hence the eye transmits through the atmosphere its own image to all the objects that are in front of it and receives them unto itself, that is to say, on its surface, whence they are taken in by the common sense.[20]

Virtually the same idea invests "A Valediction: of Weeping" with its succession of mirror replications: "When a teare falls, that thou falls which it bore / . . . / So doth each teare, / Which thee doth weare, / A globe, yea world by that impression grow."

In the elegy titled "His Picture" there are two kinds of pictured images, the one held in the heart and the other painted on a physical surface:

> Here take my Picture, though I bid farewell;
> Thine, in my heart, where my soule dwels, shall dwell.
> 'Tis like me now, but I dead, 'twill be more
> When wee are shadowes both, the 'twas before.
> When weather-beaten I come backe; my hand,
> Perchance with rude oares torne, or sun beames tann'd.
> My face and brest of haircloth, and my head
> With cares rash sodaine hoarinesse o'rspread,
> My body'a sack of bones, broken within,
> And powders blew staines scatter'd on my skinne;
> If rivall fooles taxe thee to'have lov'd a man,
> So foule, and course, as, Oh, I may seeme than,
> This shall say what I was: and thou shalt say,
> Doe his hurts reach mee? doth my worth decay?
> Or doe they reach his judging minde, that hee
> Should like 'and love lesse, what hee did love to see?
> That which in him was faire and delicate,
> Was but the milke, which in loves childish state

Did nurse it: who now is growne strong enough
To feed on that, which to'disus'd tasts seemes tough.

Whether or not this poem originally accompanied the gift of some actual portrait in miniature we do not know, but it expresses in a monologue that is dramatically conceived around such a presentation the idea that portraits possess a divine element which not only make "absent men present, as friendship is said to do, but moreover make the dead seem almost alive."[21] Indeed, there is a specific reference to this notion in lines 3 and 4. The gift also marks an occasion for speculation on the relationships of past to present and present to future, relationships that determine the structure of this conversation. In the future the face imaged in the portrait will lose much of its similarity to the speaker, who from the vantage point of this imagined future speculates on the opinions viewers will have when they see this discrepancy. The portrait thus becomes a tangible pivot on which the speaker shifts attention from present to future, and from future back to the past. In fact, it attains the same mystery of replication that so intrigued Leonardo. The man who will appear older and more weatherbeaten in the future remains the man who was once "faire and delicate." When the two "face each other exactly" in the future, "the first will be reflected in the second and the second in the first," even though unperceptive persons will be incapable of seeing it. At that time (as with the images reflected in Leonardo's two mirrors) these images will "go on to infinity," which in this poem is nothing less than an expression of eternal love. In a more subtle sense, the portrait is also a visible threshold of the soul, for it is a medium through which the soul expresses itself no less than is the face—that is, the portrait conveys forever the idea of the sitter, regardless of any physical transformations that may occur through time, for the portrait transcends time. Such, too, was the poetic portrait Donne wrote on the soul of Elizabeth Drury. This is the image that remains in the heart "where my soule dwels."

Aside from William Shakespeare, Ben Jonson was Donne's most eminent literary contemporary. And he offers a sharp contrast to Donne in his unwillingness to make concessions to the language of visible forms. In fact, his poetry exhibits as much hostility to the concept of picture as Donne's exhibits hospitality. This antipathy to art was publicly expressed in Jonson's famous quarrel with Inigo Jones. In "The Expostulation" with Jones, for example, he belittled all visual art, which in his view had abandoned the priority of the word:

And I have mett with those
That doe cry up the Machine, and the showes!
The maiesty of Iuno in the Cloudes,
And peering forth of Iris in the Shrowdes!
Th' ascent of Lady Fame which none could spy,

Not they that sided her, Dame Poetry,
Dame History, Dame Architecture too,
And Goody Sculpture, brought with much adoe
To hold her up, O Showes! Showes! Mighty Showes!
The Eloquence of Masques! What need of prose
Or Verse, or Sense t'express Immortall you?

And a few lines later he wrote:

Oh, to make Boardes to speake! There is a taske.
Painting and Carpentry are the Soule of Masque.
Pack with your pedling Poetry to the Stage.
This is the money-gett, Mechanick Age![22]

As D. J. Gordon has observed, Jonson's "more considered insults presuppose a body of doctrine: a serious doctrine of what the masque is to the poet; a serious doctrine of what the practitioner of the visual arts and particularly the architect is and does. Jonson is criticizing not only a man but a theory."[23]

Jonson believed that all *inventio* (the discovery of a subject) belonged exclusively to literary art. As he wrote in the *Discoveries*, "A *Poet* is that, which by the Greeks is call'd . . . a Maker, or a fainer: His Art, an Art of imitation, or faining; expressing the life of man in fit measure and harmony, according to Aristotle." It may be objected that in an earlier passage he quotes with apparent approval Philostratus' remark that "whosoever loves not *Picture*, is injurious to Truth." But even there Jonson is careful to add "and all the wisdome of *Poetry*." Picture may well be "the invention of Heaven," but when Jonson quotes Plutarch he is again quick to distinguish between the powers of the word and of picture: "Poetry, and Picture, are Arts of a like nature; and both are busie about imitation. It was excellently said of Plutarch, Poetry was a speaking Picture, and *Picture* a mute Poesie. For they both invent, faine, and devise many things, and accommodate all they invent to the use, and service of nature. Yet of the two, the Pen is more noble, then the pencil. For that can speake to the Understanding; the other, but to the sense."[24] This refusal to concede the value of even a "poetical portrait" may well have motivated Jonson's remark to Drummond "that Dones Anniversarie was profane and full of Blasphemies" and "that he told Mr. Donne," if it had been written of ye Virgin Marie it had been something."

Following his visit with Drummond in 1618, he wrote a piece called "My Picture Left in Scotland." Whether an actual portrait or drawing prompted this poem is unknown, even considered doubtful. But Jonson makes it clear to his Scottish host that any impression conveyed through language is to be valued far higher than one conveyed through portraiture:

I now thinke, Love is rather deafe, then blind
For else it could not be,
That she,
Whom I adore so much, should so slight me,

And cast my love behind:
I'm sure my language to her, was as sweet
      And every close did meet
   In sentence, as of subtile feet,
      As hath the youngest Hee,
That sits in shadow of Apollo's tree.
   Oh, but my conscious feares,
      That flie my thoughts betweene,
      Tell me that he hath seene
      My hundred of gray haires,
      Told seven and fortie yeares,
   Read so much wast, as she cannot imbrace
      My mountaine belly, and my rockie face,
And all these through her eyes, have stopt her eares.

Though written with a comic lilt, the poem conveys Jonson's view that he will be perfectly satisfied to have conveyed an impression to the ear, and thus through the understanding, rather than one merely to the eye. This attitude may be traced to Jonsonian self-consciousness. In contrast to Donne, who was able to step out of himself and look upon his own portrait with a certain objective fascination, Jonson repeatedly deprecates his appearance, as in the second poem of "A Celebration of Charis in Ten Lyrick Peeces":

So that there, I stood a stone,
Mock'd of all: and call'd of one
(Which with griefe and wrath I heard)
Cupids Statue with a Beard,
Or else one that plaid his Ape,
In a *Hercules*-his shape.

But in this connection, we should consider the poem called "My Answer. The Poet to the Painter," Jonson's reply to "A Poem sent me by Sir William Burlase" (which is subtitled in *The Underwood* "The Painter to the Poet"). Jonson again uses his own physical appearance as the basis for caution about the mendacity of the painted image:

Why? though I seeme of a prodigious wast,
I am not so voluminous, and vast,
But there are lines, wherewith I might b' embraced.

You are he, Jonson tells Burlase, who "can paint." And then he adds emphatically that his own preferred medium is the word:

I can but write:
A Poet hath no more but black and white,
Ne knowes he flatt'ring Colours, or false light.

Colorire, Jonson would agree, is more a rhetorical than a painterly concept. In no other place does he express more emphatically his preference for rhetorical over visual *colorire*. True expression—and he never waivers on this point—is verbal expression.

The true object of Jonson's scorn was *maniera*, or the

styled accomplishments of representational skill that comprise the major development of Renaissance art. Nicholas Hilliard, for example, spoke in conformity with the growing interest in *maniera* when he praised Albrecht Dürer and Paolo Lomazzo for their explanations of "painting perspectiue and foreshortning of lines, with due shadoing acording to the rule of the eye, by falshood to express truth in very cunning of line." [25] And when we contrast his views with Jonson's in *Discoveries*, we recognize how far the poet was from approving of an art that worked its will by *physical* deceptions. In the lines to Burlase, for example, we hear Jonson's sharp rebuttal to the following words of Lomazzo: "No painter or caruer ought in his workes to imitate the proper and naturall proportion of thinges, but the visuall proportion. For (in a word) the eie and the understanding together being directed by the Perspective arte, ought to be a guide, measure and judge of Painting and Caruing." [26] As Jonson made plain in his quarrel with Jones, he could never accept the eye as an equal partner to the understanding. As he wrote in the first of the "Ten Lyrick Peeces" to Charis, it is

The Language and the Truth,
With the Ardor and the Passion,
   and the
      Truth,
With the Ardor and the Passion,
Gives the Lover weight, and fashion.

In the epigram in *The Underwood* addressed "To a Friend, and Sonne," Jonson further asserts the superiority of the pen. After parodying the story told by Pliny of Apelles' painted horses that fooled real horses (*Nat. Hist.* 35.36), he compares visual representation with a species of immoral flattery:

But as a wretched Painter, who so ill
   Painted a Dog, that now his subtler skill
Was, t'have a Boy stand with a Club, and fright
   All live dogs from the lane, and his shops sight,
Till he had sold his Piece, drawne so unlike:
   So doth the flatt'rer, with farre cunning strike
At a Friends freedome, proves all circling meanes
   To keepe him off . . .

And in "To the Author, Thomas Wright," though he grudgingly concedes some of the power ascribed to artists by Hilliard and Lomazzo and Dolce, it is this author's verbal line—his "black and white"—that evokes Jonson's praise:

In Picture, they which truly vnderstand,
   Require (besides the likenesse of the thing)
   Light, Posture, Heightning, Shadow, Culloring,
all which are parts commend the cunning hand;
   And all your Booke (when it is throughly scan'd)
      Will well confesse; presenting, limiting,
      Each subtlest Passion . . .

Jonson's scorn for "the cunning hand" rests on his conviction that true motion or lifelikeness (*energeia*) is verbal and governed by the rules of poetry. By contrast, Paolo Lomazzo declared in his *Tract Containing the Artes of Curious Paintings* that "Perfect knowledge of this *motion* [is] accounted the most difficult part of the art, and reputed as a divine gift: insomuch as herein alone consisteth the comparison betweene *Painting* and *Poetrie*" ("The Second Booke of Actions and Gestures," p. 5).

So sharp is the contrast between Jonson and Lomazzo that some interesting ironies emerge from the fact that one of Jonson's best-known poems takes for its subject a work of visual art. This is the epigram "To the Reader," which accompanied Martin Droeshout's engraved portrait of Shakespeare in the First Folio:

> This Figure, that thou here seest put,
>   It was for gentle Shakespeare cut;
> Wherein the Grauer had a strife
>   With Nature, to out-doo the life:
> O, could he but haue drawne his wit
>   As well in brasse, as he hath hit
> His face; the Print would then surpasse
>   All, that was euer writ in brasse.
> But, since he cannot, Reader, looke
>   Not on his Picture, but his Booke.

At issue in this piece is the question of imitating nature. Specifically, is nature to be identified as what we can see, or is it more appropriate to define it in terms of intellective capacities? The figure before the reader is, for Jonson, simply an artist's fancy, a design, a substitute for the real. Shakespeare's wit is different, for wit is the force behind invention. Proper invention requires only the poet's "black and white"—not the painter's artificial "flatt'ring colours" or the engraver's "false light."

There was one occasion, though, when Jonson carried the poet's challenge directly to a painter—Sir Anthony Van Dyck—who enjoyed unrivalled prominence. The poem is "The Picture of the Body," a piece in *Eupheme* dedicated to the memory "of that Truly-Noble Lady, the Lady Venetia Digby."

> Sitting, and ready to be drawne,
>   What makes these Velvets, Silkes, and Lawne,
> Embroideries, Feathers, Fringes, Lace,
>   Where every lim takes like a face?
>
> Send these suspected helpes, to aide
>   Some Forme defective, or decay'd;
> This beautie without falshood fayre,
>   Needs nought to cloath it but the ayre.
>
> Yet something, to the Painters view,
>   Were fitly interpos'd; so new:
> Hee shall, if he can understand,
>   Worke with my fancie, his owne hand.

> Draw first a Cloud: all save her neck;
>   And, out of that, make Day to breake;
> Till, like her face, it doe appeare,
>   And Men may thinke, all light rose there.
>
> Then let the beames of that, disperse
>   The Cloud, and show the Universe;
> But at such distance, as the eye
>   May rather yet adore, then spy.
>
> The Heaven design'd, draw next a Spring,
>   With all that Youth, or it can bring;
> Foure Rivers branching forth like Seas,
>   And Paradise confining these.
>
> Last, draw the circles of this Globe,
>   And let there be a starry Robe
> Of Constellations 'boute her horld;
>   And thou has painted beauties world.
>
> But, Painter, see thou doe not sell
>   A Copie of this peece; nor tell
> Whose 'tis; but if it favour find,
>   Next sitting we will draw her mind.

Often regarded as an imitation of Anacreon's epigrams offering advice to a painter, "The Picture of the Body" is not considered an original piece. The type has been defined this way:

> In the lyric poem written as a tribute to a lady, the poet, by pretending to give directions for his subject's portrait, delineated her many charms, often imitating the manner and order of the descriptions in the Anacreontic odes from which he drew the "Advice to a Painter" device, describing, in sensuous phrasing, first her hair, and then, in order, her forehead, eyebrows, eyes, nose, cheeks, lips, neck, and body.[27]

The advice motif in Jonson's poem, accordingly, is a borrowing "directly, or indirectly, from the Anacreontea." Many have assumed that Jonson's advising a painter is therefore purely rhetorical. Such a view, however, takes no acount of the circumstances involving portraiture at the time of Venetia's death or of topical similarities between the poem and those circumstances.[28] And it ignores how current theories of portraiture and not merely description of the lady is the subject of Jonson's poem.

Venetia Digby died on May Day, 1633. One of the celebrated beauties of her time, she had married Sir Kenelm (a close friend and patron of Jonson) in 1625 after a long and well-known romantic courtship. Venetia was devoted to her husband, and he to her. And when she died quite unexpectedly, he was so bereaved that he took unusual steps to memorialize her. He had plaster casts made of her face, had her hair cut off to be preserved as a relic, and on the second day of her death had his close friend Sir Anthony Van Dyck paint a death portrait. This picture (a copy of which is in the Dulwich Gallery [fig. 13]) and the circumstances under which it was so

Figure 13. Anonymous copyist, after Sir Anthony Van Dyck, *Lady Venetia Digby on Her Deathbed.* By permission of the Governors of Dulwich College Picture Gallery.

hastily painted contain what I believe to be evidence that Jonson's poem is more than an Anacreontic imitation.

Like Van Dyck, Jonson also had a personal motive for eulogizing the wife of a friend and patron. He was writing, moreover, for a man whose own profound interest in philosophical matters would soon appear in *Two Treatises, in the One of Which, the Nature of Bodies; in the Other, the Nature of Mans Soule, is looked into* (Paris, 1644; London, 1645). Jonson's "The Picture of the Body" rejects painted, physical forms while its sequel, "Her Mind," declares the superiority of the poet. It would seem that "The Picture of the Body" is Jonson's appeal to Sir Kenelm, an appeal intended to offset Van Dyck's painting. The intellectual basis for his quarrel with Inigo Jones lends much support to such a theory.

The first three and the last stanzas frame and therefore dilute the so-called Anacreontic stanzas, stanzas 4 through 7. Certainly, "Sitting, and ready to be drawne" is not itself Anacreontic. The phrase signals nothing more than a conventional sitting in an artist's studio. However, the fact that it was a death portrait gives sig-

nificance to Jonson's pointed reference to—and rejection of—nearby "Velvets, Silkes, and Lawne." These, he says, are merely "suspected helpes." Such props, he adds, would "aide" only some *defective* form. Then Jonson makes a curious qualification: "or decay'd." Is this poem, then, related specifically to the painting made not of a living sitter but one who has just died? A subtly affirmative reply emerges from the poem when the poet says that the beauty the artist has attempted to portray needs "nought to cloath it but the ayre." We could take this line to mean that an uncommonly beautiful sitter should be painted according to the conventional iconography of the Venus *pudica* (see below, fig. 16), which would be consistent with the view that this is but another "painter" poem. But the eighth line confirms our suspicion that the subject of this painting, like those angels which so intrigued Donne ("Aire and Angels"), is now herself a pure form, pure idea, and that her corporeality is now little more than air itself. Logically, because the body is now a form "decay'd," it is poetry and not painting that offers the most appropriate mode for a memorial. After all, what claim can a painter make to capture the motions of a sitter who is dead?

Competing with Van Dyck in the spirit of the *paragone*, but reversing the order of the competition as Leonardo da Vinci had originated it,[29] Jonson asserts his strong, uncompromising views on the superiority of poetry. That this was his purpose all along becomes evident in "The Mind." Now the painter can be dismissed entirely:

> Painter, yo'are come, but may be gone,
>   Now I have better thought thereon,
>   This worke I can performe alone;
>   And give you reasons more then one.

He adds that the artist's hand can hardly be expected to "draw a thing that cannot sit," a reference to the pose given Venetia in the death portrait. Stanzas 1 and 2 of "The Body" may therefore be taken as a description of a once lively and beautiful woman now propped lifelessly with pillows for the painter to copy. Stanza 3 then suggests the need for something "fitly interpos'd." And what occurs in stanzas 4 through 7 is far more substantial than mere rhetorical instructions in imitation of Anacreon. In the first place, Jonson presents none of the particulars we associate with Anacreon's poems. Rather, the images unfold like a vast painted allegory, but it is the poet's invention through words—not the painter's through forms—that takes precedence. And the simple point is that only a verbal unfoldment could ever give the true idea of Venetia—the physical body is now nothing. Only poetry in its language of "black and white" can evoke the truth.

Though Jonson's remarks to Drummond about Donne's *First Anniversarie* reveal no particular sensitivity to the poet's goal of representing a comparable idea, Jonson has set a comparable goal for himself in the commemoration of Venetia Digby. In fact, it is illuminating to compare the "Elegie on my Muse," the final published poem in *Eupheme*, with the *Anniversarie*. Both poems belong to the ritual accommodation that mourners make with death, and both require to be read in the structural context of rites of passage associated with death.[30] Venetia, like Elizabeth Drury, enters heaven immediately with no experience of purgatory. Moreover, both poems read very much like funeral sermons, Donne's however being more impersonal and philosophical and Jonson's more personal and even theological.

Such differences spill over into the further distinctions separating Donne and Jonson. Donne's ready acceptance of the language of visible forms is a vital force behind his creative thought. Jonson, on the other hand, urges his words into ever subtler meanings, eschewing flights of pictorial fancy except to show the painter what cannot be done in oils on canvas. In fact, Jonson's only favorable poem on a work of visual art is an iconographic explication, "The Mind of the Frontispiece to a Booke," a prefatory poem to Sir Walter Raleigh's *History of the World* (1614). As a professional man of letters who had a heavy emotional stake in others' acceptance of his skills with the pen, Jonson would no doubt have felt keenly the threat posed by artists whose medium was canvas and the pencil. In an age of connoisseurs and collectors when visual art commanded increasing attention, Jonson kept his guard against competing forms. What is more, through his ability as a poet, he encouraged his patrons and friends to share and act upon that view.

3. Thomas Carew's "A Rapture" and Lord Herbert's "To his Mistress for her true Picture": Poetic Invention on Pictorial Themes

Diversity of subject seems to be the most constant feature of lyric poetry, a fact acknowledged by J. C. Scaliger in the middle of the sixteenth century. In his *Poetices, Libri Septem*, for example, he identified *lyrica* as the genre appropriate for a variety of things: praises, loves, disputes, things not done, feasts, wishes, and vows—among others. Lyrics, he observed, may narrate brief events, express desires, explain places and times, repudiate suspicions, or present invitations, though most frequently they are about love. In one of his seven books, Scaliger deals with the figures of rhetoric and identifies most as tropes, that is, figures whose effect depends upon some variation away from the ordinary meaning of a word. At the very head of his list is *tractatio*, the description of things so vividly as to place them before the eyes of the hearer or reader, and among the subtypes of this figure he includes *imago* (or *icon*), *similitudo* (or *omoeosis*), and *comparatio* (or *analogia*). From Scaliger—as from critical works by Sidney, Puttenham, and others influenced by him—it is easy to see why so many lyric poems are borderline cases spanning literature and the visual arts. The subjects they treat and their manner of treating them invite such interart cooperation.

During the seventeenth century in England the frequency of such borderline cases increases dramatically. Donne and Jonson with their respective views on the priority of picture set the pace, but this development is due to the visual preoccupations of the baroque—to the interest in both the theory and practice of visual art and to the great number of collectors who, particularly in court circles, came to see themselves as connoisseurs. As Jonson's poetic challenge to Van Dyck suggests, the similarities between portrait painting and poetic praise were not lost upon cultivated persons, many of whom would readily have understood the compatibility of the painted portrait and the Theophrastian and La Bruyerian character sketches that were then becoming fashionable. Such literature sought to be expressive in terms of *enargeia*, what Quintilian had identified as vivid illus-

tration or representation of things.[1] Such a style does not merely state a thing. Rather, it sets it forth as though it were portrayed in color, so that it seems painted rather than narrated. This interest in vivid representation through skilled use of the traditional "colors" of rhetoric explains the creative motivation behind much seventeenth-century lyric poetry. And when we add the goal of *energeia*, which refers to the pleasure-giving features of poetry and the actualization of its potency in the mind, we can understand why Jonson could be confident of the poet's superiority to the painter. For *energeia* (again Quintilian) is the evidence of vigor—of energy—and its function is to assure that nothing one says is tame.

Seventeenth-century English lyric poetry is especially rich in examples of both *enargeia* and *energeia*. Donne placed a high priority on picture, pivoting often from a literal picture to metaphoric use of picture expressing various ontological states. Jonson, despite his suspicion of picture, could never quite extricate himself from its magnetic pull. Their successors could scarcely do less, whether they were followers of the metaphysical Donne or were the Sons of Ben.

Two poems bid for attention here, not because they have traditionally been singled out as representative of the work of either poet. Rather, Thomas Carew's "A Rapture" and Edward, Lord Herbert's "To his Mistress for her true Picture" offer examples of poetic invention which begins with an iconography already established in visual art and develops through *dispositio* and *elocutio* (structure and rhetorical coloration) the kind of clear representation which is the mark of *enargeia*.[2] As a consequence, these two poems offer their readers that vicarious perception of poetic energy which we call *energeia*.

The iconographic foundation of Carew's poem lies in the erotic art of the Renaissance, visual art whose literary counterparts are those numerous poems describing beautiful women (*descriptio puellae*), the love elegies written in imitation of Horace and Catullus and Ovid, and, of course, the often libidinous *epyllia* such as Lodge's *Scylla's Metamorphosis* or Marston's *Metamorphosis of Pygmalion's Image*. Lord Herbert's "To his Mistress for her true Picture" alludes, albeit in a glancing way, to the same tradition, the request for a portrait often providing the basis for an elaborate visual fantasy. But the dominant topos in this poem is not erotic, despite the poet's calculated suggestion to the contrary. Rather, it is the well-known dance of death, popularized in the early sixteenth century by Hans Holbein's famous series and its many imitations and repeated with increasing ingenuity and frequency well into the seventeenth. In fact, the significance of this poem may be said to lie in its evocation of a threshold between eroticism and death, a threshold dramatized in such contemporary stage plays as *The Duchess of Malfi*, *The Revenger's Tragedy*, and *The Changeling*.

Both Lord Herbert and Carew traveled in Europe, Herbert extensively so and Carew to a lesser degree. Herbert's profound contemplative habits and intellectual detachment, unusual in a man so passionately devoted to military action, are abundantly manifest in his unfinished autobiography as well as his *De Veritate*, his *Dialogue between a Tutor and his Pupil*, and his *De Religione Gentilium*. We have every reason to believe that he was familiar with the iconography of death and dying so prominently displayed in tomb sculpture in European churches and equally prominent in paintings executed for individual patrons. On his embassy to Paris in May 1619 Lord Herbert was accompanied by Thomas Carew, who on yet another occasion was affiliated with Sir Dudley Carleton, ambassador from England to Venice. Whether Carew had any particular role in Carleton's well-known art negotiations for himself and for his wealthy patrons is not known, but it is evident from Carew's poetry that like Lord Herbert he found substantial stimulus in art.

Lord Herbert's poetry is often obscure, sometimes even harsh. The dominant topos is the *descriptio puella*, with its obvious parallels to portraiture, which marks the limits of his poetic, though not his intellectual, reach. Many of his poetic portraits are thus expressive in commonplace ways.[3] "A Description," for example, is a Petrarchist comparison of a lady with the cosmos: "The little World the Great shall bless;/ Sea, Earth, her Body; Heaven, her face." However, in his inversions of conventional Petrarchist portraiture Herbert displays the most originality. In such a poem as "To One Blacke, and not very Hansome, who expected comendation" his sense of the ironical and the absurd displaces convention—instead of depending for his meaning on weary stereotypes, he offers a caricature that is fresh if not entirely appealing. "The Green-Sickness of Beauty" is another such poem as are those entitled "Platonic Love," where Herbert's Neoplatonic intellectualism prevents his ever

going to such pictorial excess as did Suckling in "The Deformed Mistress."

Carew, too, wrote poems on less than appealing ladies, though he was evidently more comfortable than Herbert with such standard pictorial conventions as the blazon.[4] "To the Painter" is an *ekphrasis*, and a somewhat conventional one at that. But it does question in a thoughtful way the distinction between art and nature. "To my Friend, G.N. from Wrest" is a verse epistle that skillfully blends *topographia* with emblem. And "For a Picture where a Queen Laments" seems to be about a painting which hung in the Orchard Gallery at Whitehall. It is "yᵉ picture *pijntit opan de lijeht* of a lamenting stooping Woeman wrapt all in white linin Saide to be of Breciano"—that is, Girolomo Muziano, 1528–1592.[5] This poem is one of the very few seventeenth-century *ekphrases* that can be linked with an actual work of art. It is also one of the first examples in English poetry that reads an emotional significance into a work of art, in contrast to the large group of poems (like Jonson's "The Mind of the Frontispiece of a Booke" and the poem on Shakespeare's portrait by Droeshout) that explain the significance of emblematic designs. In "A Rapture," perhaps the most exuberant of all seventeenth-century poems of seduction, Carew relies on visual art and structures his poem according to a sequence of images based on erotic iconography.

> I Will enjoy thee now my *Celia*, come
> And flye with me to Loves Elizium:
> The Gyant, Honour, that keepes cowards out,
> Is but a Masquer, and the servile rout
> Of baser subjects onely, bend in vaine
> To the vast Idoll, whilst the nobler traine
> Of valiant Lovers, daily sayle betweene
> The huge Collosses legs, and passe unseene
> Vnto the blissfull shore; be bold, and wise
> And we shall enter, the grim Swisse denies   10
> Only tame fooles a passage, that not know
> He is but forme, and onely frights in show
> The duller eyes that looke from farre; draw neere,
> And thou shalt scorne, what we were wont to feare,
> We shall see how the stalking Pageant goes
> With borrowed legs, a heavie load to those
> That made, and beare him; not as we once thought
> The seed of Gods, but a weake modell wrought
> By greedy men, that seeke to enclose the common,
> And within private armes empale free woman.   20
>
>   Come then, and mounted on the wings of love
> Wee'le cut the flitting ayre, and sore above
> The Monsters head, and in the noblest seates
> Of those blest shades, quench, and renew our heates.
> There, shall the Queene of Love, and Innocence,
> Beautie and Nature, banish all offence
> From our close Ivy twines, there I'le behold

Thy bared snow, and thy unbraded gold.
There, my enfranchiz'd hand, on every side
Shall o're thy naked polish'd Ivory slide.   30
No curtaine there, though of transparant lawne,
Shall be before thy virgin-treasure drawne;
But the rich Mine, to the enquiring eye
Expos'd, shall ready still for mintage lye,
And we will coyne young *Cupids*. There a bed
Of Roses, and fresh Myrtles, shall be spread
Vnder the cooler shade of Cypresse groves;
Our pillowes of the downe of *Venus* Doves,
Whereon our panting lims wee'le gently lay
In the faint respites of our active play;   40
That so our slumbers, may in dreames have leisure,
To tell the nimble fancie our past pleasure;
And so our soules that cannot be embrac'd,
Shall the embraces of our bodyes taste.
Meane while the bubbling streame shall court the
    shore,
Th' enamoured chirping Wood-quire shall adore
In varied tunes the Deitie of Love;
The gentle blasts of Westerne winds, shall move
The trembling leaves, & through their close bows
    breath
Still Musick, whilst we rest our selves beneath   50
Their dancing shade; till a soft murmure, sent
From soules entranc'd in amorous languishment
Rowze us, and shoot into our veines fresh fire,
Till we, in their sweet extasie expire.
    Then, as the empty Bee, that lately bore,
Into the common treasure, all her store,
Flyes 'bout the painted field with nimble wing,
Deflowering the fresh virgins of the Spring;
So will I rifle all the sweets, that dwell
In my delicious Paradise, and swell   60
My bagge with honey, drawne forth by the power
Of fervent kisses, from each spicie flower.
I'le seize the Rose-buds in their perfum'd bed,
The Violet knots, like curious Mazes spread
O're all the Garden, taste the ripned Cherry,
The warme, firm Apple, tipt with corall berry:
There will I visit, with a wandring kisse,
The vale of Lillies, and the Bower of blisse:
And where the beauteous Region doth divide
Into two milkie wayes, my lips shall slide   70
Downe those smooth Allies, wearing as I goe
A tract for lovers on the printed snow;
Thence climbing o're the swelling *Appenine*,
Retire into thy grove of Eglantine;
Where I will all those ravisht sweets distill
Through Loves Alimbique, and with Chimmique skill
From the mixt masse, one soveraigne Blame derive,
Then bring that great *Elixar* to thy hive.
    Now in more subtile wreathes I will entwine
My sinowie thighes, my legs and armes with thine;   80

Thou like a sea of milke shalt lye display'd,
Whilst I the smooth, calme Ocean, invade
With such a tempest, as when *Jove* of old
Fell downe on *Danae* in a storme of gold:
Yet my tall Pine, shall in the *Cyprian* straight
Ride safe at Anchor, and unlade her fraight:
My Rudder, with thy bold hand, like a tryde,
And skilfull Pilot, thou shalt steere, and guide
My Bark into Loves channell, where it shall
Dance, as the bounding waves doe rise or fall: 90
Then shall thy circling armes, embrace and clip
My willing bodie, and thy balmie lip
Bathe me in juyce of kisses, whose perfume
Like a religious incense shall consume
And send up holy vapours, to those powres
That blesse our loves, and crowne our sportfull houres,
That with such Halcion calmenesse, fix our soules
In steadfast peace, as no affright controules.
There, no rude sounds shake us with sudden starts,
No jealous eares, when we unrip our hearts   100
Sucke our discourse in, no observing spies
This blush, that glance traduce; no envious eyes
Watch our close meetings, nor are we betrayd
To Rivals, by the bribed chamber-maid.
No wedlock bonds unwreathe our twisted loves;
We seeke no midnight Arbor, no darke groves
To hide our kisses, there, the hated name
Of husband, wife, lust, modest, chaste, or shame,
Are vaine and empty words, whose very sound
Was never heard in the Elizian ground.   110
All things are lawfull there, that may delight
Nature, or unrestrained Appetite;
Like, and enjoy, to will, and act, is one
We only sinne when Loves rites are not done.
    The Roman *Lucrece* there, reades the divine
Lectures of Loves great master, *Aretine*,
And knowes as well as *Lais*, how to move
Her plyant body in the act of love.
To quench the burning Ravisher, she hurles
Her limbs into a thousand winding curles,   120
And studies artfull postures, such as be
Caru'd on the barke of every neighbouring tree
By learned hands, that so adorn'd the rinde
Of those faire Plants, which as they lay entwinde,
Have fann'd their glowing fires. The Grecian Dame,
That in her endlesse webb, toyl'd for a name
As fruitlesse as her worke, doth there display
Her selfe before the Youth of *Ithaca*,
And th' amorous sport of gamesome nights prefer,
Before dull dreames of the lost Traveller.   130
Daphne hath broke her barke, and that swift foot,
Which th' angry Gods had fastned with a root
To the fixt earth, doth now unfetter'd run,
To meet th' embraces of the youthfull Sun:
She hangs upon him, like his Delphique Lyre,

Her kisses blow the old, and breath new fire:
Full of her God, she sings inspired Layes,
Sweet Odes of love, such as deserve the Bayes,
Which she her selfe was. Next her, *Laura* lyes
In *Petrarchs* learned armes, drying those eyes   140
That did in such sweet smooth-pac'd numbers flow,
As made the world enamour'd of his woe.
These, and ten thousand Beauties more, that dy'de
Slave to the Tyrant, now enlarg'd, deride
His cancell'd lawes, and for their time mispent,
Pay into Loves Exchequer double rent.

   Come then my *Celia*, wee'le no more forbeare
To taste our joyes, struck with a Pannique feare,
But will depose from his imperious sway
This proud *Vsurper* and walke free, as they   150
With necks unyoak'd; nor is it just that Hee
Should fetter your soft sex with Chastitie,
Which Nature made unapt for abstinence;
When yet this false Impostor can dispence
With humane Justice, and with sacred right,
And maugre both their lawes command me fight
With Rivals, or with emulous Loves, that dare
Equall with thine, their Mistresse eyes, or haire:
If thou complaine of wrong, and call my sword
To carve out thy revenge, upon that word   160
He bids me fight and kill, or else he brands
With markes of infamie my coward hands,
And yet religion bids from blood-shed flye,
And damns me for that Act. Then tell me why
This Goblin Honour which the world adores,
Should make men Atheists, and not women Whores.

Each of the six parts of the poem presents a stage in the speaker's unfolding efforts to seduce his Celia. Of course, the name given the lady would be sufficient to establish the poem's generic dependency upon similar pieces by Horace, Ovid, and Catullus and Donne and Jonson; that is, literary and not pictorial conventions set the reader's expectations. Nevertheless, the lover makes a clever appeal to Celia through a number of pictorial types. If she will but fly with him to "Loves Elizium" and sail defiantly between the very legs of that collusus Honour, they can escape the formalities of behavior that so effectively inhibit sexual expression. Indeed, personal expressiveness is the very basis of the lover's appeal to Celia. And to invest expression with substance, he offers in the place of social "forme" a persuasive succession of pictorial forms whose vitality and capacity to move emotions is their own justification. Honor remains behind as but "a weake modell," devised by selfish men who "seeke to enclose the common, / And within private armes empale free woman." By contrast, the speaker promises not pleasure alone but amplitude and freedom.

The image he offers of this Elizium is based on the conventional garden of love, a topos depicted in a draw-ing by Peter Paul Rubens (fig. 14) and expressed not long before by Spenser in his Bower of Bliss. Carew's lover, though, is far more a Cymochles than a Guyon. For he promises his lady that once among those "blest shades" they will both "quench, and renew [their] heates"—a promise of dalliance no less exuberant than that expressed in a drawing by Giulio Romano on the theme of *Hylas and the Nymphs* (fig. 15), which expresses through myth the dream of sexual freedom with an emphasis on feminine arousal that is entirely compatible with the goal of Carew's speaker. This drawing (actually copied at one time by Rubens and engraved on several occasions by other artists) is simply one among many depictions of the garden of love motif that were readily available during Carew's time in popular prints. And it is the expressive character of such visual images that links them to Carew's verbal expression. Where paintings, prints, and drawings of the garden of love express the idea of passion at a glance, the poet now employs rhetorical *colorire* to recreate the iconography. The rationale behind such an invention had been enunciated long before by Quintilian, who had observed the effectiveness of gesture in oratory, saying that it was very much like the silent gestures in painting which could so effectively penetrate the hearts of viewers (*Inst. orat.* 11.3.67). *Enargeia* in such cases would be a direct cause of *energeia*, a sense of shared vitality. In Carew's poem, then, the lover's promise of a very special kind of freedom depends for its persuasive effect upon an existing typology familiar alike to speaker, hearer, and reader.

His argument in part 2 turns to a suggestive description of the lady's own body, a description that has literary connections to the blazon but equally enjoys ties to one of the most popular mythological subjects of painters—the depictions of Venus. In the painting by Josef Heintz (fig. 16), for example, Venus exhibits precisely the charms anticipated by the anxious lover in this poem: a wide expanse of beautiful white skin and a profusion of golden hair. No less than the garden of love, this painting belongs to the speaker's gallery of persuasive pictures of Venus (with Mars, with Adonis, with Cupid), of Susanna (sometimes with, sometimes without the Elders),[6] and of any number of other subjects drawn from both profane and sacred sources. Similarly, the tactile effects given in lines 29 and 30 are a common motif in erotic art and are expressed most vividly in Bartolomäus Spranger's highly mannerist *Vulcan and Maia* (fig. 17). And yet it is the image of the bower itself—the cool shades of cypress, the bubbling spring, and the trembling leaves—that exerts the most persuasive appeal in the speaker's arsenal of seductive images.

The third section continues the metamorphosis of the garden of love into the body of the lady herself. Now comparing himself to a bee moving voluptuously about a "painted field," the lover delcares his intent to "rifle all the sweets" in his new-found paradise. He will dip, first,

Figure 14. Christopher Jegher, after a drawing by Peter Paul
Rubens, *The Garden of Love.* Copyright Museum Plantin-
Moretus, Antwerp.

Figure 15. Giulio Romano, *Hylas and the Nymphs.* Courtesy
of Graphische Sammlung Albertina, Vienna.

Figure 16. Josef Heintz, *Sleeping Venus.* Courtesy of Kunsthistorische Museum, Vienna.

to the rosebuds of his mistress' cheeks. He will trace the delicate blue veins on her body, which are now become "curious Mazes spread / O're all the Garden." He will taste the "ripned Cherry" of her lips. And he will linger upon her breasts, the "firm Apple, tipt with corall berry." Her belly is the Apennine way, encouraging further travel, and the passage culminates in a "grove of Eglantine," a microcosm of the garden of love itself. This metamorphosis of the garden into the body concludes with alchemical images which affirm the mystique of the transformation imagined in the foregoing lines.

The tactile expressiveness becomes still more intense in the fourth section, where this transformation of garden into body permits the lover to speak of entwining himself with his mistress in "subtile wreathes." What follows is evidently a verbal gloss on some of the world's best-known prints, the "poses" designed by Giulio Romano to accompany Aretino's *I sonetti lusuriosi.*[7] Can the lovers' "subtile wreathes" be less than an allusion to one of the more contorted and mannerist of the designs (fig. 18)? Further, can the metaphor of the ship being guided into "Loves channell" by the hand of a skilled pilot be anything but a direct reference to the image drawn for another of the sonnets (fig. 19)? Carew's undisguised reference to Aretino in part 5, lines 115-118, justifies affirmative answers. And when we read in line 121 that even the chaste Lucrece "studies artfull postures," the evidence becomes irresistible. The powerful

Figure 17. Bartolomäus Spranger, *Vulcan and Maia.* Courtesy of Kunsthistorische Museum, Vienna.

Figure 18. Friedrich von Waldeck, lithograph, after an engraving by Marcantonio Raimondi of a design by Giulio Romano. Reproduced by Courtesy of the Trustees of the British Museum.

Figure 19. Friedrich von Waldeck, lithograph, after an engraving by Marcantonio Raimondi of a design by Giulio Romano. Reproduced by Courtesy of the Trustees of the British Museum.

eroticism of these lines takes for granted the reader's familiarity with prints and drawings by Giulio Romano, Agostino Carraci, and others whose scarcity today is no indication of their unfamiliarity then.[8] Part 5 then reaffirms the power of erotic pictorialism by declaring how other women famous for their chastity also learn from Aretino's models. Even Petrarch's Laura renounces the tyrant Honour under the persuasive guidance of such pictures, paying "double rent" into "Loves Exchequer."

The poem concludes with the suggestion that Celia, no less than her lover, must now yearn for the absolute freedom of love. Such a conclusion amounts to the total rejection of a stereotype expressed with some humor in an engraving after Primaticcio (fig. 20), an artist whose works encouraged numerous popular engravings. In it, two women bear on their shoulders a reluctant third, who is about to be ravished by a libidinous satyr. The woman is a victim, one who struggles to preserve her honor, who resists libido with all her might. Carew's poem expresses the opposite view, depicted in the companion piece to this engraving (fig. 21). Now it is the satyr who resists the aggressive desires of the libidinous woman, and it is she who expresses the uninhibited state to which the lover in the poem urges his Celia.

The link between the poem and the body of visual images to which it constantly refers is a theoretical point that occurs frequently in Renaissance discussions of art and poetry. As far back as Alberti's *Della Pittura* (1435), the parallels between visual and verbal art were defined in rhetorical terms. Where the first step for Cicero's orator, for example, was *inventio*, Alberti identified invention as the initial step for the painter as well.[9] Affective gesture is as much a factor in Alberti's notion

of art as it is in Cicero's theory of rhetoric. A hundred years later Lodovico Dolce bluntly affirmed that "writers are painters, [and] that poetry is painting, history is painting, and . . . any kind of composition by a man of culture is painting." Taking his cue from Plutarch's version of Simonides' remark that the painter is but a mute poet, Dolce testifies to the conformity between painter and writer, stressing that art begins with invention, whose constituents are order and propriety—"a great necessity for writers as well—so much so, that without it they are incapable of producing anything perfect."[10] He turns next to disposition or organization and then to design, and in each case extends the comparison of the painter to the poet. By the third decade of the seventeenth century in England, the comparison of the painter to the poet had become commonplace. And in no book is the commonplace more extensively argued than in Franciscus Junius' *The Painting of the Ancients* (London, 1638), a systematic survey of rhetorical and art criticism from the ancients to its own time.

"Painters," says Junius, "do express with colours what Writers doe describe with words; so is it that they doe but differ in the matter and manner of Imitation, having both the same end." Both, he continues, "doe wind themselves by an unsensible delight of admiration so closely into our hearts, that they make us in such an astonishment of wonder to stare upon the Imitation of things naturall, as if we saw the true things themselves" (p. 54). Moreover, "both doe hold the rains of our hearts, leading and guiding our Passions by that beguiling power they have, whithersoever they list" (p. 55). And quoting Quintilian, he explains that picture "is a silent worke, and constantly keeping the same forme, doth so insinuate itselfe into our most inward affections,

Figure 20. Master L.D. (School of Fontainebleau), after Primaticcio, *Femme portée vers un satyre*. Courtesy of Musée Condé de Chantilly, Photographie Lauros-Giraudon.

that it seemeth now and then to be of greater force then Eloquence itselfe" (p. 56). Junius, naturally, would have found such a piece as Carew's distasteful. But his ready assimilation of painterly and poetic concerns explains fully the grounds upon which Carew pursued his poetic invention in pictorial terms.

"A Rapture" then, develops out of the figure *imago* (*icon*), defined in *Ad Herennium* as the comparison of one form or figure or attitude with another, implying a certain resemblance between them. The figure works because the poet can transfer to his reader some of the responsibility for such connections by assuming the reader's familiarity with the iconography of eroticism. Here George Puttenham's more exact description of the figure is useful. In *The Arte of English Poesie* he defines icon as a scheme, saying, "When we liken an humane. person to another in countenance . . . it is not called bare resemblance, but resemblance by imagerie or pourtrait, alluding to the painters terms, who yeldeth to th' eye a visible representation of the thing he described and painteth in his table."[11] In "A Rapture" Carew invites his readers to supply pictorial vividness from their own store of visual types, keys to which are offered liberally in the poem. Thus, not only does the poet's invention depend upon an established typology, but our recreation of the poem in our own minds depends upon our capacity to "read" the *similitudo* and to supply the required visual amplification. Without this foundation in the Renaissance theory that visual art supports the work of the poet, the narration and the persuasive endeavors of the speaker in this poem would lack the vigor that is requisite for *energeia*.

The association of eroticism and death has a long history in Western art and literature, but Lord Herbert brings the two together in a highly original manner in "To his Mistress for her true Picture." Like Carew's poem, this one too depends upon the reader's familiarity with a preexisting topos.

Death, my lifes Mistress, and the soveraign Queen
Of all that ever breath'd, though yet unseen,
My heart doth love you best, yet I confess,
Your picture I beheld, which doth express
No such eye-taking beauty, you seem lean,
Unless you'r mended since. Sure he did mean
No honour to you, that did draw you so;
Therefore I think it false: Besides, I know
The picture, Nature drew, (which sure's the best)
Doth figure you by sleep and sweetest rest: 10
Sleep, nurse of our life, care's best reposer,
Natures high'st rapture, and the vision giver:
Sleep, which when it doth seize us, souls go play,
And make Man equal as he was first day.
Yet some will say, Can pictures have more life
Then the original? To end this strife,
Sweet Mistress come, and shew your self to me,
In your true form, while then I think to see
Some beauty Angelick, that comes t'unlock
My bodies prison, and from life unyoke   20
My well divorced soul, and set it free,
To liberty eternal: Thus you see,
I find the Painters error, and protect
Your absent beauties, ill drawn, by th' effect:
For grant it were your work, and not the Graves,
Draw Love by Madness, then, Tyrants by Slaves,
Because they make men such. Dear Mistress, then
If you would not be seen by owl-ey'd Men,
Appear at noon i'th' Air, with so much light,
The sun may be a Moon, the Day a Night,   30
Clear to my Soul, but dark'ning the weak sense
Of those, the other Worlds Cimmeriens,
And in your fatal Robe, imbroidered
With Starr-characters, teaching me to read
The destiny of Mortals, while your clear brow
Presents a Majesty, to instruct me how
To love or dread nought else: May your bright hair,
Which are the threds of life, fair crown'd appear
With that your Crown of Immortality:
In your right hand the Keyes of Heaven be;   40
In th' other those of the Infernal Pit,
Whence none retires, if once he enter it.
And here let me complain, how few are those
Whose souls you shall from earth's vast dungeon lose
To endless happiness! few that attend
You, the true Guide, unto their journeys end:
And if of old Vertue's way narrow were,
'Tis rugged now, having no passenger.
Our life is but a dark and stormy night,
To which sense yields a weak and glimmering light; 50
While wandring Man thinks he discerneth all,
By that which makes him but mistake and fall:
He sees enough, who doth his darkess see;
These are great lights, by which less darkned be.
Shine then Sun-brighter through my senses vail,
A day-star of the light doth never fail;

Shew me that Goodness which compounds the strife
'Twixt a long sickness and a weary life.
Set forth that Justice which keeps all in aw,
Certain and equal more then any Law.   60
Figure that happy and eternal Rest,
Which till Man do enjoy, he is not blest.
Come and appear then, dear Soul-ravisher,
Heavens-light-Usher, Man's deliverer,
And do not think when I new beauties see,
They can withdraw my settled love from thee.
Flesh-beauty strikes me not at all, I know,
When thou do'st leave them to the grave, they show
Worse, then they now show thee: they shal not move
In me the least part of delight, or love   70
But as they teach your power: Be she nut-brown,
The lovliest colour which the flesh doth crown:
I'll think her like a Nut, a fair outside,
Within which Worms and rottenness abide:
If fair, then like the Worm it self to be;
If painted, like their slime and sluttery.
If any yet will think their beauties best,
And will, against you, spite of all, contest,
Seize them with Age: so in themselves they'l hate
What they scorn'd in your picture, and too late   80
See their fault, and the Painters: Yet if this,
Which their great'st plague and wrinkled torture is,
Please not, you may to the more wicked sort,
Or such as of your praises make a sport,
Denounce an open warr, send chosen bands
Of Worms, your souldiers, to their fairest hands,
And make them lep'rous-scabb'd: upon their face
Let those your Pioners, Ring-worms, take their place,
And safely hear with strong approaches got
Intrench it round, while their teeths rampire rot   90
With other Worms, may with a damp inbred
Stink to their senses, which they shall not dead:
And thus may all that e'r they prided in,
Confound them now: As for the parts within,
Send Gut-worms, which may undermine a way
Unto their vital parts, and so display
That your pale Ensign on the walls: then let
Those Worms, your Veteranes, which never yet
Did fail, enter *Pel mel*, and ransack all,
Just as they see the well-rais'd building fall: 100
While they do this, your Forragers command,
The Caterpillars, to devour their land;
And with them Wasps, your wing'd-worm-horsement,
    bring,
To charge, in troop, those Rebels, with their sting:
All this, unless your beauty they confess.

And now, sweet Mistress, let m'a while digress,
T'admire these noble Worms, whom I invoke,
And not the Muses: You that eat through Oak
And bark, will you spare Paper, and my Verse,
Because your praises they do here reherse?   110

Figure 21. Master L.D. (School of Fontainebleau), after Primaticcio, *Satyre porté vers une femme.* Courtesy of Musée Condé de Chantilly, Photographie Lauros-Giraudon.

Brave Legions then, sprung from the mighty race
Of Man corrupted, and which hold the place
Of his undoubted Issue; you that are
Brain-born, *Minerva*-like, and like her warr,
Well-arm'd compleat-maile-jointed Souldiers,
Whose force *Herculean* links in pieces tears;
To you the vengeance of all spill-bloods falls,
Beast-eating Men, Men-eating Cannibals.
Death-priviledg'd, were you in sunder smit
You do not lose your life, but double it: 120
Best framed types of the immortal Soul,
Which in your selves, and in each part are whole:
Last-living Creatures, heirs of all the earth,
For when all men are dead, it is your birth:
When you dy, your brave self-kill'd Generall
(For nothing else can kill him) doth end all.
What vermine-breeding body then thinks scorn,
His flesh should be by your brave fury torn?

Willing, to you, this Carkass I submit,
A gift so free, I do not care for it: 130
Which yet you shall not take, untill I see
My Mistress first reveal her self to me.

Mean while, Great Mistress, whom my soul admires,
Grant me your true picture, who desires,
That he your matchless beauty might maintain
'Gainst all men that will quarrels entertain
For a Flesh-Mistress; the worst I can do,
Is but to keep the way that leads to you,
And howsoever the event doth prove,
To have Revenge below, Reward above;   140
Hear, from my bodies prison, this my Call,
Who from my mouth-grate, and eye-window bawl.

The lover's request for his mistress' portrait forges an immediate link with that genre of painting considered by many in the Renaissance to be one of the most expressive of human nature. A true as opposed to a false portrait would thus be one where a transcendent reality displaces mere appearance, one that exhibits things only the painter can detect and mediate for others through art. A true portrait, then, is one that is above all expressive of its subject; mere replication of a facial image will never do. As Nicholas Hilliard said in his *Arte of Limning*, an artist undertakes to represent the motions—to "catch those louely graces, witty smilings, and those stolne glances which suddainely like lighting passe and another countenance taketh place except hee behould, and very well noate and conceit to lyke."[12] This is why Hilliard advises the painter to "be in hart wisse" and, as well, to be "amorous." Since the limner is to a great extent a purveyor of love tokens, he must be sensitive to the feelings of love and must know firsthand the longing which his portrait is designed to satisfy.[13]

The yearning and longing attitude of the lover is the dominant expressive mode of Herbert's poem. But the originality of the piece rests in the poet's substitution of Mistress Death for the more conventional Celia. This particularization of death succeeds because the poet's prosopopoeia endows death with tangible presence and

Figure 22. Hans Baldung Grien, *The Three Ages of Woman.* Courtesy of Kunsthistorische Museum, Vienna.

a character: death is expressed in terms of motion which lends it *enargeia.* Here poetry demonstrates capacities less easy to achieve in the medium of picture, which usually tends to the universal rather than the particular. For example, one may experience revulsion, even fear, as one ponders the implication of Holbein's series of woodcuts or any of the conventional images that belong to the typology of death. But one does not find in the conventional representations of the dance of death a personal point of view. Death, pictured only as a skeletal form and lacking the usual marks of personal identification, visits the plowman as readily as he dances within the hollow crown of the king. The first seven lines of Herbert's poem establish a rhetorical and verbally designated perspective and contrast this point of view with the conventional iconography of death, which the speaker declares must be misleading. If these well-known images derived by artists to express the fact of death are false, he declares, then it must be Nature who offers the proper image: "Besides, I know / The picture, Nature drew, (which sure's the best) / Doth figure by sleep and sweetest rest." The competition between art and nature—a familiar one in both visual art and literature—resolves immediately into a comparison of their respective abilities to image death: on the one hand the iconography of the famous dance, on the other the motif of the sleeping beauty.

Here our previous experience with Van Dyck's strange, perhaps even a bit unnerving, death portrait of Venetia Digby and with Josef Heintz's *Sleeping Venus* can help us to appreciate the ambiguity expressed in these two "natural" images invoked by the poet. To speak of the sleep of death permits one to harbor the notion of death as but a peaceful continuation of life's beauties. And here the respective iconographies of eroticism and death overlap.

In Holbein's, as in most other representations of death, there is no provision for the idea of gender. Death is as neuter as it is impersonal. Herbert, though, addresses death as a woman, invoking thereby another prominent image in the iconography—the ages of man and the ages of woman. In the latter, as in the painting by Hans Baldung Grien (fig. 22), the progression of the ages culminates in death after having passed through the stage of beauty associated with youth. In this painting, the mature woman on the left tries in vain to turn the mirror into which the younger woman gazes with apparent narcissistic pleasure at her own erotic appeal, but youth refuses to heed the spectral presence of death even when it is just over her shoulder. From the ages of man and woman it was but a short step to visual depictions of death as a woman, as the engraving by Gerhardt Altzenbach (fig. 23) reveals. Herbert's literary invention of female death, then, had ample precedent.

In the poem, the speaker declares however that the "Painters error" has been to depict Death by its effects.

The traditional skeletal form is an ill-conceived image because it depicts only the effects of the grave, not the actual mystery of death—the threshold of an irreversible passage. Better, Herbert declares, to "Draw Love by Madness" or "Tyrants by Slaves," invoking thereby the rhetorical coloration of metonymy. The poet then images Death in a robe embroidered with star characters, an invention that undoubtedly owes something to Cesare Ripa, whose *Iconologia* (1603) suggests that Death wears a robe, though not one decorated with stars. Ripa also writes of the crown of immortality worn by Death, a prominent feature of Herbert's description in line 39. The majestic image in lines 40–42, where Death holds in its right hand "the Keyes of Heaven" and in its left "those of the Infernal Pit," seems also to be indebted to Justus Sadeler's *Speculum Vitae Humanae*, where Death stands upon a landscape pointing up to heaven with its right hand, and with its left pointing toward hell.

By giving Death the role of a "true Guide," Herbert invokes one of the most prominent of all depictions of the way of life motif: the *Tabula Cebetis* mentioned in chapter 2, where the passage from life to death is imaged in topographical terms. In it, to win a glimpse of Truth in defiance of what Donne in his third satire called "the hill's suddenness," to strive so (again in Donne's words) "that before an age, death's twilight," one's soul might rest, "for none can work in that night," suggests in its awfulness the need for a guide. And in contrast to Donne, Herbert casts Death in precisely that benign role. Thus, when the speaker in Herbert's poem asks Death to show him "that Goodness which compounds the strife," to "Set forth that Justice which keeps all in aw," and to "Figure that happy and eternal Rest," his requests suggest that Death accompanies one in each of the stages of life represented in the various levels of the *Table*.

In line 71 he returns to portraiture, both visual and literary, speculating that Death is surely a nut-brown maiden, a variation on the literary theme of the brown beauty. But in a surreal fashion, the erotic suggestiveness momentarily conveyed by this allusion to idealized portraits and their real-life models yields to the speculation that Death is "like a Nut, a fair outside / Within which Worms and rottenness abide." Death, then, is not after all the consequence of decay; it is the condition of decay itself. Thus the skeletal form depicted by the painters misses the point, and it is up to the poet to create the proper portrait through words. The passage devoted to worms (ll. 81–105) is gruesome and perhaps more distasteful to modern readers than it was to Herbert's contemporaries. We, however, lack exposure to the iconographical tradition in which tomb sculpture often depicted worms destroying the body and in which painters such as Matthias Grünewald made a moral point by depicting *The Damnation of Lovers* (fig. 24). And as an anonymous poem from an unpublished early seven-

Figure 23. Gerhardt Altzenbach, engraver, *Death as a Woman.* Courtesy of Humanities Research Center, The University of Texas at Austin.

teenth-century manuscript makes plain, there was also a literary complement to the pictorial grounds for Herbert's invention.[14] He is again startling, though, in his witty metamorphosis of those very worms into the Muses (l. 108), and in his amplification of the point through the affirmation that these "Brave Legions" are "sprung from the mighty race / Of Man corrupted."

In this poem, invention, structure, and rhetorical coloration all depend upon motifs and themes conventionally expressed in visual art. At the level of *inventio*, acknowledged by poets and painters alike in the Renaissance to be the ground for what post-Romantics call creativity or genius, Herbert's poem has obvious roots in visual iconography. Clearly, the poet assumes his reader's familiarity with the iconography of death man-

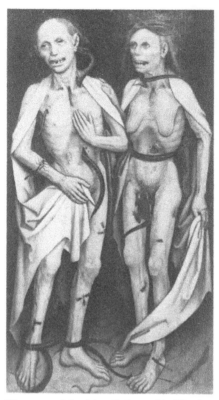

Figure 24. Matthias Grünewald, *The Damnation of Lovers.* Courtesy of Musée de Strasbourg.

Figure 25. William Simpson, engraver, "O wretched Man that I am," from Francis Quarles, *Emblemes* (1635). Courtesy of Humanities Research Center, The University of Texas at Austin.

ifest in the traditional danse macabre; without it the speaker's motives in the poem would surely be obscure. Structurally, the development of the poem (what the painters termed *dispositio*) emerges from the speaker's efforts to redefine the role and image of Death, a redefinition that would likewise lose point were a reader unfamiliar with the theoretical goals of portraiture and with the persuasive uses of portraits in the social arts of lovemaking. It is by means of this *dispositio* or rhetorical arrangement that the speaker creates an intimate, personal vision of Death as the Great Mistress. For through the rhetorical coloration—the persuasive design of the poem—he effects a link between the evocative power of the word and the illusory quality of the painter's *colorire*. And throughout the poem there is an intimate and profoundly ironic relation between speaking and exhibiting. Indeed, in the final ten lines the visual and vocal functions blend in an uncanny and witty way that fully internalizes and personifies the otherwise universal and impersonal image of death.

The dominant image in these last ten lines is one made famous by Francis Quarles in his *Emblemes* (1635) (fig. 25), which depicts the body as a cage from which the imprisoned soul aspires to escape. Vowing now in chivalric fashion to defend the honor of his new-found mistress " 'Gainst all men that will quarrels entertain / For a Flesh-Mistress," Herbert's speaker obliquely anticipates his own death and declares that his "Call" for his Mistress' true portrait emanates from within his "bodies prison," from "my mouth-grate and eye-window." In this startling turn of wit, the speaker affiliates himself with the very same skeletal representation of Death that he had earlier rejected. Now, however, he has himself become the very icon of death, speaking all the foregoing words from deep within his own condition of mortality. Pictorially, the image of death emerges in an altogether new and different perspective. For where it was formerly an image viewed objectively in the manner of the danse macabre, it is now seen subjectively as the condition of the speaker himself.

Without preexisting pictorial themes, it is doubtful whether this poem or the one by Carew would have been written. Each develops out of an invention grounded in pictorial themes. Each is structured according to a specific alignment of visual types, the word becoming the vehicle for a creative and imaginative use of those types. Neither has become prominent in the critical discussion. But when each is placed in its appropriate visual tradition, it emerges from the interart comparison with a new vitality that strictly literary approaches to poetry are ill equipped to explain.

4. Richard Crashaw: The "Holy Strife" of Pencil and Pen

The reader who in 1646 took up a copy of Richard Crashaw's *Steps to the Temple* would have discovered upon turning the title page a preface written by one identified only as "The Author's Friend." Had curiosity led him to read beyond the salutation to the "Learned Reader," he would have found the opinion that the poet whose works were before him was no less than "Herbert's second, but equall," a poet "who hath retrieved Poetry of late, and return'd it up to its Primitive use." These poems, the preface adds, are "Steppes for happy soules to climbe heaven by."

The poet was "excellent in five Languages (besides his mother tongue)." And "amongst his other accomplishments in Accademick (as well pious as harmlesse arts) hee made his skill in Poetry, Musicke, Drawing, Limming, graving (exercises of his curious invention and sudden fancy) to bee but his subservient recreations for vacant houres, not the grand businesse of his soule." Of the prominent poets who followed Donne and Jonson and preceded Milton and Dryden, Richard Crashaw alone seems to have had a significant double (if not a triple) talent, in addition to his substantial learning. Thomas Flatman, one of the best miniature painters of his time, would eventually publish his *Poems and Songs* in 1674. But during the earlier decades of the century, Richard Crashaw stands alone in his ability to express himself in picture and music as well as through the word.

Surprisingly little has been said about Crashaw in relation to this double talent. Though there have been general comments about his indebtedness to emblems and impresas, there have been few specific discussions of the way pictorial ideas and structures affect his poetic performance. Ruth Wallerstein, for example, located Crashaw's unique capacity for visual expressiveness in the tradition of emblem and impresa, saying that "with him the images, however they begin in mere rhetoric, become the thought; and to study the process by which they are filled and given meaning is to study the growth of his spirit." Pictures, she says, were the means by which Crashaw ordered sensations and emotions in relation to each other, "apart from mere random fancy or fragmentary ecstasy."[1] Austin Warren found in Crashaw's poetry the same energetic spirit that he found in "the painting of Coreggio, El Greco, Rembrandt, Rubens, Guido Reni, and the Carracci, in the sculptures of Bernini [and] in the emblem books of the Jesuits and Benedictines."[2] But it was not until Louis Martz identified a direct relation between *The Flaming Heart* and Gerhard Seghers' *The Piercing of St. Theresa's Heart* (fig. 26) that anyone made specific connections between a poem of Crashaw's and a work of visual art.[3]

Crashaw's known work as a painter is still largely unexplored. In the account book of St. John's College, Cambridge, there occurs the following entry: "Given by the M^r of Seniors appoint to Sr Crashaw of Pembroke Hall for drawing three pictures in the booke of Benefactors to the Library July 11, 1625, xiij^l vj^s viij^d.[4] These pictures, each about twelve inches by nine inches, are still to be found in the *Liber memorialis* of St. John's College. One is a portrait of King Charles (fig. 27), another is of Archbishop Williams (fig. 28), and the third is of Lady Margaret (fig. 29). Together they indicate that Crashaw, though hardly a Nicholas Hilliard or an Isaac Oliver, was a competent draftsman and a reasonably good interpreter of individual facial appearances. The design, color, and execution of these portraits, even if we allow for the remote possibility that they were copied from existing portraits, show more than an amateur's skill. The figures are all placed in believable and expressive poses, the relationships between bodily form and the picture plane being in each case compatible with the rules of verisimilitude. Though indications of rank and status are evident, especially in the portraits of the king and the archbishop, the painter has not relied upon institutional identities for his effects. The faces "speak," especially that of Lady Margaret, whose wrinkled complexion shows her age to be a mark of honor.

We are fortunate, too, to be able to see the vivid color in these paintings in addition to the evidence they give of Crashaw's sense of design. Color, as we have already

Figure 26. Gerhard Seghers, *The Piercing of St. Theresa's Heart.* Courtesy of Koninklijk Museum voor Schone Kunsten/Musée Royal des Beaux-Arts, Antwerp.

Figure 27. Richard Crashaw, *King Charles.* Courtesy of the Masters and Fellows of St. John's College, Cambridge.

seen in connection with Donne's poems, is a major concern of any artist, and it is also (after design) the technical point on which the artist stands or falls. Not only is coloring a dominant topic in all the treatises on art that were beginning to emerge during the first half of the century,[5] but artists were individually responsible for making their own colors through mixing, grinding, blending, and so forth. Dolce, for example, states that "one needs to keep one's eye fixed on the tones, primarily those of the flesh areas, and on softness. For many artists render some of these areas so that they seem made of porphyry, both in color and hardness; their shadows are too harsh and most often end in pure black. Many make the same areas too white, and many too red." In addition, "one needs to know how to imitate the color of draperies, silk, gold, and every kind of material so well that the hardness or softness seems to be communicated to the greater or lesser degree which suits the quality of the material."[6] When such criteria are applied to the coloration in Crashaw's portraits, one perceives that in addition to his understanding of *disegno* he also possessed ample technique as a colorist. Both flesh tones

and the textures of cloth are rendered convincingly.

Finally, Crashaw shows considerable sensitivity to physiognomy. The features of his sitters are not formulaic, they are individual. And from this we may infer that he knew something about the kinds of things Nicholas Hilliard had to say about facial details. "The eye," he said, "showeth most life, and nosse the most fauor, and the mouth the most liknes, although liknes is contained in euery part, euen in euery feature, and in the cheekes, chinne, and forhead, with the compasse of the face, but yet cheefly in the mouth."[7] Complexion, proportion, and countenance are those features that contribute to what he calls "fauor." "But the goodnes of picture after the life," he reiterates, "standeth cheefly vppon three points

1 Life		Eye
2 Fauor	which cheefly consist in	Nose
3 Liknes	these three features	Mouth."

The Delights of the Muses, like *Steps to the Temple* also published in 1646, contains the intriguing poem "With a Picture sent to a Friend."[8] This poem offers the

Figure 28. Richard Crashaw, *Archbishop Williams*. Courtesy of the Masters and Fellows of St. John's College, Cambridge.

Figure 29. Richard Crashaw, *Lady Margaret*. Courtesy of the Masters and Fellows of St. John's College, Cambridge.

only evidence from the poet-painter himself that on at least one occasion he composed a self-portrait:

> I paint so ill, my peece had need to bee
> Painted againe by some good Poesie.
> I write so ill, my slender Line is scarce
> So much as th' Picture of a well-lim'd verse:
> Yet may the love I send be true, though I
> Send nor true Picture, nor true Poesie.
> Both which away, I should not need to feare,
> My Love, or *Feign'd* or *painted* should appeare.

And aside from its factual interest, the poem suggests that at the time of composition Crashaw seems to have placed an equal value on pencil and pen as instruments of personal expressiveness.

Like William Blake who, a hundred years later, would combine the role of poet and maker with those of the calligrapher and the *historieur* who painted the accompanying pictures, Crashaw apparently contributed his own designs for *Carmen Deo Nostro* (1652). Thomas Car in his prefatory poem to the book specifically commends the poet for his skill at pictures:

AN EPIGRAMME

Vpon the pictures in the following Poemes which the
    Authour first made with his owne hand, admirably
    well, as may be seene in his Manuscript dedicated
    to the right Honorable Lady, the L. Denbigh.

Twixt pen and pensill rose a holy strife
Which might draw vertue better to the life.
Best witts gaue votes to that: but painters swore
They neuer saw peeces so sweete before
As thes: fruites of pure nature; where no art
did lead the vntaught pensill, nor had part
In th' worke.
The hand growne bold, with witt will needes contest.
Doth it preuayle? ah no: say each is best.
This to the eare speakes wonders; that will trye
To speake the same, yet lowder, to the eye.
Both their aymes are holy, both conspire
To wound, to burne the hart with heauenly fire.
This then's the Doome, to doe both parties right:
This, to the eare speakes best; that, to the sight.

THOMAS CAR.

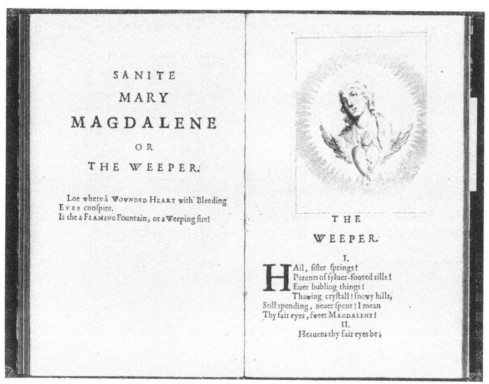

Figure 30. Engraved headpiece to "The Weeper," from
Richard Crashaw, *Carmen Deo Nostro* (1652). This item is
reproduced by permission of The Huntington Library, San
Marino, California.

Despite Car's remarks, literary critics have been reluctant to admit that Crashaw contributed anything more
than the poems for this volume. L. C. Martin, for example, said that Car exaggerated Crashaw's role in the
production of the book's illustrations, citing as evidence
the fact that all but a couple of them are signed by the
engraver, Jean Messager.[9] Martin and others, however,
have ignored the evidence of Crashaw's double talent
and have failed to take into consideration the fact that
Car makes specific reference to a holograph copy of the
Carmen—now lost—which the poet himself designed
and illustrated for the sister of the duke of Buckingham,
Lady Denbigh, who we may assume was conversant
with visual art. And since the engraved illustration
which heads that much maligned and often misun-
derstood poem "The Weeper"[10] is generally conceded to
be by Crashaw and not Messager, there are legitimate
grounds to assume that even in the printed version of
that poem we can see the creative fruits of Crashaw's
"holy strife" between pencil and pen.

In "The Weeper," the position of the figure (fig. 30) is
graphically complex. The Magdalen's head, for example, lies at an unusual angle in relation to the picture
plane. The viewer is positioned slightly below, and to
the left of the figure. She in turn faces slightly to her

right. The position of her head means that if a line were
drawn along *her* line of sight, it would bisect somewhere
to the left of the viewer a level line passing (also left-
ward) across both the viewer's eyes. In defiance of this
triangulation, however, the Magdalen's eyes seem to be
cast upward, above the point toward which her face is
directed. The pose is common enough in the iconography of the Penitent Magdalen, and is evident, for
instance, in Titian's version which is dated 1554. The
upward glance of the eyes in Crashaw's picture complements the position of the wings, a sign of ascent, upon
the flaming heart beneath. Again, we find a sharp visual
contradiction. For the upward thrust of the wings and
the eyes is countered by the falling tears and the falling
blood at the bottom of the heart. Naturally, the standard iconography of the bleeding heart dictated the general type. But the artist's own invention, coupled with
his own draftsmanship and design of the Magdalen in
relation to the image of the heart, was responsible for
the intricate disposition of angles in this seemingly un-
studied picture. Even in the engraved version where we
have the benefit of neither the color nor the flourishes
that must have appeared in the freehand version, we are
given a complex visual experience before we read the
comparably complex poem. This experience places a

heavy emphasis on our imaginative role in the completion of the poem's meaning; we think visually as well as verbally.

The "holy strife" between pencil and pen begins in stanza 1, where the reader perceives that the engraving is a reference point, as it is in virtually each stanza. Here it is the very tears represented in the picture:

> Hail, sister springs!
> Parents of syluer-footed rills!
>   Euer bubling things!
>   Thawing crystall! Snowy hills,
> Still spending, neuer spent! I mean
> Thy fair eyes, sweet Magdalene!

It is reasonable to see jubilance in these lines, but it is misleading to read the accumulation of images as an illustration of "the poet's sense of inadequacy in expressing divine truths."[11] The inadequacy can only be that of the reader who fails to sustain the connection between the verbal and visual images. For just above are those very same "springs," "rills," "bubling things," "Thawing crystall," and "snowy hills." And not only does "Still spending" refer to the limitless source of these tears, but the double meaning of "Still" as motionless or frozen in time maintains the prominence of the pictured image. Stanza 3 suggests that the tears pictured above only "seem to fall." And acknowledging the counterpoint of downward and upward movement already expressed pictorially, the fourth stanza affirms, "Vpwards thou dost weep," the significance being the ultimate transcendence of the weeper's spirit as it yearns for God. The pictured image of the Magdalen's face remains before the reader in stanza 6 ("Not in the evening's eyes / . . . / Sitts sorrow with a face so fair"), and in the seventh the "brightest majesty" of her sorrow is a concept already announced by the radiant nimbus that frames the Magdalen in the picture.

It is generally acknowledged that stanza 19 is the central stanza of the poem. There are numerous parallels in the works of other poets to what one critic has termed the extraordinary "bad taste" of these lines:[12]

> And now where're he strayes,
> Among the Galilean mountaines,
> Or more vnwellcome wayes,
> He's follow'd by two faithfull fountaines;
> Two walking baths; two weeping motions;
> Portable, & compendious oceans.

But if they are taken as an emblematic tableau they can no longer seem so outrageous as they might when read too literally and without reference to the constant presence of the pictured image.[13] Fountain, bath, ocean—each is a metonymy for tears. And the whole of which each term is but a part has already been pictured at the beginning of the poem. Here the term "compendious" offers a clue to the proper reading, for anything compendious contains all essentials in brief, just as this stanza contains the essentials presented in the picture, or as the picture contains those presented in the poem.

The most common charge against "The Weeper" has been its seeming lack of coherence, its beads-upon-a-string character manifest in a succession of images that offer few rational clues to their literal basis. How, readers ask about the troublesome nineteenth stanza, can it be said that Christ is "follow'd by two faithfull fountaines"? And how is it possible to make sense of those fountains as "Two walking baths"? The clue is established in the opening stanza, where the picture offers the basis for each successive term: springs, rills, and thawing crystal. At the verbal level, the poem articulates the picture. The Magdalen's eyes, looking upward in the engraving, "follow" Christ; their copious weeping makes them "fountaines," and their movement (expressive of grief and devotion alike) rationalizes into "walking baths" and "compendious oceans." The picture, in other words, dictates to the poem, whose images in turn become *speaking* pictures with enormous expressive, but hardly literal, potential.

There can be no question, though, that some of Crashaw's poems seem to challenge taste as well as ingenuity. The challenge to taste, however, dissolves when the reader takes into account the pictorial counterpoint that the poet so often employs. An apt example is the famous epigram based on Luke 11:27. After Christ had cast devils from a number of persons, "A certain woman of the company lifted up her voice, and said unto him, Blessed is the womb that bare thee, and the paps which thou hast sucked." On this text Crashaw wrote one of his most puzzling—and evidently to some, most offensive—epigrams:

> Svppose he had been Tabled at thy Teates,
> Thy hunger feeles not what he eates:
> Hee'l have his Teat e're long (a bloody one)
> The Mother then must suck the Son.

The epigram presupposes one's familiarity with two specific images whose iconographic identification is essential if one is to grasp the profound condensation of ideas in this poem. The first is the "Madonna lactens," painted on literally countless altarpieces and meditational objects, which represents the infant Jesus at his mother's breast. And the second is the Last Supper, which would be equally familiar and which depicts the temporal counterpart to the first. Where the Madonna nourishes her infant son from her own breast, at the Last Supper the son bestows the gift of grace (symbolized by the food) upon his disciples. The rich interplay of concepts pertaining to nourishment and grace that interanimate these two lies at the core of Crashaw's epigram and finds graphic confirmation in the painted images to which the poem makes allusion (figs. 31, 32). There the nursing child is quite literally beside a table

Figure 31. Adriaen Isenbrant, *Madonna and Child.* Collection of The Art Institute of Chicago.

Figure 32. Joos van der Beke Cleve (the Elder), *Holy Family with St. Joseph Reading.* Collection of The Art Institute of Chicago.

bearing fruit. The poem is "spoken" from the perspective of one who overhears and who muses in the first two lines (perhaps it would even be permissible to say meditates) on the mystical difference between human and spiritual sustenance. Despite the ardor of the woman's exclamation and the sincerity of her blessing, no mere human can perceive "what he eates." But this, too, has condensed double (if not triple) meaning, for, says the speaker, Christ shall soon enough taste death, an experience which inaugurates the endless nature of his life but which, ironically, comes to the mortal aspect which has drawn sustenance from an earthly mother. After his death the mortal mother must rely for her own (spiritual) nourishment upon the grace of her son. To call this "a revolting joke on Jesus and Mary," a grotesque invocation of "incest, perversion, cannibalism," is to miss the implicit presence of the pictured images associated with these themes.[14] The "holy strife" of picture and word depends equally upon picture, which imposes a visible discipline on otherwise wayward words. It is only when the words are deprived of their iconographic controls that their meanings slip to the lowest human denominator.

Throughout his entire career as a poet, Crashaw shows a consistent interest in the apt assimilation of vi-

sual art into verbal forms. Even in "Upon the gunpowder treason," a possible schoolboy exercise, he attempts to verbalize color and form. One couplet, for example, reads:

> Nor should wee need thy crisped waues, for wee
> An Ocean could haue made t'haue drowned thee.

Waves are "crisped" only to the eye that has learned to see the *image* of waves in oils upon a canvas; the image had to have been taken from painterly and not from either natural or literary experience, such as the "painted meddows" that he mentions later in the poem. "Eyes are vocall," he would later write in "Vpon the death of a Gentleman"; "Teares haue tongues, / And there be words not made with lungs." And in "Wishes. To his (supposed) Mistresse," which appeared in *Delights of the Muses,* there is a stanza which allows neither the verbal nor the visual medium exclusive rights in the representation of his lady:

> Her flattery,
> Picture and Poesy,
> Her counsell her owne vertue bee.

Two poems, though, are especially pertinent to Crashaw's perception of relations between visual and verbal images. Both, like Jonson's poems on the Droeshout engraving of Shakespeare and the frontispiece for Raleigh's *History of the World*, belong to that seldom discussed seventeenth-century genre of poems explaining the iconographic intricacies of frontispieces and pictorial title pages. The first is "Vpon Bishop Andrewes his Picture before his Sermons," which appeared with the engraved portrait of Andrewes in *XCVI Sermons* (1631). The second is "On the Frontispiece of Isaacsons Chronologie Explained."

Crashaw accords to the engraved portrait of Bishop Andrewes a hieroglyphic status (fig. 33). It is not merely another portrait, but an emblem:

> This reverend shadow cast that setting Sun,
> Whose glorious course through our Horrizon run,
> Left the dimme face of this dull Hemisphaeare,
> All one great eye, all drown'd in one great Teare.
> Whose faire illustrious soule, led his free thought
> Through Learnings Vniverse, and (vainely) sought
> Roome for her spatious selfe, untill at length
> She found the way home, with an holy strength
> Snatch't her selfe hence, to Heaven: fill'd a bright
> place,
> Mongst those immortall fires, and on the face
> Of her great maker fixt her flaming eye,
> There still to read true pure divinity.
> And now that grave aspect hath deign'd to shrinke
> Into this lesse appearance; If you thinke,
> Tis but a dead face, art doth here bequeath:
> Looke on the following leaves, and see him breath.

The portrait is a "reverend shadow" cast by the last reflections of the bishop's exemplary life, the final perceptible beams of a "setting Sun." The poet's choice of image is consistent with the notion that the Idea or first form is revealed to artists and, in the words of Giovio Pietro Bellori, "enters the marble and the canvas. Born from nature, it overcomes its origins and becomes the model of art; measured with the compass of the intellect it becomes the measure of the hand; and animated by fantasy, it gives life to the image."[15] In an image reminiscent of the walking baths in "The Weeper," Crashaw then contracts the multitudes who mourn the bishop's death into "one great eye, all drown'd in one great Teare." This eye then becomes a metonymy for the earth itself, now imaged as a hemisphere which mourns its setting sun. The new image introduces a significant visual contrast between the terrestrial and the celestial. Andrewes' expansive soul has now led his thoughts upward through "Learnings Vniverse," seeking "Roome for her spatious selfe." On the basis of this terrestrial-celestial contrast Crashaw guides the mind's eye of the reader in a manner comparable to the way one would scan a vast, triumphant skyscape. It is a verbal equivalent to the iconography common to such ascension scenes as Rubens' secular *Apotheosis of James I* (de-

signed for Inigo Jones' banquet hall) or his sacred *Assumption of the Virgin Mary* (1620). In scenes such as these the beholder experiences an illusion of enormous spatial depth, a perspective enhanced by the suggestion of receding planes. In "The Weeper" and "Blessed be the paps," Crashaw's verbal evocation of the meaning inherent in the portrait offers an example of the importance of the pictorial component in his poems. Here the Idea of the subject is said to reside within the engraved presentation. "That grave aspect" has been shrunk by art "Into this lesse appearance." But when the Idea contained by the picture is engaged with the breath or inspiration of soul expressed in the "following leaves," picture and word achieve a synthesis and are no longer independent vehicles for expression. For Crashaw, perhaps more than for any other seventeenth-century poet, picture is the very incarnation of the logos.

This principle also informs the poem explaining the title page of Isaacson's *Chronologie*. To the casual viewer whose attention is directed to the text, the pictorial details may seem decorative rather than substantive. But

Figure 33. John Payne, engraver, from Bishop Lancelot Andrewes, *XCVI Sermons* (1631). Courtesy of Rare Book and Manuscript Library, Columbia University.

substantive they indeed were, and the practice of introducing books through such emblematic title pages and frontispieces became widespread from roughly 1550 to 1650, falling off thereafter as book production increased. Conversely, what has often been termed a manuscript culture decreased[16] with the advent of print during the era of the Tudors and the technological improvements in bookmaking that occurred during the seventeenth century.[17] And during the rapid expansion in book production publishers relied upon the engraver's ability to convert picture space to page space, providing thereby a distinct threshold experience for a reader.[18]

Emblematic introductions were supposed to provoke speculation and comment. And they were designed to give formal expression to the transition from oral and conversational communication to the reading of a text, an activity requiring skills whose techniques are related to but abstracted from the gestural, intonational, and social features of speech.[19] Reading, of course, is a non-

social act. The written word communicates across noncooperating links in a chain, and except in such instances where the author will orally discuss his words, a concept cannot be checked with questioning.[20] Thus the emblematic title page or frontispiece gives the effect of pictorially summing up the text of a book in advance. It sets up expectations crucial to a reader's understanding of the book. It is no wonder, then, that books purporting to explain universal mysteries—books such as Raleigh's *History of the World* and Henry Isaacson's *Saturni Ephemerides*—should offer their readers pictorial introductions in advance of the text. And the addition of such poems as Jonson's and Crashaw's would simply be further insurance that the pictures would be understood.

In *Saturni Ephemerides* three figures appear at the top of what seems to be an architectural structure (fig. 34). In fact, the page gives the appearance of a façade, through which one "enters" the text. Time, personified as Saturn, surmounts a globe at the center. He is flanked by figures of a slightly more abstract character labeled Historia and Chronologia. Below the former is a rising sun; below the latter, darkness. In front of the façade appear two pyramids comprised of heavy bound volumes. At their respective tops are globes representing the celestial and terrestrial worlds. Panels at their base represent Creation and the Last Judgment, while in the center at the bottom, directly beneath Saturn, is the Tower of Babel. This design by William Marshall, whose design for Robert Herrick's *Hesperides* is discussed in chapter 6, may be scanned and interpreted in a number of ways. Thus, Crashaw's poem not only provides the necessary iconographic identifications, but it offers a systematic explanation of the relationships between the various images:

> Let hoary *Time's* vast Bowels be the Grave
> To what his Bowels birth and being gave;
> Let Nature die, if (*Phoenix*-like) from death
> Revived Nature take a second breath;
> If on *Times* right hand, sit faire *Historie*;
> If, from the seed of empty Ruine, she
> Can raise so faire an *Harvest*: Let Her be
> Ne're so farre distant, yet *Chronologie*
> (Sharpe sighted as the *Eagles* eye, that can
> Out-stare the broad-beam'd Dayes Meridian)
> Will have a *Perspicill* to find her out,
> And, through the *Night* of error and dark doubt,
> Discerne the *Dawne* of Truth's eternall ray,
> And when the rosie *Morne* budds into Day.
>   Now that *Time's* Empire might be amply fill'd,
> *Babels* bold *Artists* strive (below) to build
> Ruine a Temple; on whose fruitfull fall
> *History* reares her Pyramids more tall
> Then were th' *Ægyptian* (by the life, these give,
> Th' *Egyptian Pyramids* themselves must live:)
> On these she lifts the *World*; and on their base

Figure 34. William Marshall, engraver, title page of Henry Isaacson, *Saturni Ephemerides* (1633). Courtesy of Humanities Research Center, The University of Texas at Austin.

Figure 35. Peter Paul Rubens, *Peace and War*. Reproduced by courtesy of the Trustees, The National Gallery, London.

Shewes the two termes and limits of *Time's* race:
That, the *Creation* is; the *Judgment*, this;
That, the World's *Morning*, this her *Midnight* is.

Through the coordinated efforts of the engraver-designer and the poet, picture space yields to page space and visible images with symbolic associations yield to the text whose purpose has already been "framed" by the elaborate façade. The method is virtually the same as that for "The Weeper," where logos depends from the visible image which in turn establishes the iconographic constant in a complex artistic event.

"Upon the Kings coronation," composed presumably in 1628 but not included in any of the printed collections of Crashaw's poems, offers a further example of the poet's pictorial awareness. In fact, this poem offers the reader a veritable string of speaking pictures, which the poet characterizes as "perfect Emblemes of Divinity":

Doe I not see joy keepe his revels now,
And sitt triumphing in each cheerful brow?
Vnmixt felicity with silver wings
Broodeth this sacred place.

. . . .

Doe I not see a Cynthia, who may
Abash the purest beauties of the day?

. . . .

Doe I not see a constellation,
Each little beam of wch would make a sunne?

Deploying the gods of ancient mythology in that vastness of space which baroque art had made their visual preserve, Crashaw compels his reader to project these verbal images upon the canvas of a thoroughly classicized imagination. Indeed, in each of these emblems he has devised an allegory capable of competing with such contemporary works of the visual imagination as Rubens' *Saint George and the Dragon* (1630) at Buckingham Palace or the more famous *Peace and War* (1629) (fig. 35). The theme of the latter painting was very much in the air, and Crashaw would employ it himself in the poem "Vpon the Duke of Yorke his Birth: A Panegyricke," composed in 1630.

A poem of over one hundred lines, it too evokes a spectacular vision in the mind's eye in the manner of a vast mythological painting:

Brittaine, the mighty Oceans lovely Bride,
Now stretch thy selfe (faire Ile) and grow, spread wide

Thy bosome and make roome . . .

The infant Charles is greeted as the "sweet dawne of a glorious day."

> If this were Wisdomes God, that Wars sterne father,
> 'Tis but the same is said, *Henry* and *James*
> Are *Mars* and *Phoebus* under divers Names.
> O thou full mixture of those mighty soules,
> Whose vast intelligences turn'd the Poles
> Of Peace and Warre . . .

So great a birth can be ascribed only to the supreme artificer, Nature itself:

> From the same snowy Alablaster Rocke
> These hands and thine were hew'n, these cherryes
>   mocke
> The Corall of thy lips. Thou art of all
> This well-wrought Copy the faire Principall.
>   Iustly, Great Nature, may'st thou brag and tell
> How even th'ast drawne this faithfull Parallel,
> And matcht thy Master-Peece . . .

Crashaw's visual repertoire is not all in the expansive mode of panegyric, though. In "Death's Lecture at the Funeral of a Young Gentleman" which appeared in *Sacred Poems* (1652), he offers a sequence of speaking pictures which depict the mutual contraction of soul and body at the moment of death. Composed according to the dance of death motif, the poem charts a fearsome spiraling course across the spaces of the visual imagination:

>   Come man;
> Hyperbolized NOTHING? know thy span;
> Take thine own measure here: down, down, & bow
> Before thy self in thine idaea; thou
> Huge emptynes! contrast thy self; & shrinke
> All thy Wild circle to a Point. O sink
> Lower & lower yet; till thy leane size
> Call heaun to look on thee with narrow eyes.
> Lesser & lesser yet; till thou begin
> To show a face, fitt to confesse thy Kin,
> Thy neighbourhood to NOTHING.
> Proud lookes, & lofty eyliddes, here putt on
> Your selues in your vnfaign'd reflexion,
> Here, gallant ladyes! this vnpartiall glasse
> (Though you be painted) showes your true face.

Crashaw's preoccupation with spatial *dispositio* is also evident in the panegyric "Upon the birth of Princesse Elizabeth," composed in 1635 shortly after he had completed the donor portraits for St. John's College. This poem opens on a conventional note of literary invocation. But it is clearly not Crashaw's intention to sustain praise in a purely literary manner. He soon shifts into the modality of pictorial beholding:

> But such is the caelestiall Excellence,

> That in the princely patterne shines, from whence
> The rest pourtraicted are, that 'tis noe paine
> To ravish heauen to limbe them o're againe.
> Wittnesse this mapp of beauty; euery part
> Of wch doth show the Quintessence of art.

Terms like "patterne," "pourtraicted," "limbe," and "mapp of beauty" create an unusual metaphoric effect. Because the subject is but an infant, the poet could hardly expect the conventional topoi of praise, particularly praise of womanly beauty, to sound convincing. So through the use of terms that offer a conventional visual matrix, Crashaw creates a believable image of the ideas as *though* it were a visible portrait. The following lines (41–52) are central to the panegyric intent of the poem. But because they are borrowed from the familiar *descripto puellae* tradition and could easily seem too artificial, the poet frames them within the foregoing terms of image making:

> Poore earth hath not enough perfection,
> To shaddow forth th' admired Paragon.
> Those sparkling twinnes of light should I now stile
> Rich diamonds, sett in a pure siluer foyle;
> Or call her cheeke a bed of new blowne roses;
> And say that Ivory her front composes;
> Or should I say, that with a scarlet waue
> Those plump soft rubies had bin drest soe braue;
> Or that the dying lilly did bestow
> Vpon her neck the whitest of his snow;
> Or that the purple violets did lace
> That hand of milky doune.

Here we find no rhetorical advice to a painter, no debt to Anacreon, and only a formal debt to such *descripto puellae* pieces as that of Alcina's beauty in *Orlando Furioso* (canto 7) or Sidney's "What tongue can her perfection tell."[21] In addition to the language of portraiture used in the previous passage, Crashaw now includes a virtual burst of color. Relying upon his experience as an artist, he presents a verbal picture *of* a picture, and then permits his verbal creation to enjoy its status as an emblem of the newborn princess.

Richard Crashaw thus forged for himself a strong bond between poetry and painting. Not only was he sensitive to the emblematic habit of thought, but the *inventio* and *dispositio* of his poems show him to have been acutely sensitive to spatial design as well. The loss of the illustrated *Carmen Deo Nostro* is particularly sad, for we can now only speculate on a very hypothetical and tentative basis about his ultimate synthesis of art and poetry. Nevertheless, evidence from the donor portraits and the poems vindicates the anonymous preface to *Steps to the Temple* and adds important substance to Thomas Car's remark that in the work of this remarkable poet-painter "twixt pen and pensill rose a holy strife."

5. Richard Lovelace, Edmund Waller, and the Flowering of English Art

During the 1630s and 1640s the status of art at the Caroline court was enormously enhanced by the presence of Anthony Van Dyck. Four years before Charles came to the throne, Van Dyck had visited England briefly under the sponsorship of the earl of Arundel. The most brilliant of Peter Paul Rubens' pupils, he had undoubtedly come to the earl's attention during the latter's travels in 1617, or even perhaps at the time when Lady Arundel sat for Rubens in Antwerp in 1620. His first stay in England was short—he appears to have done little more than one portrait of the earl (now in possession of the duke of Sutherland),[1] although he did collect a grant of one hundred pounds from the king "by way of regard for special services." In 1630 Charles purchased Van Dyck's *Rinaldo and Armida* from Endymion Porter, who had commissioned it two years earlier for seventy-two pounds.[2] The painting thus entered the royal collection, to which had just been added the preceding year the famous Mantuan collection that had been negotiated for the king by Daniel Nys. By 1632, Van Dyck's reputation had so advanced that he was invited to enter royal service, not only with a knighthood and yearly pension but with a large studio in Blackfriars. There he began painting or directly supervising the numerous portraits that would constitute a unique record of the Caroline world.[3]

Among his contributions to English interest in art, Van Dyck brought a thorough understanding of Titian and the Venetian artists of the preceding century. Having been a student in Venice, Van Dyck was able to enjoy in England direct access to the finest collection of Titians ever assembled. Accordingly, he began converting the great Venetian's techniques of color and design to his own use, thus introducing to English art a new idiom and new conventions.[4] Carew's poem "To the Painter" seems to allude not only to the new style of portraiture but also to Van Dyck: "Great Master though thou be," Carew says, "canst thou . . . tell how to paint a vertue?" The question assumes the capacity of the virtuoso painter to render an abstract quality no less successfully

than the poet. Further, the question implies familiarity with Ausonius' well-known epigram (translated by Richard Lovelace):

> Vain Painter why dost strive my face to draw,
> With busy hands a Goddess eyes nere saw?
> Daughter of Air and Wing; I do rejoyce
> In empty shouts (without a mind) a Voice.
> Within your ears shrill echo I rebound,
> And if you'l paint me like, then paint a sound.[5]

In Carew's poetic comment on Van Dyck, there is recourse to both a literary formula and to the poet's personal assessment of Van Dyck's genius, for then he writes:

> Besides (if all I heare be true,)
> 'Tis taken ill by some that you
> Should be so insolently vaine,
> As to contrive all that rich gaine
> Into one tablet, which alone
> May teach us superstition.

Carew's assessment of Van Dyck's skill does not stand alone in the early seventeenth century in England. Edmund Waller is more enthusiastic still in his commendation of the artist's capacity to bring art up to the very borders of nature. Partly *ekphrastic* and partly panegyric, "To Van Dyck" situates the reader before one of the artist's portraits:

> RARE Artisan, whose pencil moves
> Not our delights alone, but loves!
> From thy shop of beauty we
> Slaves return, that entered free.
> The heedless lover does not know
> Whose eyes they are that wound him so;
> But, confounded with thy art,
> Inquires her name that hath his heart.
> Another, who did long refrain,
> Feels his old wound bleed fresh again
> With dear remembrance of that face,

10

Where now he reads new hopes of grace:
Nor scorn nor cruelty does find,
But gladly suffers a false wind
To blow the ashes of despair
From the reviving brand of care.
Fool! that forgets her stubborn look
This softness from thy finger took..
Strange! that thy hand should not inspire
The beauty only, but the fire;   20
Not the form alone, and grace,
But act and power of a face.
Mayst thou yet thyself as well,
As all the world besides, excel!
So you the unfeigned truth rehearse
(that I may make it live in verse)
Why thou couldst not at one assay,
That face to aftertimes convey,
Which this admires. Was it thy wit
To make her oft before thee sit?   30
Confess, and we'll forgive thee this;
for who would not repeat that bliss?
And frequent sight for such a dame
Buy with the hazard of his fame?
Yet who can tax thy blameless skill,
Though thy good hand had failed still,
When nature's self so often errs?
She for this many thousand years
Seems to have practised with much care,
To frame the race of women fair;   40
Yet never could a perfect birth
Produce before to grace the earth,
Which waxed old ere it could see
Her that amazed thy art and thee.
   But now 'tis done, O let me know
Where those immortal colours grow,
That could this deathless piece compose!
In lillies? or the fading rose?
No; for this theft thou hast climbed higher
Than did Prometheus for his fire.[6]   50

The comparison of the artist with Prometheus begs more serious consideration than Carew's comparison of the viewer with Pygmalion. If we step into this speaker's situation and role, gazing at the assumed portrait with his eyes, we acknowledge the painter's pencil to have moved not only delight (the pleasure all may find in skillful representation of appearances) but "loves" (a far more subtle response). The "shop of beauty"[7] where this effect occurs is in all likelihood Van Dyck's own Blackfriars studio. And it is to that location "we / Slaves return, that entered free," a simple but eloquent statement about the magic Van Dyck worked upon the Caroline consciousness. However, to validate this visual experience through words requires dramatic realization. Waller provides this realization by imagining two viewers. One is a "heedless lover." Even though he does not

know the sitter, his eyes are wounded by the emanations from the portrait. The other once loved the lady but has long refrained. Both viewers fall victim to the painter's skillful illusion of life, the "false wind." And both accept the illusion though her "stubborn look" is immobile.

The poem is a fair piece of art criticism, and the crux lies in lines 19–22. The painter's hand (with its delicacy of touch, its elegant layering of paint on canvas, and its control over light and color) can all but breathe ("inspire"). To the average person who views a picture, such beauty may well lie only in appearance. But to the connoisseur who prides himself or herself on an understanding of the relation between art and nature, the "fire" Van Dyck lights in the portrait transports art directly into the realm of life. The reason is simply that the artist understands the mystery in the "act and power of a face," which was, of course, Sidney's preoccupation in the *New Arcadia*, where Musidorus falls in love with the portrait of Philoclea. And Waller uses this same idea again in his poem "On my Lady Dorothy Sidney's Picture."

Even though Waller writes a number of other poems on paintings—"To the Queen, Occasioned upon sight of her Majesty's Picture," "The Night Piece," "On the Picture of a fair youth, taken after he was dead," "To a Lady, from whom he received the foregoing copy," "Under a Lady's Picture," "Of the misreport of her being painted," and "On the discovery of a lady's painting"— he simply does not present evidence that the work of the painters had an organic effect upon his own creativity. Presently, we shall return to "Instructions to a Painter," the poem in which Waller made a serious effort to incorporate the effects of art and revealed a substantial interest in the underlying notions of literary pictorialism lacking in these pieces. But we shall appreciate that poem better after considering the poems on art by Richard Lovelace.

Two considerations indicate that Richard Lovelace was responsive to visual thinking: Lovelace was a close friend of Sir Peter Lely and he was admitted (like Lely) to the Freedom of the Painter's Company, an honor reserved for those with demonstrable interest in art.[8] We do not know if Lovelace actually painted, however. Two of the dedicatory poems to *Lucasta* (1649) are particularly useful in this connection, for in them Frances Lenton and W. Rudyerd not only offer important contemporary critical insight into Lovelace's poetry, but each praises his particular kind of literary pictorialism.[9] They both acknowledge him to be a painter with words, one whose verse surpasses even "Sydneyes Prose"—an indication that the kind of literary pictorialism discussed in chapter 1 continued to find responsive readers well into the middle of the seventeenth century. Lenton and Rudyerd confirm the prevailing view that Lovelace incorporated the visual dialogue into his verbal perfor-

mance, that he spoke as a connoisseur and amateur artist should speak—namely, with visual as well as verbal
literacy.

The poem "Princesse Löysa drawing" confirms such
a view:

I Saw a little Deity,
Minerva in Epitomy,
Whom *Venus* at first blush, surpris'd,
Tooke for her winged wagge disguis'd;
But viewing then wereas she made
Not a distrest, but lively shade
Of *Eccho*, whom he had betrayd,
Now wanton, and ith' coole oth' Sunne
With her delight a hunting gone;
And thousands more, whom he had slaine,
To live, and love, belov'd againe:
Ah this is true Divinity!
I will un-Gŏd that Toye! cri'd she;
Then markt she *Syrinx* running fast
To *Pans* imbraces, with the haste
Shee fled him once, whose reede-pipe rent,
He finds now a new *Instrument*.
Theseus return'd, invokes the Ayre
And windes, then wafts his faire;
Whilst *Ariadne* ravish't stood
Halfe in his armes, halfe in the flood.
Proud *Anaxerate* doth fall
At *Iphis* feete, who smiles of all:
And he (whilst she his curles doth deck)
Hangs no where now, but on her neck.

　Heere *Phoebus* with a beame untombes
　Long hid *Leucothoe*, and dombes
Her Father there; *Daphne* the faire
Knowes now no bayes but round her haire;
And to *Apollo* and his Sons
Who pay him their due Orisons,
Bequeaths her Lawrell-robe, that flame
Contemnes, Thunder and evill Fame.

　There kneel'd *Adonis* fresh as spring,
Gaye as his youth, now offering
Herselfe those joyes with voice and hand,
Which first he could not understand.

　Transfixed *Venus* stood amas'd,
Full of the Boye and Love, she gaz'd;
And in imbraces seemed more
Sencelesse and cold, then he before.
Uselesse Childe! In vaine (said she)
You beare that fond Artillerie:
See heere a Pow'r above the slow
Weake execution of thy bow.

　So said, she riv'd the Wood in two,
Unedged all his Arrowes too,
And with the string their feathers bound
To that part whence we have our wound.

See, see! the darts by which we burn'd
Are bright Löysa's pencills turn'd;
With which she now enliveth more
Beauties, then they destroy'd before.

Princess Louise, the granddaughter of King James I, was
one of the most successful pupils of Gerard Honthorst.[10]
Her self-portrait at Coombe Abbey reveals no excep-
tional ability, but it does indicate that Lovelace's priv-
ileged role of onlooker in this poem is not fantasy. The
image of the girl drawing in her studio is itself a picture
one can readily frame in the mind's eye by a window or
door. The framing narrative is itself delicate and amus-
ing as Lovelace relates how the girl's inventive recasting
of the Ovidian tales puts Venus' nose quite out of joint.
What the poet himself has drawn is a composite view of
the transforming powers of art, a sense of what happens
when the eye takes hold of visible images and invests
them with motion. "So powerfully you draw when you
perswade," says Rudyerd of Lovelace. And the delicate
nuances on the Princess Louise support that judgment.

"Amyntor's Grove, His Chloris, Arigo, and Gratiana.
An Elogie" offers more convincing proof that "Poets,
and Painters have some near relation, / Compar'd with
Fancy and Imagination." Here "the picture of the Mind"
that Lenton praises in Lovelace's work is vivid. The
poem opens in a conventional pastoral setting, like the
first book of the *New Arcadia*. Soon, however, it brings
the reader indoors where the eye is struck by a variety of
visual riches:

It was *Amyntor's* Grove, that *Chloris*
For ever Ecchoes and her Glories;
Chloris, the gentlest Sheapherdesse,
That ever Lawnes and Lambes did blesse;
Her breath like to the whispering winde,
Was calme as thought, sweet as her Minde;
Her lips like coral-gates kept in
The perfume and the pearle within;
Her eyes a double-flaming torch
That alwayes shine, and never scorch:
Her selfe the Heav'm in which did meet
The *All* of bright, of faire and sweet.

　Here was I brought with that delight
That seperated Soules take flight;
And when my Reason call'd my sence
Back somewhat from this excellence,
That I could see; I did begin
T' observe the curious ordering
Of every Roome, where'ts hard to know
Which most excels in *sent* or *show*:
Arabian gummes do breath here forth,
And th' *East's* come over to the *North*;
The Windes have brought their hyre of sweet
To see *Amyntor Chloris* greet;
Balme and Nard, and each perfume

To blesse this payre chafe and consume;
And th' *Phoenix*, see! already fries!
Her Neast a fire in *Chloris* eyes!

   Next the great and powerful hand
Beckons my thoughts unto a stand
Of *Titian, Raphael, Georgone*
Whose *Art* ev'n *Nature* hath out-done;
For if weake *Nature* only can
Intend, not perfect what is man,
These certainely we must prefer,
Who mended what *She* wrought, and *Her*;
And sure the shadowes of those rare
And kind incomparable fayre
Are livelier, nobler Company,
Then if they could or speake, or see:
For these I aske without a tush,
Can kisse or touch, without a blush,
And we are taught that *Substance* is,
If uninjoy'd, but th' shade of blisse.

   Now every Saint Clearly divine,
Is clos'd so in her severall shrine;
The Gems so rarely, richly set,
For them wee love the Cabinet;
So intricately plac't withall,
As if th' imbrodered the Wall,
So that the Pictures seem'd to be
But one continued Tapistrie.

   After this travell of mine eyes
We sate, and pitied Dieties;
Wee bound our loose hayre with the Vine,
The Poppy, and the Eglantine;
One swell'd an Oriental bowle
Full, as a grateful, Loyal Soule
To *Chloris*! *Chloris*! heare, Oh heare!
'Tis pledg'd above in ev're Sphere.

   Now streight the Indians richest prize
Is kindled a glad Sacrifice;
Cloudes are sent up on wings of Thyme,
Amber, Pomgranates, Jessemine,
And through our Earthen Conduicts sore
Higher then Altars fum'd before.

   So drencht we our oppressing cares,
And choakt the wide Jawes of our feares,
Whilst ravisht thus we did devise,
If this were not a Paradice
In all, except these harmelesse sins;
Behold! flew in two *Cherubins*
Cleare as the skye from whence they came,
And brighter then the sacred Flame;
The Boy adorn'd with Modesty,
Yet armed so with Majesty;
That if the Thunderer againe
His Eagle sends, she stoopes in vaine;
Besides his *Innocence* he tooke
A Sword and Casket, and did looke

Like *Love* in *Armes*; he wrote but five,
Yet spake eighteene, each *Grace* did strive,
And twenty *Cupids* thronged forth,
Who first should show his prettier worth.

   But Oh the Nymph! did you ere know
Carnation mingled with *Snow*?
Or have you seene the Lightning shrowd,
And straight breake through th' opposing cloud?
So ran her blood, such was it's hue;
So through her vayle her bright Haire flew,
And yet its Glory did appeare
But thinne, because her *eyes* were neere.

   Blooming Boy, and blossoming Mayd,
May your faire Sprigges be neere betrayd
To eating worme, or fouler storme;
No Serpent lurke to do them harme;
No sharpe frost cut, no North-winde teare,
The Verdure of that fragrant hayre;
But may the Sun and gentle weather,
When you are both growne ripe together,
Load you with fruit, such as your Father
From you with all the joyes doth gather:
And may you when one branch is dead
Graft such another in it's stead,
Lasting thus ever in your prime
'Til 'th' Sithe is snatcht away from *Time*.

This poem, with its suggestions of Kalandar's picture gallery, begs comparison as well with Jonson's "To Penhurst" and Carew's poem to Saxam, but with the major difference that the present owner's impressive cabinet of paintings has led the mind of the poet to the sophisticated delights of art and not to the natural appearances of the estate. It is probable that the grove is an allegory for Woodhall, the country house of Endymion Porter. Hazlitt, for example, suggested that Amyntor might be identified with Porter, and if this is correct, Chloris is Porter's wife, Olive, while Arigo and Gratiana are the youngest children, James (b. 1638) and Lettice (b. 1631). In his notes to "Amyntor" Wilkinson noted that no record showed Porter as the owner of paintings attributed to Titian, Raphael, and Giorgione. However, we know now that Porter oversaw many of King Charles' acquisitions of paintings by these artists, and that he himself had a sizable collection both at his London house and at Woodhall. Indeed, Porter's biographer speculates that he spent some two thousand pounds on that collection, "a big sum in days when a full size Van Dyck cost only £100, and when a Titian could be bought for the same price."[11] Lovelace's poem may be a quite accurate appreciation of Porter's country house and collection, whose "Pictures seem'd to be / But one continued Tapistrie."

"Upon the Curtaine of Lucasta's Picture, it was thus wrought" is a playful little piece which is based on assumptions that might be brought to any portrait; it hints

Figure 36. Sir Peter Lely, *Charles I and the Duke of York.*
Syon House, Brentford. Courtesy of His Grace, The Duke of
Northumberland.

at the sudden flash whereby the image of the soul (some
might call it the real picture) is perceived mystically. But
it is Lovelace's two poems to Peter Lely that ultimately
define his understanding of visual art. "To my Worthy
Friend Mr. Peter Lely: on that excellent Picture of his
Majesty, and the Duke of York, drawne by him at
Hampton-Court" (fig. 36) is one of the best-known
seventeenth-century poems on a work of art.

See! what a *clouded Majesty*! and eyes
Whose glory through their mist doth brighter rise!
See! what an humble bravery doth shine,
And griefe triumphant breaking through each line;
How it commands the face! so sweet a scorne
Never did happy misery adorne!
So sacred a contempt! that others show
To this, (oth' height of all the wheele) below;
That mightiest Monarchs by this shaded booke
May coppy out their proudest, richest looke.

  Whilst the true *Eaglet* this quick luster spies,
And by his *Sun's* enlightens his owne eyes;
He cares his cares, his burthen feeles, then streight
Joyes that so lightly he can beare such weight;

Whilst either eithers passion doth borrow,
And both doe grieve the same victorious sorrow.

  These my best *Lilly* with so bold a spirit
And soft a grace, as if thou didst inherit
For that time all their greatnesse, and didst draw
With those brave eyes your *Royall Sitters* saw.

  Not as of old, when a rough hand did speake
A strong Aspect, and a faire face, a weake;
When only a black beard cried Villaine, and
By *Hieroglyphicks* we could understand;
When Chrystall typified in a white spot,
And the bright Ruby was but one red blot;
Thou dost the things Orientally the same,
Not only paintst its colour, but its *Flame*:
Thou sorrow canst designe without a teare,
And with the Man and his very *Hope* and *Feare*;
So that th'amazed world shall henceforth finde
None but my *Lilly* ever drew a *Minde*.

Prior to this no English poet had so consciously committed himself to the close *ekphrastic* analysis of a
painting. Lovelace was familiar with both Giorgio Vasari's *Lives of the Painters* and Karel Van Manders' *Het*

Schilder-Boeck (Harlem, 1604), and from such sources he certainly had learned concepts of *ekphrasis* that support his performance in this poem.[12] But Lovelace had access to an English source for such ideas as well, Franciscus Junius' *The Painting of the Ancients* (London, 1638). In this work he could have read that "livelinesse of great spirits [will] issue forth, whilest every one doth most readily expresse in his workes the inward motions of his most forward minde."[13] Like the painting to which Lovelace's poem must be read as a companion piece, the poem is "busie about the shapes and deeds of the Worthies," expressing in word what the painter has expressed in color. "Picture," Junius had said, "is nothing else in it selfe but a delusion of our eyes" and a "reviving of our minde." Certainly, it is the quality of fancy that, according to Lovelace, so enlivens the artist's colors with a "Flame." The poem locates the reader in that situation of "retiredness" familiar to anyone who has seriously studied a picture. Junius had spoken about this phenomenon of imaginative beholding, saying that "the reason is at hand, and may be drawne out of our former discourse, where we doe shew that solitary and silent places doe mightily helpe and nourishe our Phantasie, the only means Artificers doe worke, and lovers of Art doe judge by."

The poem that best reveals Lovelace's grasp of art and his perception of the relations it enjoys with poetry is "Peinture. A Panegyrick to the best Picture of Friendship. Mr. Pet. Lilly." It is also the most extensive contemporary assessment of Peter Lely's work, and is thus an important document in art criticism.

> If *Pliny* Lord High Treasurer of all
> Natures exchequer shuffled in this our ball;
> *Pincture*, her richer Rival, did admire,
> And cry'd she wrought with more almighty fire,
> That judg'd the unnumbered issue of her Scrowl,
> Infinite and various as her Mother Soul
> That contemplation into matter brought,
> Body'd *Idæa's*, and could form a thought:
> Why do I pause to couch the Cataract,
> And the grosse pearls from our dull eyes abstract?
> That pow'rful *Lilly*, now awakened, we
> This new Creation may behold by thee.

> To thy victorious pencil, all that Eyes
> And minds can reach, do bow; the Deities
> Bold *Poets* first but feign'd, you do, and make
> And from your awe they our Devotion take.
> Your beauteous Pallet first defin'd Loves Queen
> And made her in her heav'nly colours seen;
> You string the Bow of the Bandite her Son,
> And tipp'd his Arrowes with Religion.
> *Neptune*, as unknown as his Fish might dwell,
> But that you seat him in his throne of Shell.
> The thunderers Artillery, and brand
> You fancied *Rome* in his fantastick hand.

> And the pale frights, the pains and fears of Hell,
> First from your sullen Melancholy fell.
> Who cleft th' infernal Dog's loath'd head in three,
> And spun out *Hydra's* fifty necks? by thee
> As prepossess'd w' enjoy th' *Elizian* plain,
> Which but before was flatter'd in our brain.
> Who ere yet view'd Airs child invisible,
> A hollow Voice, but in thy subtile skill?
> Faint stamm'ring *Eccho*, you so draw, that we
> The very repercussion do see.

> Cheat *Hocus-pocus*-Nature an Essay
> O' th' Spring affords us, *Præsto* and away;
> You all the year do chain her, and her fruits,
> Roots to their Beds, and flowers to their Roots.
> Have not mine eyes feasted i' th' frozen *Zone*,
> Upon a fresh new-grown Collation
> Of Apples, unknown sweets, that seem'd to me
> Hanging to tempt as on the fatal Tree;
> So delicately limn'd I vow'd to try
> My appetite impos'd upon my Eye.

> You Sir alone, Fame and all conqu'ring Rime,
> Files the set teeth of all devouring time.
> When Beauty once thy vertuous paint hath on,
> Age needs not call her to Vermilion;
> Her beams nere shed or change like th' hair of day,
> She scatters fresh her everlasting Ray;
> Nay, from her ashes her fair Virgin fire
> Ascends, that doth new massacres conspire,
> Whilst we wipe off the num'rous score of years,
> And do behold our Grandsires as our peers,
> With the first Father of our House, compare
> We do the features of our new-born Heir;
> For though each coppied a Son, they all
> Meet in thy first and true Original.

> Sacred Luxurious! what Princesse not
> But comes to you to have her self begot?
> As when first man was kneaded, from his side
> Is born to's hand a ready made up Bride.
> He husband to his issue then doth play,
> And for more Wives remove the obstructed way:
> So by your Art you spring up in two moons
> What could not else be form'd by fifteen Suns;
> Thy Skill doth an'mate the prolifick flood,
> And thy red Oyl assimilates to blood.

> Where then when all the world pays its respect,
> Lies our transalpine barbarous Neglect?
> When the chast hands of powe'rful *Titian*,
> Had drawn the Scourges of our God and Man,
> And now the top of th' Altar did ascend,
> To crown the heav'nly piece with a bright end;
> Whilst he who to seven Languages gave Law,
> And always like the *Sun* his Subjects saw,
> Did in his Robes Imperial and gold,
> The basis of the doubtful Ladder hold.
> O *Charls*! A nobler monument then that,

Which thou thine own Executor wert at.
When to our huffling *Henry* there complain'd
A grieved Earl, that thought this honor stain'd;
Away (frown'd he) for your own safeties, hast,
In one cheap hour ten Coronets I'l cast:
But *Holbeen's* noble and prodigious worth,
Onely the pangs of an whole Age brings forth.
Henry! a word so princely saving said,
It might new raise the ruines thou hast made.

    O sacred *Peincture*! that dost fairly draw
What but in Mists deep inward *Poets* saw;
'Twixt thee and an Intelligence no ods,
That art of privy Council to the Gods,
By thee unto our eyes they do prefer
A stamp of their abstracted Character;
Thou that in frames eternity dost find,
And art a written and a body'd mind;
To thee is Ope the *Juncto* o' th' *Abysse*,
And its conspiracy detected is;
Whilest their Cabal thou to our sense dost show,
And in thy square paint'st what they threat below.

    Now my best *Lilly* let's walk hand in hand,
And smile at this un-understanding land;
Let them their own dull counterfeits adore,
Their Rainbow-cloaths admire, and no more;
Within one shade of thine more substance is
Than all their varnish'd Idol-Mistresses:
Whilst great *Vasari* and *Vermander* shall
Interpret the deep mystery of all,
And I unto our modern Picts shall show,
What due renown to thy fair Art they owe,
In the delineated lives of those,
By whom this everlasting Lawrel grows:
Then if they will not gently apprehend,
Let one great blot give to their fame an end;
Whilst no Poetick flower their Herse doth dresse,
But perish they and their Effigies.

Contrasting nature and art, Lovelace declares that the randomness of the former is epitomized by Pliny's treatment in the *Natural History*. "Pincture" on the other hand has now become Nature's rival, and the "Pow'rful *Lilly*" is chief among the painters. The poet writes to cast aside the "Cataract" that obscures the "new Creation" the artist has wrought. His purpose is to raise the English consciousness of art and, by implication, to dispel the view that painting is subordinate to poetry.

He turns first to a group of subject paintings. Art historians know Lely as a portraitist, not as a subject painter.[14] And this fact lends particular importance to Lovelace's ascription to Lely of a Venus and Cupid, a Neptune seated upon a shell, a Jupiter, a Hercules, a landscape, and a picture of Echo. From the catalogue of Lely's own collection we know that he owned a Titian *Venus and Adonis* as well as one ascribed to Giorgione, a Rubens *Hero and Leander*, *A Satyr and Nymph* by

Martin de Vos, and a Tintoretto *Vulcan and Cupid*. But we have only Lovelace's word that Lely worked in this vein himself.[15]

In each case the artist's skill is said to defy the limitations of his medium, clear evidence of the value then placed in the skillful illusion of reality. For a modern it is difficult to sort out conventional hyperbole from genuine critical criteria, but the following remarks from an anonymous late seventeenth-century manuscript on the rules for painting offer a clue to Lovelace's poem. "The life & true force of a picture lies nott in a childish niceity of smooth stroakes, fair coulors, neate ornaments & a scrupulous exactness in the imitation of every trifle. And thearfore my master told me once the whole businis is but to know: its easy then to doe itt; wh. I interprett thus, that if a man knows where in the true force & life of a picture doth consist it will be easie enoff for him to express that force."[16] Lovelace's assertion that Lely can give the viewer "The very repercussion" of Eccho and (Apelles-like) can impose the appetite upon the eye in a still life is analogous to this "life & true force."

Because Lely possesses that special knowledge, he can with Fame as well as "all-conqu'ring Rime" disarm time, that Saturnian horror who traditionally consumes his offspring (see fig. 34). When he speaks of the painter's unique creativity as "Sacred Luxurious," Lovelace offers particular insight into the Caroline passions for portraits. Only through his skills is it possible to "behold our Grandsires as our peers," for Lely's portraits mysteriously capture an entire family history in a single frame. The English, however, have traditionally failed to value art. Comparing "our transalpine barbarous Neglect" with the reverence accorded to the painters of Italy, Lovelace hints at firsthand familiarity with Titian's *Crowning of Thorns* (fig. 37). To remedy that neglect he devotes the closing section of the poem to the affinities between poetry and painting. "Peincture" displays "What but in Mists deep inward Poets saw." And by invoking both Vasari and Van Mander, who "Interpret the deep mystery of all," Lovelace becomes the first English poet to declare his familiarity with the two most popular writers on art of his time.

If we add to the poems by Lenton and Rudyerd these by Lovelace himself, it becomes evident that "Aramantha. A Pastoral" as well as a number of the shorter pieces to Lucasta and on such varied subjects as "The Snayl" and "The Ant" may be more indebted to visual thinking than modern critics have acknowledged. In "Aramantha," for example, there is a strong emphasis on color and texture. Verbal portraiture blends into floral landscape until the title figure is transformed into Flora herself. As the poem progresses the mythological allusions each have their pictorial complements, while the grove owes more to landscape than to the word alone. Soon Lovelace presents his reader with still life comparable to what he praised in Lely's art, and by the

Figure 37. Titian, *Crowning of Thorns.* Courtesy of Alte Pinakothek, Munich.

close of the poem the reader is left to wonder what has been most impressive: the thin narrative lines or the succession of lush pictures, those Lenton had characterized as "the Pictures of the Mind / In purer Verse."

Richard Lovelace's talent for poems that describe and critique works of art has much in common with the ability of his contemporary Edmund Waller to emulate a pictorial style. Waller's "Instructions to a Painter" is probably the best-known seventeenth-century poem incorporating the visual arts with literature. As the subtitle of the expanded version tells us, the poet wrote it "for the drawing of the posture and progress of His Majesty's forces at sea . . . together with the battle and victory over the Dutch, June 3, 1665." It is a topical piece and subject on that account to the charge that it suffers the imaginative liabilities of occasional poetry. However, when the nature of its relation to visual art is made apparent, the "Instructions" appears far more original than we have been accustomed to believe. Commonly read as an extended imitation of Anacreon's epi-

grams ("Painter, by unmatch'd desert" and "Draw my Fair as I command"),[17] the poem is far better understood as a literary analogue to seventeenth-century decorative painting of the sort found in public buildings and palaces on the Continent. The poem requires to be read, therefore, against the background of a rapidly accelerating interest in visual art and a persistent English yearning for indigenous art that might rival Continental splendor.

As early as 1621, Peter Paul Rubens was singled out to paint the vast ceiling of the banqueting hall at Whitehall, the construction of which was to be completed in March 1622. Rubens' paintings were not installed until 1636, but in spite of the fourteen-year interval they amply fulfilled royalist expectations with their magnificent tribute to the infallibility of Stuart government. By 1638 Sir Anthony Van Dyck was proposing another ambitious decorative scheme. To complement the Rubens paintings on the ceiling, he would decorate the walls with a succession of scenes illustrating the history of the Order of the Garter. The scale of these paintings can only be inferred from the one existing sketch, which shows King Charles in the center of a stately procession of all the Knights of the Garter. Charles, however, could not afford to finance the scheme, and so it came to naught— a disappointment to Van Dyck that may have well played a part in his efforts to seek employment away from the English court. Soon, though, negotiations were opened with Jacob Jordaens, through Sir Balthasar Gerbier, for a series of canvasses to decorate the cabinet in the queen's house. There were to be nine for the ceiling and thirteen for the walls. Several of these paintings seem to have been completed, but all have now disappeared and nothing is known of the subject matter of this ambitious scheme. Still later, in 1651, Gerbier and George Geldorp, along with Sir Peter Lely, proposed yet another scheme, one designed to complement the parliamentary politics of the day. With Lely as master painter, they would decorate Whitehall with oil paintings depicting all the memorable achievements since the Parliament's first sitting, but once again the scheme failed to develop.[18]

These and lesser schemes for decorative painting on the grand heroic scale show a persistent feeling that English exploits should also be visually depicted in the style commonly employed by baroque artists on the Continent, a feeling that would persist well into the nineteenth century when a national commission was established to select artists and subjects for the newly built Houses of Parliament. By the mid-seventeenth century, travelers abroad were fully aware of such examples as the Veronese ceiling in the Venetian church of S. Sebastiano or Rubens' Medici series at the Luxembourg Palace in Paris. But England was destined to wait for Antonio Verrio and Louis Laguerre, who would appear at the very end of the century, and for Sir James Thorn-

Figure 38. Pietro Liberi, *La Battaglia dei Dardanelli.* Courtesy of Alinari/Editorial Photocolor Archives.

hill, who would emerge well into the next, before it could boast of extensive decorative painting on the heroic scale.

In what was felt among the connoisseurs and virtuosos of the mid-century to be an artistic vacuum, an obscure translator named Thomas Higgons published in 1658 an English version of Gian Francesco Busenello's poem "Prospettive Del Nauale Trinto Riportata dalla Republica Serenissma contra il Turco. Al Signor Caualier Pietro Liberi Pittore Insigne, e Famoso." This panegyric celebrating the Venetian victory over the Turkish fleet in the Dardanelles in 1656 was a verbal analogue to precisely the kind of painting some of the English had long sought to have established in their own land. It was composed to praise a painter who was commissioned to do an elaborate *istoria* of the battle to be hung in the doge's palace. Indeed, the painting is there to this day (fig. 38).[19] Higgons prefaced his translation with a letter of dedication to Lord Henry, earl of Peterbourgh. This was followed by a commendatory poem by the translator's friend, Edmund Waller. The translation was something of a catalyst for "Instructions to a Painter," but the true nature of this interaction between art and literature can best be appreciated if we examine Higgon's letter to his patron.

"You, my Lord, who have so refined a taste, who know the nature and propriety of everything, will be best able to determine" the worth of this poem. Addressing the earl as a connoisseur of art, a virtuoso, Higgons sets the tone for his translation by directing it at the art consciousness of his patron. To reinforce this tone he adds that the beauty of Busenello's poem "lies not in the matter, but in the words, in the aire and dresse." It requires not "judgment onely, but invention too." As a connoisseur who has had ample experience with art, his patron could be expected to invent the spirit of the original picture imaginatively (and correctly) on the basis of words alone. "With the English, I have sent your Lordship the Originall, that you may not onely judge, whether it be *well painted* [my italics], but whether it be a faithful Copy, and imitate the Italian life."[20] Higgons plainly thought of Busenello's poem as a verbal copy of Liberi's painting, just as he considered his translation a verbal painting. He was not disturbed, as we are now apt to be, by the ontological differences between a verbal performance and a physical painting.[21] The reason is that he accepted the principle of interrelated correspondences whereby verbal reference to standard iconography or motifs would be a sufficient shorthand for the informed reader.[22] Busenello's *energeia*, which Higgons hopes he has captured in English, is an analogue to Liberi's visual *desegno* and therefore an appropriate medium through which one may mentally perceive the motion in the painting. Though Higgons does not specifically use the term *energeia*, the following passage makes it plain that this is his main criterion:

Besides the noble Persons which are here celebrated, there is something else . . . that will entertain your Lordship. I imagine, you will be pleased to hear Busenello discourse to Liberi, the rareness of his art, and the incredible things that are done by Painting; to see such a description of Colours, expressing Nature to the Life; and then Words with as great a life, expressing those Colours. Methinks here is no ill Idea of those two noble Sisters, Poesy and Picture, the Sciences of Words and Colours. And which of them my Lord, in your judgment, deserve to be preferd? which of them, shall we believe, imitates Nature best and which has the advantage of the other, silent, or talking painting? But I will leave your Lordship with Busenello, to determine that question, and beg pardon for my confidence in this Addresse.[23]

Some key terms in this passage require explanation. Busenello "discourses" on the things that can be achieved by painting: the celebration of "noble Persons" and the achievement of "rareness" and "incredible" things done by painting. But in addition to telling his reader about art, he endows his words "with as great a life." The key idea is that through the poet's rhetorical *colorire* a reader may vicariously witness colors as they appear in nature. Color in the language of visible forms has its equivalent in written language and even in music. In the work of painters, such colors express "Nature to the Life," and words enjoy "as great a life, expressing those Colours." This "science" of words and colors is nothing less than what Paolo Lomazzo had called the principle of motion: "It is generally confessed of all men, that all such motions in pictures . . . doe most neerely resemble the life."[24] As Lomazzo says, motions such as these are the common ground "Betweene Painting and Poetrie." Painting, he had declared, "is an instrument vnder which the treasure of the memory is contained, insomuch as writing is nothing else, but a picture of white and black" (an idea echoed by Ben Jonson in "My Answer. The Poet to the Painter"). Truly those pictures are in black and white upon the page, but in the reader's imagination they may be transformed (through the poet's control of *energeia*) into vivid colors.

Busenello's poem and Higgons' explanations of it to Lord Peterbourgh are two of the major keys to Waller's poem. An additional factor lies in the instructional rhetoric of the increasing number of works in English that appeared in the seventeenth century offering to teach drawing and painting. One such work is Henry Peacham's *The Compleate Gentleman* (1634). In the thirteenth chapter we find the following: "To begin a Picture, first draw the Eye, the white thereof make of white Lead with a little Charcoale black; having finished it, leave from the other Eye the distance of an Eye, then draw the proportion of the Nose, the compasse of the Face, after that make the Mouth, the Eare, the Haire, &c." The blunt didactic tone has not changed at all from the initial appearance of these instructions in Peacham's earlier *Drawing with the Pen* (1606): "Con-

cerning these directions I haue giuen, they are such as I thought in respect of their breuity & plainnesse, fit for the capacity of the young learner, for whom they were first and principally intended." "But if (Reader) thou shalt find any thing herein worthy thy practise of likeing, I care not what the others say."[25] Accordingly Peacham gives precise orders, first for drawing a face and then for drawing an entire body. Perhaps more pertinent to the kind of instruction we find in later seventeenth-century poems are Peacham's rules for doing landscapes: "*You shall alwaies* in your Landtskip *shewe* a fair Horison, *and expresse* the heauen more or less either ouercast by clouds, or with a cleare sky, *shewing* the sunne rising or setting ouer some hill or other; *you shall seldome*, except vpon necessity, *shew* the moone or stars, because we imagin al things to be seene by day." And finally, "if you laie your Landskip in coulours, the farther you goe, the more *you must lighten* it with a thinne and aiery blew, *to make it seeme* farre off. . . ." In depicting drapery, "*you must not vse* much folding where the garments ought to fit close," and "to make a chamlet, *you shall draw* but fiue lines waued ouerthwart."[26]

Comparison of the instructional rhetoric that had become so familiar in writings on art with the rhetoric of Waller's poetic "Instructions" speaks quite adequately for itself:

First *Draw* the Sea, that portion which between
The greater World and this of ours is seen
Here place the British, there the Holland Fleet,
Vast floating Armies, both prepar'd to meet.

    Draw the whole World, expecting who shall Raign
After this Combat, o're the conquer'd Mayn;
Make Heav'n concern'd, and an usual Star
Declare th' importance of th' approaching War.

    Make the Sea shine with Gallantry, and all
The English Youth flock to their Admiral
The valiant DUKE whose early Deeds abroad
Such Rage in Fight, and Art in Conduct show'd.
His bright Sword, now, a dearer Int'rest draws,
His Brothers Glory, and his Country's Cause.

    Let thy bold Pencil Hope and Courage *spread*
Through the whole Navy by his Highness led;
Make all appear, where such a Prince is by,
Resolv'd to Conquer, or resolv'd to Dye.[27]

This passage also exhibits assumptions about art and poetry identical to those discussed in Higgon's dedication to Lord Peterbourgh: the celebration of "noble Persons," a "discourse" on the "rareness" of art and the "incredible things that are done by Painting," and a "description of Colours, expressing Nature to the Life." By "expressing Nature," neither Higgons nor Waller means what a modern might think. Where we would expect realistic representation or description, they think in terms of iconographic and symbolic givens. Waller's poem does not call for photographic realism. Instead, he assumes his reader's familiarity with such iconographic commonplaces as Fame, Valor, Rage, Heroic Virtue, Glory, and the like. Such details are offered by Cesare Ripa in his *Iconologia* (1603). There, Fame (*fama bvona*) is depicted as a woman holding a trumpet in her right hand and an olive branch in her left; she wears a necklace of gold and a white cape billowing out from her shoulders. The trumpet signifies the sound of Fame, which is universally heard (the iconographic expression of which occurs in the title page to Raleigh's *History of the World* and is glossed by Jonson); the olive branch indicates the sincerity we expect of a truly famous person. Valor (*valore*) bears iconographic resemblance to Hercules, for it is personified as a naked man who has the skin of a lion wrapped around him in the manner of a cape. Rage (*furore superbo*) is depicted as a man armed and wearing a cuirass and helmet; he has a fiery expression and bears a sword in his right hand, a shield in his left. Finally, Glory (*gloria*) is a woman wearing a crown of gold and, like Fame, holding a trumpet. She proclaims the triumph of a principle.

Even abbreviated in this manner, Ripa's descriptions help us to understand how Waller's verbal painting could speak. His readers would have had a clear sense of the symbols necessary to body forth the concepts conveyed. Using the language of visible forms, Waller, in Higgons' words, could conflate "Poesy and Picture, the Sciences of Words and Colours." He could assume (again in Higgons' words) that neither had "the advantage of the other, silent, or talking painting." And he could expect his readers to understand that in either the imagined or the real painting there would be "study of designe, more variety of Colouring, more Art and invention, and more patience and dilligence then in any picture by the Life, which is the worke of a few dayes onely."

The last remark appears in Edward Norgate's *Miniatura*, in the discussion of the "Lymning of Histories." In histories, Norgate declares, "there are many figures, and those of different Complexions and ages, wherein the passions of the mind as well as the lineaments of the body are to be exprest." And he adds that "there must be in the workman a prompt and ready hand, and Invention . . . well read in study, and something of the poet."[28] We see how faithfully Norgate states Waller's assumptions. Poetry must aid painting, and painting must flesh out the concepts presented in poetry.

Higgons, Norgate, and Waller—the translator, the man writing instructively about art, and the poet—each spoke in his respective voice to the issue that England deserved heroic and decorative art comparable to that found on the Continent. The common theme for each is summed up in the term *istoria*, a genre whose rules have been developed as far back as Alberti's *On Painting*. "The greatest work of the painter," Alberti had said, "is

Figure 39. Hans (Johannes) Liefrinck, Caricatures after Leonardo da Vinci. Copyright Museum Plantin-Moretus, Antwerp.

the *istoria*." To him the term connoted monumentality and dramatic content, but it also meant intellectual depth. The ordering of themes and figures through variety and richness had to be accomplished with restraint, verisimilitude, and dignity. Alberti did not, however, present a rigid set of rules. He merely declared that "composition is that rule of painting by which the parts of the things seen fit together in the painting. The greatest work is not a colossus, but an *istoria*. *Istoria* gives greater renown to the intellect than any colossus." And when proper variety and verisimilitude are presented by the painter, "the *istoria* will move the soul of the beholder."[29]

Indeed, the criterion of motion, of movement or *energeia*, is dominant in Higgons' remarks about Busenello. And because those remarks appear to lie at the foundations of Waller's poem it is worth keeping in mind Alberti's further comments on the subject:

When we have an *istoria* to paint, we will first think out the method and the order to make it more beautiful; we will make our drawings and models of all the *istoria* and every one of its parts first of all; we will call our friends to give advice about it. We will force ourselves to have every part well thought out in our mind from the beginning, so that in the work we will know how each thing

Figure 40. Sir Peter Lely, *Anne Hyde, Duchess of York*. Courtesy of Scottish National Portrait Gallery, Edinburgh.

ought to be done and where located. In order to have the greatest certainty we will divide our models with parallels. In the public work we will take from our drawings just as we draw maxims and citations from our private commentaries.[30]

Alberti's advice reads almost like a blueprint for what we may now suspect Waller to have done in preparation for his "Instructions to a Painter." Waller took what he could from the poem by Busenello, recasting it in the light of Higgons' remarks to Lord Peterbourgh and then applying the motif to the current event. While Anacreon may have supplied a comparable topos, Waller's efforts were aimed at the much richer, more complex idea of Alberti's *istoria*.

For the first sixty-five lines of the expanded version of his poem, Waller gives his reader a vicarious experience with "drawings and models" of the *istoria* and, incidentally, a preview of those "incredible things" that Higgons said "are done by Painting." Verbal coloring (*colorire* in the painter's manuals but *energeia* in the manuals of verbal style) thus becomes the poet's way of assimilating "Poesy and Picture." And it is on this foundation that Waller begins, in line sixty-seven, to narrate, not draw, the fable of the battle. Shifting entirely to a

verbal presentation, he concedes to poetry the sole capacity to give a beginning, middle, and end to the *favola*. But in keeping with the presumed parallel between his poem and the imagined painting, the narration unfolds through a sequence of variants. The effect is supposed to parallel the details that might appear in the foreground, middle ground, and background of a large heroic painting comparable to those found in the banqueting hall at Whitehall. When we perceive what Waller has done, we are less apt to criticize him for dropping the advice motif. He has, in fact, dropped nothing. Instead, he has shifted into a more strictly *literary* procedure to suggest through words the experience a viewer would have in scanning a complex painting such as Liberi's from one side to the other. Verbal narration belongs to his plan which includes painting *and* poetry, which is apparent when he explains in the final lines, "Painter! excuse me if I have awhile / Forgot thy art, and *used another style*" (italics added). Because the Muses (in Higgons' words) "instruct us how to write," their dictates have had to assume temporary priority over the artist's "famed pencil." But at the poem's conclusion Waller has resumed "drawing" and concludes in the mode with which he began: "Last draw the Commons at his royal feet."

Waller's "Instructions" led to an anonymous "Second Advice" in 1667. This was followed in that same year by a "Third" and then by a "Fourth." The mode now, however, was satiric rather than panegyric. A "Fifth" appears at last to have encouraged Andrew Marvell to write "The Last Instructions to a Painter." Marvell demonstrates how poetry and painting continued to enjoy a close relationship in spite of the new mode the genre had assumed. Where Waller took his pattern secondhand from an Italian *istoria*, Marvell found a visual analogue in a Dutch engraving celebrating Holland's victory at Chatham on June 9, 1667.[31] Closer inspection shows him also to have written according to the lessons offered by that uniquely seventeenth-century invention, caricature.[32]

In scale and effect, caricature is the opposite of the heroic. And Marvell offers a brilliant example in his depiction of Sir Edward Turnor, speaker of the Commons. Though Turnor wears a "golden gown" and exhibits "Bright hair, [and] face," the poet instructs the painter to do his head as though it were a solid, wooden mace. Depicted in turn as a smoke-puffing cook in an apron and a swelling "squatted toad," Turnor's appearance in the reader's inner eye conforms closely to what the seventeenth-century had learned from Leonardo (fig. 39), from Guercino, and, of course, the Carracci brothers. And Turnor is not Marvell's only victim to be exposed to visual imagination. St. Albans (Henry Jermyn) is to be "painted" with "Drayman's shoulders, butchers Mein, / Member'd like Mules, with Elephantine chinne" (ll. 33–34). And the duchess of York (ll. 49–63) is to be painted "with Oyster lip, and Breath of Game." Instead of the feminine figure portrayed by Lely (fig. 40), she is to have a "Wide mouth that Spargus may well proclaim" and a "Chanc'lor's Belly, and so large a Rump."

By the end of the seventeenth century the satiric impulse in poetry seems to have gained ascendancy over the heroic, and an increased number of poems on the so-called ugly-woman theme began to appear. Just at the time when the art of portraiture achieved its most cherished goals under the brushes of Van Dyck and Lely, the art of caricature began to compete successfully with it.[33] In fact, we shall not be far from the mark in looking for a reciprocal development between poetry and painting. William Sanderson remarked, for example, in his *Graphice* (London, 1658) that Van Dyck was the "first painter that 'er put Ladies dresse into a carelesse Romance" (p. 39). Once the canons of attractiveness and seductiveness were relaxed to include the *disordine*, Robert Herrick's "Delight in Disorder" and Lovelace's "To Aramantha, that she would Dishevel her Hair" took up the identical theme. It was then a simple matter to take the next step and to play more and more openly with total repulsiveness. Accordingly, the stinking old hag who propositions a young man in Horace's infamous eighth *Epode* ("Rogare longo putidam te saeculo") finds her counterpart in John Cleveland's "A Young Man to an Old Woman Courting him." But Cleveland's poem proves no match for John Suckling's inversion of pictorial, to say nothing of Petrarchist and poetical, ideals in "The Deformed Mistress."

Waller's "Instructions to a Painter epitomizes some major critical assumptions of the age. It is a watershed in the development of taste which gradually shifted from the heroic to the satiric. But even with this shift, satirists relied heavily on the language of visible forms then developed by caricaturists. And John Dryden gave the dependence of high art in poetry upon comparably high art in painting the strongest possible stamp of approval in his preface to Alphonse du Fresnoy's highly influential *De Arte Graphica*. In that preface, titled "A Parallel of Poetry and Painting," Dryden declared that "the art of painting has a wonderful affinity with that of poetry; and that there is betwixt them a certain common imagination. For, as the poets introduce the gods and heroics, and all those things which are either majestical, honest, or delightful, in like manner the painters, by the virtue of their outlines, colours, lights, and shadows, represent the same things and persons in their pictures."

It is perhaps vain to speculate whether these lines would have been written had there not been such a flowering of English visual art in the seventeenth century. But Lovelace and Waller wrote with a refined sense of graphic organization and employed the grammar of seeing as skillfully as any one of their contemporaries. Their poems emanate from an art-conscious society, and we must read their works with a mind (as well as an eye) to the brilliant visual art of Rubens, Van Dyck, and Lely as well as to the achievements of such great collectors as Charles I, Buckingham, Endymion Porter, and a host of others.

6. Herrick's Hesperidean Garden:
Ut pictura poesis Applied

"The most pleasant of all outward pastimes," Robert Burton declares, is "to walk amongst orchards, gardens, bowers, mounts, and arbours, artificiall wildernesses, green thickets, arches, groves, lawns, rivulets, fountains, and such like pleasant places."[1] Though he has little to say in this connection about comparable inward pastimes, one need look no farther than such miscellanies as *Briton's Bowre of Delights* (1591, 1597), *The Arbor of Amorous Devises* (1597), *England's Helicon* (1600, 1614), and *Bel-vedere: or the Garden of the Muses* (1600) to realize that for the seventeenth-century reader a book of poems was often the verbal equivalent of a garden. Indeed, an experience within such a verbal universe was often regarded in horticultural terms, and for this there was ample mythological precedent in the Hesperidean garden of the Muses.

Henry Hawkins, who sees the physical garden in which Burton would have us walk as an emblem of universal harmony, begs his Genius in *Partheneia Sacra* (1633) to lead the reader into a similar poetic garden: a "goodlie Amphitheatre of flowers, upon whose leaves delicious beauties stand, as on a stage, to be gazed on and to play their parts."[2] In its blend of emblematic image with poetry, *Partheneia Sacra* offers both a series of visible "stages" and lines to be delivered on them. Its visual as well as verbal multiformity is thus compatible with Burton's further advice when he recommends "inspection alone of those curious iconographies of temples and palaces." And when he adds the recreations of both country and city, the "May-games, feasts, wakes, and merry meetings" where men "solace themselves," Burton prescribes in 1628 much that was to appear in the collected poems of Robert Herrick.

By 1648 there was good reason for that poet to call his large and multiplex collection *Hesperides*. G. C. Moore Smith remarked many years ago that the name is conventionally enough used to mean, not the nymphs of the gardens, but the gardens themselves.[3] And Roger Rollin has remarked more recently that "Herrick's book itself [is] the new Hesperides, a garden whose golden fruits take the shape of poems."[4] For of all the poets who wrote and published their verse during the first half of the seventeenth century, Robert Herrick was most consistently conscious of his work as a verbal succession of pictures. Even the design of his book acknowledges the compatibility of painting and poems, and when we add to the visual message of the frontispiece the broad image of subjects announced in "The Argument of his Book" it readily becomes apparent that *Hesperides* is a verbal garden nurtured and sustained by the concept of picture—*ut pictura poesis* applied. It is time to explore it in the light of Horace's *Ars poetica* (ll. 361 ff.).

In 1675 Edward Phillips wrote that what is "chiefly pleasant in these poems [i.e. *Hesperides*] is now and then a pretty Floury and Pastoral gale of Fancy, a vernal prospect of some Hill, Cave, Rock, or Fountain; which but for the interruption of other trivial passages might have made up one of the worst Poetic Landskips."[5] The unimaginative Phillips missed the artistry of Herrick's lyric achievements, although he identified a major generic feature of the poems, that of landscape. "Landskip," writes Henry Peacham in *The Art of Drawing with the Pen and Limning in Water Colours* (London, 1606), "is a Dutch word & it is as much as we shoulde say in English landship, or expressing of the land by hills, woodes, Castles, seas, valleys, ruines, hanging rocks, Cities, Townes, &c, as farre as may bee shewed within our Horizon." Notably, though, landscape is only seldom drawn "by it self, but in respect & for the sake of some thing els." For this reason, "it falleth out among those thing[s] which we call *Parerga*, the accessory elements in a properly subordinated landscape." In a section called "Of the Fairest and Most Beautiful Landskips in the World," which appeared first in the 1612 edition, Peacham explains that landscape is properly associated with traveling because it takes a variety of subjects. Indeed, his list of subject matter for the landscape artist is quite wide:

If you draw your Landskip according to your invention, you shall please very well, if you shew in the same, the faire side of some goodly Cittie, haven, forrest, stately house with gardens. I ever took delight in those peeces that shewed to the life a countrey village, faire or market, *Bergamascas* cookerie, *Morrice* dancing, peasants together by the eares, and the like.[6]

It is a short step from this to Herrick's declared intention to sing "of *May-poles, Hock-carts, Wassails, Wakes, / Of Bridegrooms, Brides,* and of their *Bridallcakes,*" to say nothing of his writing "of *Youth,* [and] of *Love.*" The step is particularly short when we make it with Burton's encouragement "to walk amongst orchards, gardens, bowers . . . and such like places" and to enjoy "may-games, feasts, wakes, and merry meetings." The notion of variety and diversity, the mixture of pure scene with the activities of those who dwell naturally and properly in such a scene, the juxtaposition of fertile and barren, of smooth and rough, of near and far, of mountains and lowlands—all are present in Herrick's lyrics just as they are in the landscapes of the late sixteenth and early seventeenth centuries. In short, there is a strong parallel to the theories and effects of the visual arts in the works of this English poet. To discuss this parallel requires discussion of (1) the pertinence to a reading of *Hesperides* of William Marshall's engraved frontispiece to the 1648 edition, (2) the inferences that may be drawn from the several poems that relate directly to painters and painting, and (3) Herrick's apparent fascination with the visual experience and with the ideas stimulated by iconic and *ekphrastic* poetry.

The frontispiece to *Hesperides* (fig. 41) shows us the bust of a curly-headed man in profile, which emphasizes his prominent nose and mustache. The landscape setting for the bust includes the Hill of Parnassus, the Spring of Helicon, Pegasus about to soar from the hill, trees, and a group of nine naked figures who may be intended to represent the Muses. Two of these winged figures fly with wreaths of flowers (presumably from the Garden of the Hesperides) and prepare to crown the bust of the poet. Two others, holding branches of bay or olive leaves, sit in the foreground and point to a Latin poem inscribed on the pedestal where the bust resides, while five others circle in a dance beneath the largest tree.

It has been questioned whether "the engraver . . . intended this to portray Herrick" and suggested that "the picture may well be merely a generalized representation of the poet."[7] And there are further questions that arise in connection with this frontispiece. First, does Marshall's engraving have a genuine relation to the contents of the book? Or is it simply an addendum, a piece of random decoration? Second, is there some emblematic cue in this engraving to what a reader might expect to find, some forecast as to the nature and genre of his poetry and to the experience one may anticipate having with it?

The frontispiece has an organic relation to the contents of the book, as the previous discussion of Ben Jonson's

Figure 41. William Marshall, engraver, frontispiece to Robert Herrick, *Hesperides* (1648). Courtesy of Humanities Research Center, The University of Texas at Austin.

and Richard Crashaw's poems explaining frontispieces should indicate. Merely decorative as these pictorial images may seem to us, they were taken seriously and symbolically by contemporary readers. And in the *Hesperides* such an organic relationship is seen in "The Pillar of Fame," the penultimate poem, which clearly seems to echo the visual monument of the frontispiece in both its statement and in its topiary character. As was explained in chapter 4, in addition to their symbolic and hieroglyphic nature these frontispiece and title page designs also offered a visible threshold separating reading experience from lived experience. Alfred Johnson, for example, observed that "the title-page had ceased to be purely decorative and has become a thing of emblems and allegories. The scheme was frequently based on the Roman arch flanked by symbolic figures; in the case of the Greek and Roman classics, the heroes of antiquity; in Bibles, we have Old and New Testament characters; in books of travel, Turks, Persians, and the like. In that age of metaphysical poets a number of symbolic scenes were often imposed on an architectural framework.[8] What Johnson failed to point out is that this visible

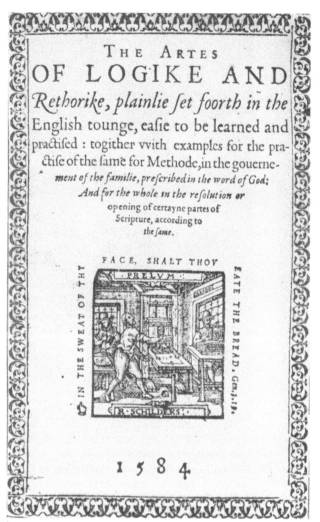

Figure 42. Title page of Dudley Fenner, *The Artes of Logike and Rethorike* (1584). Courtesy of Humanities Research Center, The University of Texas at Austin.

sense of an outside and an inside separated by a mediating threshold was as common in illuminated manuscripts as it became in printed books. The written word communicates across noncooperating links in a chain. The reception of a concept cannot, then, be checked by questioning except where the author will orally discuss his words. Consequently, the presentation of written words must include a measure of formal redundancy, an assurance of continuity. Title pages and frontispieces belong to this category of deliberate redundancy, for they facilitate readers' imaginative entry into the mental space of a book by keying them—through a combination of words and pictures—to the appropriate expectations. Readers not only know what information or persuasion they are reading for, but they know that reading stands in a certain relation to speech. It is perhaps not so well known in this connection that rubrics and title pages in illuminated manuscripts as well as printed

books frequently make visual allusion to the link between speaking and reading, to the identification of the written word as an extension of the spoken.[9] In such cases, even before readers begin to read the words of the text they are offered pictures either of a person reading or a scribe writing. These are visual representations of a concept that would require a great deal of verbal circumlocution. Moreover, they are redundancies that specifically denote the relation of words on the page to words from the mouth.

A charming little example of this visual redundancy is the woodcut colophon on the title page of Dudley Fenner's *The Artes of Logike and Rethorike* (fig. 42). In the foreground is a printer who is vigorously pulling at the handle of a press. Behind him a compositor sets type at a nearby table, while in front of him another worker inks a prepared tray of type. The book was clearly not intended for sophisticated readers. Its title is clearly homiletic, to say nothing of self-conscious in its efforts to justify its existence. These characteristics suggest that the woodcut not only identifies the printer (R. Schilders of Middleburg) but spells out in visual terms the chain of events whereby the spoken word becomes the written, which is then converted to print by means of a mechanical device. The printer's role thus stands in sharp relation to that of the reader and the author. Like the countless rubrics that depict a man holding an open book, a scribe writing in his cell, or a reader interpreting a text to a small audience, this image bridges a chasm that is more formidable to those with minimal reading skills than those practiced in silent reading.

Such unsophisticated examples of reader preparation through pictorial images and threshold symbols help us to perceive the function of a complex frontispiece like that opposite the title page of *Hesperides*.[10] And in view of the mediating function of this pictorial page, we are on secure ground in assuming the poet to be a representation of Robert Herrick, even if we understand the frontispiece to be something of an emblematic tableau. For the character of such tableaux is such that they combine naturalistic representation with some organization in space which is not naturalistic but artificial, schematic, or diagrammatic. In allegorical tableaux, moreover, the verbal element with all its capacity for weighted intensification is quite equal to the visual element in its often quite unrealistic spatial frame. This is to say that the space inside the pictorial element is denaturalized and is subordinated to the overall scheme of picture and word. While "all real or dramatic actions take place in time, real or imagined, respectively," in the allegorical tableau there is no human time element at work. It may well involve figures pictured in some sort of action, but it remains "basically a diagram felt as committed to space in such a way as to be free of time, like a geometrical triangle or square."[11] If the portrait in *Hesperides* is in fact a representation of Herrick—that is, a representation of nature—then its presence in the emblematic field of this tableau informs readers that they may anticipate a continuing relation between the poet's own Hesperidean fiction and its informing realities, a relation displayed in another mode by the poet's own assimilation of the visual in the verbal. The blend of realism and allegory in the frontispiece warns against any simplistic reading of the poems and suggests that they do in fact seek a balance between the modalities of naturalism and allegory.

Since there appear to be no other portraits of Herrick, the test of verisimilitude must lie in the assumption that portraits by William Marshall offer reasonably accurate representations. An approximate example is Marshall's frontispiece to Sir John Suckling's *Fragmenta Aurea*

(1646) (fig. 43). The visual accuracy of this engraving can readily be compared with that of Van Dyck's portrait (fig. 44). Marshall has captured the essential features of Suckling's face: the direct and frank look about the eyes, the set of the mouth, and the structure of the cheekbones and nose. Though there is admittedly a degree of idealization in each picture, Marshall's portrait is clearly an attempt at a natural likeness. Further examination of Marshall's other engravings, such as those of Robert Baron, Charles I, George Villiers, John Hall, and William Lilly, reveals his close attention to the idiosyncratic features of individual faces.[12] The engraving of Herrick appears, then, to be a genuine portrait—and not only *a* portrait, but the *only* portrait of the poet. We may conclude that the visual complexity of the frontis-

Figure 43. William Marshall, engraver, frontispiece to Sir John Suckling, *Fragmenta Aurea* (1646). This item is reproduced by permission of The Huntington Library, San Marino, California.

Figure 44. Sir Anthony Van Dyck, *Sir John Suckling.* Copyright The Frick Collection, New York.

Figure 45. William Marshall, engraver, bust of Henry Carew, frontispiece to J. F. Senault, *The Use of Passions* (1649). This item is reproduced by permission of The Huntington Library, San Marino, California.

piece was intended to complement (and perhaps even define) the poet's achievement in his poems.

As we scan the frontispiece (fig. 41) we perceive that a large bust of the poem rests upon an ornate pedestal occupying the entire foreground of the picture. The bust and pedestal rest, in turn, upon a stone slab that bears a commendatory Latin inscription by John Harmar. The practice here is in keeping with including inscriptions in works of visual art to intensify the significance of the visual.[13] To insure our attention to the verses, two *putti* (each bearing a laurel branch symbolic of eternity and triumph) point to the inscription, and the juxtaposition of picture and word immediately characterizes the piece as an allegorical tableau. We are not, therefore, to ex-

pect natural representation in the picture, although we may assume that the bust does depict Herrick.

Our perception of the frontispiece "occurs" within a perceived setting between the visual and the verbal, a condition that is especially propitious for creativity.[14] The garden in which the memorial statue is placed is denaturalized, and yet it retains trees, groves, rolling hills, a pleasant valley, and a spring—the visual components of a *locus amoenus*. Here the iconology of the picture takes precedence over any traditional notion of landscape. We know that the hill must be Helicon and that the spring flowing from its base is Hippocrene, the waters of which are released by the hard hoof of Pegasus and are sacred to the nine Muses. We notice that it is toward Helicon that the bust of the poet faces. And perhaps with equal appropriateness it is toward Herrick that Pegasus himself faces as he rears majestically on Helicon. The interrelatedness of these images of the poet, the mountain, and the winged horse promotes the viewer's conscious perception of having crossed boundaries normally denoted by time and space. Instead of framing the poet in a conventional cartouche (as he had done with the portrait of Suckling), instead of leaving the bust in a starkly unadorned and unframed setting (as he had done with the bust of Henry Carew, earl of Monmouth [fig. 45]), and instead of using the far more conventional architectural setting, Marshall has framed the image of Robert Herrick with symbols that define the *condition* the poet has achieved through his poetry: inspired composition (the association with Pegasus), responsiveness to classical traditions and conventions (the association with Helicon and the Muses), eternal fame (the association with the *putti*, and again with Pegasus). In so doing, Marshall has in effect linked the frontispiece of *Hesperides* with "The Pillar of Fame" at its conclusion. There, in a topiary poem that combines the visual and the verbal, thus contrasting with the engraving's combination of the verbal and the visual, Herrick writes:

> FAmes pillar here, at last, we set,
> Out-during *Marble, Brasse,* or *Jet,*
>   Charm'd and enchanted so,
>   As to withstand the blow
>   Of overthrow:
>   Nor shall the seas,
>   Or OUTRAGES
>   Of storms orebear
>   What we up-rear
>   Tho Kingdoms fal,
>   This pillar never shall
>   Decline or waste at all;
> But stand for ever by his owne
> Firme and well fixt foundation.

We do not see the memorial statue of Robert Herrick in a representation of the Garden of Hesperides. For one thing, there is none of the traditional Hesperidean iconography in the picture—nothing about the famous apples, the eleventh labor of Hercules, the dragon, and so on. But as we ponder the title that faces this picture, we come gradually to the recognition that Herrick's Hesperides is the poetic collection that follows and toward which the poet's gaze directs us as we turn over the facing leaf and commence to read.

As we walk about (i.e., "read") this garden, we anticipate that our experience will be the verbal equivalent to seeing, a perception which rests squarely on the Horation doctrine *ut pictura poesis*. A preponderance of the poems are to be read as speaking pictures, as "landskips," where scenes of village life and rustic pleasures mingle with the tales of the fairy kingdom and descriptions of trees and flowers, or read simply as iconic poems in which the poet contemplates an already formed graphic representation. In still another sense, the large number of epigrams that pervade *Hesperides* also argue for the principle of poetry as speaking picture, especially if we call to mind the inscriptive nature of that poetic genre, which was to make some object to "speak" to the beholder. In this respect, nearly all the "Julia" poems function as individual inscriptions elaborating the image of Julia.

Herrick's apparently conscious application of the *ut pictura poesis* principle to his poetry may be argued, initially, on the basis of the poem addressed to his nephew—himself an artist—in which the poet identifies an impressive group of major painters; the list is comparable to nothing in the works of contemporary poets. Second, it is arguable from his friendship with and patronage by Endymion Porter, whose prominence in the collection and patronage of art has been discussed in chapter 5. Third, it is arguable on the basis of "To his Honoured Kinsman, Sir Richard Stone," which poses the tantalizing possibility that Herrick took as his primary schema the famous statue-gallery of the earl of Arundel. And finally, it is arguable from the advice-to-a-painter poems in which Herrick demonstrates uncommon skill in manipulating the reciprocal demands of the verbal and the visual.

"To his Nephew, to be prosperous in his art of Painting" is addressed in all probability to Henry Stone, a son of Nicholas Stone of Devon, who was the outstanding English mason-sculptor of the period.

> ON, as thou has begunne, brave youth, and get
> The Palme from *Urbin*, *Titian*, *Tintarret*,
> *Brugel* and *Coxie*, and the workes outdoe,
> Of Holben, and That mighty Ruben too.
> So draw, and paint, as none may do the like
> No, not the glory of the World, Vandike.

Henry was baptized in London on July 15, 1616; he died there on August 24, 1653. The inscription on his tomb states that he "passed the greatest part of 37 years in Holland, France, and Italy." He returned to England from Italy in 1643. Henry is not to be confused with the Simon Stone who specialized in copies of Van Dyck, Titian, and other prominent Renaissance artists. Rather, he appears to have been better than a mere copyist, and it is even possible that Henry painted some of the pictures thought to be by the celebrated William Dobson.[15] He also composed a modest treatise called *The Third Part of the Art of Painting*, which we may legitimately suspect was known to his uncle, the Dutch painter Thomas De Keyser at Amsterdam, to whom he was apprenticed as a young man. From the unusual familiarity with the prominent artists of his time that Herrick exhibits in this poem, we may surmise that he, like so many of his contemporaries, learned much from the art trade of connoisseurs. Indeed, we should have sufficient basis for this surmise in Herrick's friendship with Endymion Porter.

He evidently enjoyed a close relationship to this well-known patron of both poets and painters. Porter seems to have encouraged Herrick as much as he encouraged such painters as Anthony Van Dyck, Daniel Mytens, and Orazio Gentileschi. Certainly, Endymion Porter figures prominently in Herrick's poems, four of which are addressed to him and one of which includes his voice in a pastoral dialogue[16]—and the house described in Herrick's "The Country Life, to the honoured Mr. End: Porter" is quite possibly Porter's own elegantly furnished home, Aston-sub-Edge, whose cabinet of paintings is described in Richard Lovelace's "Amyntor's Grove."

Through his friendship with Porter, Herrick could also have enjoyed access to the earl of Arundel's collection. Indeed, one of his poems, "To his Honoured Kinsman, Sir Richard Stone," suggests this to have been the case:

> TO this *white Temple* of my *Heroes*, here
> Beset with stately Figures (every where)
> Of such rare *Saint-ships*, who did here consume
> Their lives in sweets, and left in death perfume.
> Come thou *Brave man*! And bring with Thee a Stone
> Unto thine own *Edification*.
> High are These Statues here, besides no lesse
> Strong then the Heavens for everlastingnesse:
> Where build aloft; and being fixt by These,
> Set up Thine own *eternall Images*.

The basic image in this poem, that of a "*white Temple* of . . . *Heroes*"—figuring significant achievement and the honors attendant upon that achievement—may depend upon the very same pictorial formula used in the portrait of the earl of Arundel in his famous statue-gallery by Daniel Mytens, who was also patronized by Endymion Porter (fig. 46). It may be a visual schema developed in Italy and used by artists elsewhere[17] rather than a representation of the earl's collection, but it is certainly true that by the late thirties of the seventeenth century

Figure 46. Daniel Mytens, *Thomas Howard, Earl of Arundel.* Courtesy of the Tate Gallery, by permission of His Grace the Duke of Norfolk.

tial bits of evidence suggesting Herrick's awareness of the pantheon of painters and, perhaps, of the statue gallery—itself an important visual metaphor—dedicated to the fame of heroic men. But in his two poems written according to the instruction-to-a-painter topos, we may witness Herrick's ability to bridge the demands of the two arts. The first of these is "To the Painter, to draw him a Picture," one of the earliest English poems of its kind: [19]

> Come, skilfull *Lupo*, now, and take
> Thy *Bice*, thy *Umber*, *Pink*, and *Lake*;
> And let it be thy Pensils strife,
> To paint a Bridgeman to the life:
> Draw him as like too, as you can,
> An old, poore, lying, flatt'ring man:
> His cheeks be-pimpled, red and blue;
> His nose and lips a mulbrie hiew,
> Then for an easie fansie; place
> A Burling iron for his face:
> next, make his cheeks with breath to swell,
> And for to speak, if possible:
> But do not so; for feare, lest he
> Sho'd by his breathing, poyson thee.

The speaker's direct address to Lupo immediately locates the event in human or dramatic time. A person has approached the artist with instructions for the composition of a picture. Our attention goes rather automatically to the verbal event (perhaps even the narrative event) in which we are only vicarious participants. "Come," "take," and "let" are spoken within the precincts of this narrative framework. But a curious thing happens after "let." It is to be "thy Pensils strife, / To paint a Bridgeman to the life." By putting the emphasis on the pencil, the instrument, Herrick removes attention from the person, the artist; to a degree, the artist fades from view while the pictorial creation achieves an autonomy. In line 5, "Draw" momentarily returns us to an awareness of the dramatic event. But the ensuing description of the proposed portrait exerts an unavoidable pull toward the iconic. Lines 5–9, then, are virtually *ekphrastic*. They describe an object that resides in the stilled ("still" to use the pun employed by Keats in his "Ode on a Grecian Urn" and Eliot in "Burnt Norton") world of plastic forms. Indeed, the language of the poem is the device whereby the effect of stillness is created and maintained. Spatial concerns have overcome for the moment all temporal concerns: before us we see the face of an old, poor, lying, flattering man with pimpled cheeks discolored as much by the outer elements as by the inner disease of a mean and crafty disposition. In line 9 the imperative, "place," temporarily reasserts the dominance of the original dramatic moment, and in line 11 "make" reinforces our sense of resumed temporal progression of events. But the suspense generated in lines

Arundel House had reached the height of its splendor, the sculpture collection being said to have comprised "no less than thirty-seven pieces, one hundred and twenty-eight busts and two hundred and fifty inscriptions, as well as large number of sarcophagi, altars and fragments. And the sculpture was, of course, only part of what the house could boast." [18] Whether or not Mytens' painting is the representation of a place, it is certainly the visual equivalent to Herrick's panegyric. Mytens, like the poet, invites the beholder to see a pantheon—a white temple of heroes where statuary towers over one's head. And Herrick, like Mytens, suggests an actual place (Arundel House?) through "this" temple of heroes that is "here / Beset with stately Figures."

Neither of these two poems conveys an inner sense of the *ut pictura poesis* dictum. They are only circumstan-

11–12 is based almost wholly on visual perception vicariously entertained. We are expected to see in our mind's eye the painter's ultimate, anticipated triumph—that of creating an illusion which seems on the verge of actually speaking. This, after all, was the achievement attributed to Zeuxis, who, according to tradition, painted a thoroughly lifelike image of Helen, and of Apelles and Praxiteles, who both rendered perfect and all-but-breathing images of Phryne. But it is at just this point that the speaker in the dramatic, temporal framework of the poem hesitates. Reversing direction, which has been toward the iconic creation of a living picture in the tradition of Philostratus' *Imagines*, that an image so true to life "Sho'd by his breathing, poyson thee." In doing so he calls us back from *pictura* to *poema*.

All the theoretical ingredients of the *ut pictural poesis* formula are here: the doctrine of imitation, the doctrine of invention, and the doctrine of expression. Verbally, we have followed the imitation of a dramatized event. But closely associated with that event, we have been invited to participate vicariously in a visual *compositione*. The *dispositio*, or blocking out of the poem's rhetorical course, has paralleled the *circonscriptione*, or the outline drawing of the caricature as it is created by the "Pensils strife." And in the *elocutio* of the poem—its actual spoken performance—we learn that such an accurate visual likeness as has emerged through words comes dangerously close to being as disgusting as the model in person.[20] The description of the painting, the iconic element, has also brought the reader vicariously into the midst of the most popular of the Renaissance *paragone*, the strife between nature and art (see also fig. 4). The visual and the verbal have fought it out here, and the verbal appears to have won. But it is only because the visual threatens to reproduce actuality so vividly that the capacity of art to sustain illusion would be destroyed.

"The Eye" is Herrick's only other poem using the instructions-to-a-painter topos. But here, instead of framing the instructions within a clearly dramatized situation, Herrick launches immediately into them:

Make me a heaven; and make me there
Many a lesse and greater sphaere.
Make me the straight, and oblique lines;
The Motions, Lations, and the Signes.
Make me a Chariot, and a Sun;
And let them through a Zodiac run:
Next, place me Zones, and Tropicks there;
With all the Seasons of the Yeare.
Make me a Sun-set; and a Night:
And then present the Mornings-light
Cloath'd in her Chamlets of Delight.
To these, make Clouds to poure downe raine;
With weather foule, then faire againe.
And when, wise Artist, that thou hast,

With all that can be, this heaven grac't;
Ah! what is then this curious skie,
But onely my *Corinna's* eye?

As we read this poem, the precise *descriptio* calls instantly to mind a well-known set of visual topoi commonly termed "le monde et les creatures." The subject of hundreds of broadside engravings and woodcuts, to say nothing of emblems, the composite subject of Herrick's proposed "picture" includes, either directly or indirectly, the seven planets, the seasons, the months, and day and night. In addition, it includes the four elements, the signs of the Zodiac, and popular meteorology.[21] As the conventional diagram of the universe begins to unfold, the cyclical progression of the seasons is compounded by the cycles of day and night until at last we reach that circle beneath the moon where clouds "poure downe raine." Not until the fourteenth line of the poem is the dramatic frame of reference established by the speaker's recognition of the "wise Artist" who presumably stands before him. And, in an interrogative that unfolds in leisurely, rhetorically periodic manner before us, we learn that this carefully structured and infinitely manifold universe is "onely my *Corinna's* eye."

The method here is comparable to that of an emblem, which required that poems be speaking pictures and that pictures be visual poems. The first thirteen lines are deliberately and systematically iconic, recalling such standard depictions of the universe as that on the title page of Robert Fludd's *Metaphysica, Physica atque Technica Historia* (Oppenheim, 1617), where we find a vivid emblem of what Herrick called "Times transshifting" (fig. 47). But instead of describing a picture that imitates reality in its natural form, it describes a hieroglyphic image. When we read the final line of the poem, the unmistakable symbol of the universe is metamorphosed into Corinna's eye, which becomes (in both senses of the term) the universe. After achieving the proper symbolic image, Herrick turns to the resources of language—in this instance the calculated effect of the interrogative mode—to reveal the significance of the emblem. Once again we should be lost without the *ut pictural poesis* maxim. For Corinna's eye, "The Eye," is itself a multiplex picture that speaks several messages simultaneously. Each element in the emblem *is* an aspect of the universe. And the manifold universe cannot help but manifest itself in the singleness of this beautiful eye.

Thus far we have prepared ourselves to walk about in Herrick's Hesperidean garden to the extent that we know to see as well as to read. From the emblematic frontispiece to the two painter poems we have learned that to relate to Herrick's verbal world we should perform the poems vicariously in a manner that allows verbalization to blend subtly with verisimilitude.[22] Indeed, it is just such a blend that Herrick himself found so pleasing in Sir John Denham's "Cooper's Hill," a poem that he praised in "To Master Denham, on his Prospective Poem." And once we have learned the technique, we see that it has been the poet's intention from the beginning for us to move vicariously about in this poetic world. In the much discussed "Argument of his Book," for example, he systematically proceeds through the links in the conventional great chain of being from the world of inanimate to animate nature, then to the world of humanity, to the world of God's mysteries of cause and effect, and to the realms of hell and heaven. He has signaled that this garden of poetry—the virtual realm—figures the realm of actuality even to the extent of expressing the way one perceives actuality. That is to say, his poems are not so much about anything; rather, they are experiences in and of themselves which relate us to the actual experience we have with the surrounding universe and even with the pictures of the universe. This is

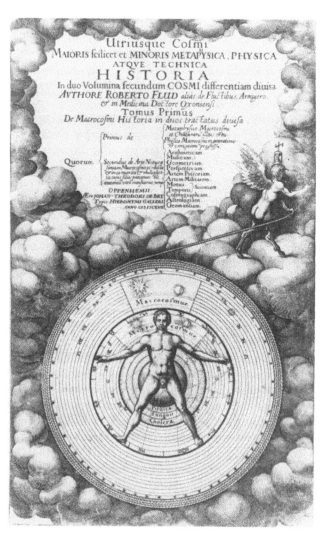

Figure 47. Title page of Robert Fludd, *Metaphysica, Physica atque Technica Historia* (1617). Courtesy of Humanities Research Center, The University of Texas at Austin.

why one's perambulations in the Hesperidean garden depend so much upon a reciprocal interplay of the visual and the verbal, the one being perceptual and the other being conceptual. The difference between Herrick and, say, Donne or Cleveland is not so much that between one who is a Cavalier and others who are Metaphysicals. Rather, it is to be seen in Herrick's deliberate foreshortening of visual conceits which Donne and Cleveland tend to leave deliberately unresolved. For such poets as those, catachresis commonly prevents images from coming together on a common ground; the compass image from "A Valediction: forbidding mourning" is illustrative. In a subtle way, Robert Herrick also brings many disparate things into the precincts of a poem. But instead of catachresis, Herrick employs the more radical principle of *ut pictura poesis*, whereby it is the visual and the verbal that are yoked together and not, as Samuel Johnson complained of the Metaphysicals, "heterogeneous ideas . . . yoked by violence together." And so smoothly does he miter the joints in this fusion of the visual and the verbal that the reader interested only in nature poetry misses the art altogether.

By way of conclusion, we may look briefly at some of the more exquisite subtleties of Herrick's blend of the visual and verbal in the "Oberon" poems, in the "Julia" poems, and in a sampling of others where his poetry embraces topoi common to the painting of the period. Andrew Marvell most fully developed the *ekphrastic* potential of poetry during the seventeenth century in England, and some have made a strong case for Marvell's use of the Horatian maxim in the composition of such poems as "The Gallery," "The Unfortunate Lover," "The Garden," and "Upon Appleton House."[23] But no one has observed that Robert Herrick often works in comparable poetic ways, particularly in the "Oberon" poems. What is remarkable is that he is doing so many years before Robert Hooke's *Micrographia* (1665) with its theme of "small things seen as great."

In Herrick's dedication of "Oberons Feast" to Thomas Shapcott, he identifies his interest in "things that are / Curious, and un-familiar." In the very first line of the poem proper he is able to begin the *ekphrasis* with "A Little mushroome table spred." It is too easy, perhaps, from our own modern perspective to view the scene as something in a doll's house, a plaything. But such a view would be misleading, for Herrick has embarked on the creation of a particular illusion through words. As he proceeds through the miniature delicacies of the feast—the "Moon-parcht grain of purest wheat," the "pure seed-Pearle of Infant dew," the "nornes of paperie Butterflies," and the "little Fuz-ball-pudding," the "late fatned" moth, and "The unctuous dewlaps of a Snaile"—we respond to the verbal pictures precisely because they link something of normal size in the actual world to the item in the fairy world. Cows in our world do have dewlaps; they are also sizable creatures, and

Figure 48. Jan Brueghel, *Sight*, from *The Five Senses Suite.*
Courtesy of Museo del Prado, Madrid.

their dewlaps have considerable bulk and weight. To speak of the dewlaps of snails is to require significant proportional adjustment on the part of the reader. At once we must visualize ourselves to be so small that the snail becomes the equivalent of a cow. This is no less spectacular than Marvell's imagined grasshoppers who peer down from grass that waves above one's head, but in Herrick's poem a tiny object in the actual world has been magnified in a consciously dislocative and disruptive way. As *pictura*, "Oberons Feast" requires a significant optical adjustment, which we now take for granted as a consequence of our telescopes, microscopes, and close-up lenses.

In "King Oberon his Cloathing," which I believe to have been written by Herrick and not sir Simeon Steward,[24] we find the same *ekphrastic* impulse and the same scalar disruption. But there is also a tactile element that intensifies the verisimilitude of the verbal picture: one of Oberon's waistcoats is made "Of the Trowt-flies guilded wing," but it is discarded because those dressing the king fear that "euen with its weight" it will "make him sweat." As in the previous poem, where the reader was invited to project a scalar self-image into the poem, we are here invited to imagine how delicate we must be for the wings of trout-flies to make us sweat. And when we

read that the lace on Oberon's doublet is "Drawne by the unctuous Snailes slow trace" and that his "Roabes for Reuelling" are "a cob-webb shirt more thinne / Then euer spider yet could spinne," we are compelled to adjust ourselves to a world of relativity where something so insubstantial in our experience assumes great substance in the world of pure verisimilitude.

The effects created by Herrick parallel those created by Jan ("Velvet") Brueghel in his vivid flower paintings as well as in his landscapes. In "The Fairie Temple," for example, the following lines manifest a clarity of object, a vividness of texture and color, and a tightly woven sense of spatial interdependencies. Of the tiny altar we read that its

. . . Linnen-Drapery is a thin
Subtile and ductile Codlin's skin;
Which o're the board is smoothly spred,
With little Seale-work Damasked.
The Fringe that circumbinds it too,
Is Spangle-work of trembling dew,
Which, gently gleaming, makes a show,
Like Frost-work glittring on the Snow.

Further, "the Fairie-Psalter [is] Grac't with the Troutflies curious wings, / Which serve for watched Ribbanings." Herrick's perceptual grasp of surfaces, textures, and proportional relationships rewards comparative reading with the painter's *Five Senses Suite* from the Prado (fig. 48). Indeed, the theme in these very detailed paintings prompts the question whether the *Hesperides* is not also a tour of the senses that combines pastoral scenes, imaginary landscapes, pictures within pictures, perspectives, mythological creatures, and still life. Certainly, Herrick's vivid flower-poems—"To Cherry-blossomes," "How Lillies came white," "To Pansies," "On Gelli-flowers begotten," and the remarkably colorful "The Lilly in a Crystall"—reflect an awareness of an interest in still life done by Brueghel and other artists of the Dutch school (fig. 49).

And there is a great deal more of an *ekphrastic* nature in the poems to Julia. "On Julia's Picture" is a purely iconic poem in which Herrick's sensuality depends upon textures, surfaces, and intimate physical detail. It is also about a picture and not the subject of the picture:

How am I ravisht! When I do but see,
The Painters art in thy *Sciography*?
If so, how much more shall I dote thereon,
When once he gives it incarnation?

Figure 49. Jan Brueghel, *Little Bouquet in a Clay Jar*. Courtesy of Kunsthistorische Museum, Vienna.

On the basis of the strong visual element in the "Julia" poems, we may wonder if when Herrick declares his intention "to sing of cleanly-Wantonness" he is doing so on the grounds that in iconic poetry the visual illusion is sustained only by the fragile temporality of language (the very epitome in art of "Times trans-shifting"). Notably, this epigram ("How I am ravisht") relies upon the same principle that we observed in "To the Painter, to draw him a Picture." Through the art of the painter, it is assumed that the image will suddenly spring into life; it will assume a natural life through the medium of art. And when he writes,

Fain would I kiss my Julia's dainty Leg,
Which is as white and hair-less as an egge.

or

Display thy breasts, my Julia, there let me
Behold that circummortall purity:
Between whose glories; there my lips Ile lay,
Ravisht, in that faire *Via Lactea*.

We are made aware that the declaration and the image are indeed so far apart that they are forever prevented from losing the delicacy of illusion—of artful representation—that is the universal hedge against pornography.

Thematically, *Hesperides* is a large and complex "landskip" which the poet is at pains to define in "The Argument of his Book" and to redefine by the poetic experiences he holds up to his readers. Like the painted landscapes of the seventeenth century,[25] Herrick's poems encompass natural scenes,[26] objects seen in a natural setting,[27] celebrations and village environs,[28] and pastorals.[29] And interspersed about this poetic landscape are several hundred epigrams, poems in a genre derived from the lineated inscription which, as we have seen in Sidney's *New Arcadia*, could appear anywhere in the stylized environment of pastoral—upon tablets, shields, and plaques as well as upon temporary structures made for pageants and processions. They also appeared in seventeenth-century paintings as cryptic, impresa-like messages like the well-known "Et in arcadia ego" in Nicholas Poussin's paintings by that title.

In the midst of this variety and poetic ripeness, Herrick's Hesperidean garden is one whose golden fruits take the form of poems. It is a garden created according to the ancient formula *ut pictura poesis*, and one in which we may "walk amongst" the verbal equivalent of "bowers, mounts, and arbours, artificiall wildernesses, green thickets, rivulets, fountaines and such like pleasant places."

7. Lady Drury's Oratory: The Painted Closet from Hawstead Hall

From Kalander's picture gallery in the fictitious Arcadia to John Donne's collection of paintings to Anthony Van Dyck's "shop of beauty" to Richard Lovelace's encomium to Endymion Porter's paintings in "Amyntor's Grove," the evidence is abundant that Renaissance art had found a receptive audience among the English. The evidence is likewise abundant that this fascination with visual expression had important bearings on poetry. It seems appropriate that the final chapter in this discussion of relations between *pictura* and *poesis* take up a virtually unknown instance of the visual and verbal synthesis, a room from Hawstead Hall, Suffolk. This room, used evidently as an oratory by Lady Anne Drury, mother of Elizabeth Drury whom Donne eulogized in his *Anniversaries*, is a rare instance—perhaps unique in England—where the emblem was transferred from its customary medium, the printed book, and applied to the walls of a chamber as an aid to contemplation or perhaps even devotion.[1]

One of the most expressive combinations of the visual and the verbal in Renaissance culture, the emblem is a synoptic genre whose very comprehensiveness led to its long neglect by scholars and critics. E. N. S. Thompson, for example, relegated the emblem to what he called the "literary bypaths" of the Renaissance, emphasizing the difficulty experienced by most scholars with a genre that could not readily be categorized according to the familiar types of literature. More recently emblems have come to be seen as an apt medium for the expression of serious concerns.[2] For us they are a window through which we may look back on the way people of the Renaissance thought about the world and their place in it. Through emblems we have access to Renaissance recreative thought, for they are ultimately invitations to readers to apply visual signals to their reception of the word and to viewers to apply verbal messages to the pictured image—an image that seldom pretends to represent things as they are in nature. Emblems may thus be regarded as a combined visual and verbal record of a habit of mind indigenous to the Renaissance no less than as

evidence of the Renaissance hierarchy of values where a metaphysical truth took precedence over a purely physical one.

In consideration of the importance in Renaissance thought of the relationship between sight and the imagination—a relationship established in faculty psychology and sustained in the work of literary critics and those writing manuals on the theory and practice of the visual arts—it is odd that relatively little attention has been paid to the "sensible" rhetoric of the emblem books. While the semantics of emblems have been the object of study, emblems have yet to benefit from the interest in visual epistemology we have encountered in the backgrounds for Sidney's *Arcadia*. In *Batman uppon Bartholome, his Booke De Proprietatibus Rerum* (London, 1582), we read that "the soule sensible . . . giveth feeling" and that "the soule Rationalis . . . giveth reason. For the being and the working of the soule, that is Sensibilis, is dependent of the bodie, that it is in, and maketh it perfect." In spite of its vulnerability to deception, the sensible soul is capable of "many noble workings and dooings. For it maketh the bodies of beastes to have feeling, and maketh perfect the inner kinde and the utter knowing. . . . Also it dealeth & spreadeth his vertue into all parts of the body" (fol. 15'). One has only to read the chapter in Robert Burton's *The Anatomy of Melancholy* (Oxford, 1628) devoted to the "Sensible Soul" to become aware of a basic assumption which appears to have supported the emblematists' appeal to their audience through the combined force of image and word: "Of these five senses, sight is held to be most precious, and the best . . . ; it sees the whole body at once; by it we learn and discern all things, a sense most excellent for use" (pt. I, sec. 1, mem. 2, subs. 6). As the most direct and morally superior route to the so-called inward senses (common sense, fantasy, and memory), sight was believed to be the instrument par excellence for reaching the understanding and the will. Perhaps no other manifestation of Renaissance culture exhibits so clearly as do emblem books the efficacy of the Horatian dictum *ut pictura poesis* and its occasional inversion *ut rhetorica pictura.* In this regard the painted closet from Hawstead Hall makes its appeals to the eye, to the ear, and to a rich collective imagination stocked with classical allusion and the humanists' concern for the betterment of the whole person.

In the small room from Hawstead Hall, the meditative stimulus of enigmatic pictures and their accompanying mots transforms the chamber from a mere room into something like a memory theater employed for the recall and contemplation of particular truths.[3] Indeed, the mnemonic potential of this tiny room is enormous, for each of the pictures seems to be intended to put the viewer in mind of principles applicable alike to mental and spiritual well-being.

In this room, no less than in the emblem books to which it is so clearly indebted, the appeal to sight—the challenge to a viewer to scan and to read the visible image before turning to any kind of verbal explanation—confirms the priority given to sight by the Renaissance. As we have seen in chapter 1, Philip Sidney devoted considerable theoretical attention to visual thinking in his *Defence* and then practiced such thinking in his *Arcadia.* The painted chamber from Hawstead Hall bears comparison with Kalander's picture gallery, for each is a pictorial inducement to thought. The function of each is defined by Sir Francis Bacon in his remarks on the retention of knowledge in his *Advancement of Learning:* "This art of memory is but built upon two intentions; the one prenotion, the other emblem. Prenotion dischargeth the indefinite seeking of that we would remember, and directeth us to seek in a narrow compass, that is, somewhat that hath congruity with our place of memory. Emblem reduceth conceits intellectual to images sensible, which strike the memory more; out of which axioms may be drawn much better practique than that in use; and besides which axioms, there are divers more touching help of memory, not inferior to them" (bk. 2, XV, 3). The painted closet is just such an instance of "prenotion" and "emblem." It is a physical implementation of pictorialism distinguishable from literary implementation. A similar idea emerges in Helkiah Crooke's *Microcosmographia* (London, 1618). "The eyes," Crooke says, "are the discoveries of the mind, as the countenance is the Image of the same; by the eyes as by a windoe, you may looke euen into the secret corners of the Soule." And in a long poem titled *Microcosmos. The Discovery of the Little World, with the government therof* (London, 1603), John Davies of Hereford writes the following lines:

> Amonge the *pleasures* which are sensuall,
> The vilst is that we *feele,* by that we touch;
> Because it is the Earthli'st *sense* of all:
> The *Tast's* of better temper, though not much:
> *Smelling* is light, and lightly more will grutch

> At vnsweete Savors, then in sweete will ioye;
> The *Hearing* is more worthie farre then such,
> Sith it's more *Airey* and doth lesse annoy,
> Whereby we gaine the *Faith* which we enioy.

> But *Seeing,* (*Sov'raigne* of each outward *sense*)
> Holds most of *Fire,* which is in nature neere
> To the *Celestiall Nature's* radience;
> Therefore this *sense* to *Nature* is most deere,
> As that which hath (by *Nature's* right) no *Peere.*
> Thus much for *pleasures* which these *senses* giue,
> Whereof the *best* must needs most *base* appeare
> Compared to the *worst* our *Soules* receave,
> Whose *powres* haue much more pow'r to take and
>   giue.[4]

These remarks suggest that the pictorial appeal of emblematic illustrations is more complex than one might at first think. Illustration is not mere decoration; rather it is an aid to thought. Taken collectively, the foregoing remarks have a bearing on the status of the word in relation to visual images. Words are initially spoken—and thus heard. And hearing, these natural philosophers assert, is subordinate to sight. By implication, then, the written word (which is a substitute for words that would otherwise be spoken) is subordinate to the visual image, as it indeed is in virtually all emblem books. No doubt it was in recognition of this hierarchy of perception that the publishers of books during the first hundred years of mechanized book production devoted so much attention to the preparation of illustrated frontispieces and title pages. And this well-defined relationship in emblem literature carries over into the expressive scheme developed for Lady Drury's oratory.

This little room (figs. 50–51), dismantled in about 1612 and moved to Hardwick House, Suffolk, was moved a second time (after the 1924 sale of that house) to the Branch Museum, Christchurch Mansion, Ipswich. There it may still be seen. Three of the walls contain painted panels, recently cleaned of a heavy coat of varnish applied in the nineteenth century. By whom they were executed it is impossible to say. Hawstead was the home of Sir Robert Drury, who commissioned Donne to write the poem commemorating his daughter's untimely death, but there is no evidence that Donne was ever at Hawstead, or that he even knew about the paintings.[5] Certainly, there is no link between them and any of his writings. Lady Drury was a niece of the enormously accomplished artist Sir Nathaniel Bacon; it is possible that she practiced art on an amateur basis and might have painted these panels. At the very least they appear to have been done at her bidding, perhaps even according to her design and invention. For almost two centuries the only available discussion of the paintings has been Sir John Cullum's *The Histories and Antiquities of Hawstead* (1784). The only iconographic record has been the crude and often inaccurate engravings he in-

Figure 50. Lady Drury's oratory. Branch Museum,
Christchurch Mansion, Ipswich. Photography by N. J. &
L. Cotterell. Copyright Ipswich Museum Committee.

cluded in his book, which was an amateur labor of love.

Of the physical appearance of the room where they were in the eighteenth century and of the general nature of the pictures, Cullum wrote:

> Contiguous to one of the bedchambers was a wains-coted closet, about seven feet square; the panels painted with various sentences, emblems, and mottos. It was called *the painted closet*; at first probably designed for an oratory, and, from one of the sentences, for the use of a lady. The dresses of the figures are of the age of James I. This closet was therefore fitted up for the last Lady Drury, and perhaps upon her direction. The paintings are well executed; and now put up in a small apartment at Hardwick House. As some of these emblems are per-haps new, and mark the taste of an age that delighted in quaint wit, and laboured conceits of a thousand kinds, I

shall set them down, confessing myself unable to un-ravel some of them.[6]

While the pictures were done with moderate compe-tency in a primitive or provincial style, their significance lies in their subject matter. Some are obviously decora-tive (if for some unknown reason they were not simply left incomplete). Fifteen panels at the bottom are of trees and landscape with stylized pictures of flowers. Three on the left wall are also decorative. Seven panels at the top contain mottoes within elaborate cartouches. But the large majority—forty-three to be exact—are em-blematic. Some are imitations of contemporary emblems and impresas; one or two suggest familiarity with hiero-glyphic lore. Cullum identified two immediate ana-logues: Joachim Camerarius' *Symbolorum et Emblema-*

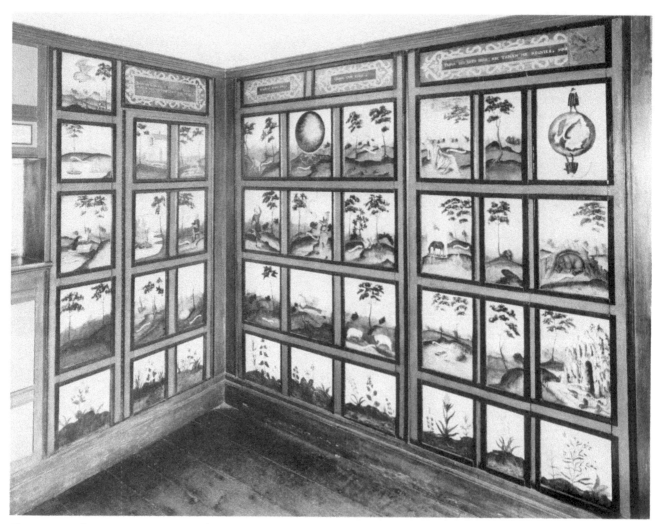

Figure 51. Lady Drury's oratory. Branch Museum,
Christchurch Mansion, Ipswich. Photography by N. J. &
L. Cotterell. Copyright Ipswich Museum Committee.

tum . . . Centuriae (Nuremberg, 1590–1604) and
Claude Paradin's *Heroical Devises* (1551; English translation 1591). However, he only casually associated two
of the panels with these analogues, and he restricted
himself to a brief descriptive list of subjects and mottoes. The task, then, is to restore these emblematic and
impresa-like paintings to their historical analogues, to
give them a history as it were. In this regard we must
keep in mind the Renaissance dependence upon such au-
thorities as Aristotle, Aelian, Lucretius, and Pliny. At
the time when this room seems to have been illustrated,
there was an inclination to believe that elephants had no
joints in their legs and that the left legs of badgers were
longer than their right, that the chameleon could live on
no other substance but air, and that ostriches could
readily digest the iron thought to be a staple of their
diet. Sir Thomas Browne's enormous *Pseudodoxia Epi-*

*demica, or Enquiries into very many Received Tenets
and Commonly Presumed Truths* would not appear until 1650. The natural world, then, harbored allegories
no less expressive than Davies of Hereford's "little
world of man." And one who entered this room for the
purpose of meditation or contemplation could, first
through the faculty of sight and then through the faculty
of mind, discover this narrow little place to be a virtual
everywhere.

The starting point and progression of the panels remain a mystery. The sentences written upon the topmost
panels suggest a possible progression whose starting
point is on one's left immediately upon entering the
room. But this order of progression (if there ever was
one) can be questioned, for no one knows whether the
arrangement of the panels was changed during their two
removes. And Cullum's numbering follows no apparent

order—at least the way the room is presently constituted.

Immediately upon entering the room, on an upper panel just to the left (fig. 50), one finds the following sentence: "Frustra nisi Dominus" (In vain without the Lord).[7] Beyond the small intervening window (which was obviously not a part of the original room), the next upper panel (fig. 51) bears the message "Quod sis esse velis, nihilque malis. Summam nec metuas diem, nec optes" (Wish to be what you are, and wish to be nothing more. Neither fear your day, nor long for it). Proceeding to the right once again, the eye falls upon the next upper panel (fig. 51) which reads "Nunquam minus sola" (Never less alone), followed by "quam cum sola" (than when alone), the feminine singular indicating that the room was used by a lady. The fourth panel (fig. 51) reads "Parva, sed apta mihi: nec tamen hic requies" (Small, but fit for me: and yet there is no rest here), a statement which seems to affirm the nature of that mental effort carried out in this room. The fifth panel (fig. 50) relates to all the foregoing: "Amplior in coelo domus est" (A larger home in heaven). And so likewise does the sentence on the final upper panel (fig. 50), "Quae copio, haud capio" (I do not get what I desire).

Directly beneath the sentence "Frustra nisi Dominus" are eight pictures, two on the bottom decorative and those above emblematic. The one on the top left (fig. 52) shows a bee scap surrounded by several bees and the mot "Cum melle aculeus" (With honey a sting). The obvious message, that no good thing comes without difficulty, is an appropriate modification of the sentence above. But comparison of this panel with a related emblem from Geoffrey Whitney's *A Choice of Emblems* (Leiden, 1586) (fig. 53) enables us to understand that the picture pertains also to the labors of the bees and their "worke of arte" which no person can duplicate. They bring honey to their rooms as a deeply religious person would bring spiritual fruits into this room. The symbolism of the bee is extensive.[8] A passage from *The Hieroglyphics of Horapollo* explains that the Egyptians drew bees "to show the people obedient to the king." Alone among the animals, continues Horapollo, "the bees have a king whom the rest of the bees follow in a body, just as men obey their king. And they suggest from the honey . . . from the center of vital power . . . that it is a good thing to be vigorous towards. . . ." Further, "by the picture of a bee making honey, they [i.e.,

Figure 52. Bee scap, "Cum melle aculeus." Lady Drury's oratory. Photography by N. J. & L. Cotterell. Copyright Ipswich Museum Committee.

Figure 53. "Patria cuique chara," from Geoffrey Whitney, *A Choice of Emblems* (1586). Courtesy of the Rare Book and Special Collections Division, Library of Congress.

Figure 54. Mermaid combing her hair, "Spem fronte." Lady Drury's oratory. Photography by N. J. & L. Cotterell. Copyright Ipswich Museum Committee.

Figure 55. Flaming wreath, "Quid ergo fefellit." Lady Drury's oratory. Photography by N. J. & L. Cotterell. Copyright Ipswich Museum Committee.

the ancient Egyptians] indicate a king, showing by this symbol that a ruler must have both sweetness and yet a sharp sting."[9] And the concept of reverence is evident in Pliny's remarks on the bee and the perfect commonwealth of the bee kingdom (*Nat. Hist.* 11.7). This panel appears, then, to promote contemplation of proper reverence.

Directly beneath the bee scap is the picture of a mermaid gazing into a mirror and combing her hair, with the mot "Spem fronte" (She has hope in her forehead) (fig. 54). Biform creatures such as mermaids, centaurs, and satyrs are commonly used in emblems to represent the human and the animal. Mermaids occasionally came to be confused with Sirens among seafaring men who believed they could be lured onto the rocks by their songs. Why this particular mermaid should exhibit hope may be explained by the natural desire for betterment, in this case transformation into being wholly human. If this is the correct message, then the mirror may be intended to symbolize prudence. However, the mirror may also denote pride—a notion conveyed by the way she combs her hair. If *this* is the true signal of the painting,

then there is irony in the mot, for pride of hope would be counterproductive. The emblem and mot, therefore, may be a warning against a proud assumption that spiritual metamorphosis is inevitable.

Beneath the mermaid is the picture of a wreath in flames with the mot "Quid ergo fefellit" (What, then, was the deception?) (fig. 55). Pictures of a burning wreath seem not to occur in emblem literature,[10] but wreaths in various connections are abundant. Pliny (*Nat. Hist.* 21.25) was but one classical source for commentaries, and Cesare Ripa's *Iconologia* (though not properly an emblem book) assigns a flaming wreath to Carita to stress her ardent nature. The Hawstead mot implies that the view of the wreath as a symbol of achievement lacks validity, that the wreath is vulnerable to flames and, by extension, is consumed by the fires of high spiritual desire. Further, the mot is an interrogative and thus a stimulus to inquiry into private motives.

At the top of the second row of paintings we come to the picture of a chimney on fire with the mot "Alte, sed extra locum" (On high, but beyond its place) (fig. 56). This image seems to continue the motif from the burning wreath, thus lending substance to the possibility that we are intended to read down rather than across. A similar picture occurs in an impresa said by Paolo Giovio to have been designed by Odesto di Fois (fig. 57). Samuel Daniel, in his *The Worthy Tract of Paulus Iovius* (London, 1585), translates Giorio's commentary thus: "It was a large chimney, and therein a great fire, with this mot 'Dou' e gran fucco e gran fumo,'" the inference being that "where there is a fiery courage ioyned with Nobilities, there must also be a great smoke of pryde: Wherefore it is necessarie, that great estates, take especial regard that they commit nothing to cause them to bee hated of the common people" (sig. F5ᵛ). Fervor, the Hawstead emblem seems to suggest, must be directed on high and must be located as well in the intellect; however, fervor must be controlled and disciplined because pride (expressed in the mermaid panel) is a detriment to fervor.

Self-abnegation is further expressed just below in the panel depicting a well with the bucket evidently descend-

ing (fig. 58). Here the mot is "Descendendo adimpleor" (By descending, I am filled). A similar picture appears in Henry Peacham's *Minerva Britanna* (London, 1612) (fig. 59). Though of a later date than the Hawstead picture, it has analogues in several earlier books including Nicholas Reusner's *Emblemata . . . Partim Vero Historica & Hieroglyphica* (Frankfurt, 1581). Peacham's verse permits us a glimpse at a probable relation between the emblem of the well and the sentence above it. Repeated descent into the waters of spiritual regeneration not only affirms the continued sweetness of the waters, but is also an antidote to pride and vanity, which deflect spiritual appetites. The exercise of wit, as expressed in the second stanza, is also apt in connection with the message conveyed by the fire and the chimney above.

In the following emblem (fig. 60) the bucket is completely drawn up. This image appears with the mot "Haud facile emergit" (It does not emerge easily), suggesting the difficulty of retrieving the waters of spiritual

Figure 56. Burning chimney, "Alte, sed extra locum." Lady Drury's oratory. Photography by N. J. & L. Cotterell. Copyright Ipswich Museum Committee.

Figure 57. From Paolo Giovio, *Dialogo dell'Imprese Militari et Amorose* (1574). Courtesy of Princeton University Library.

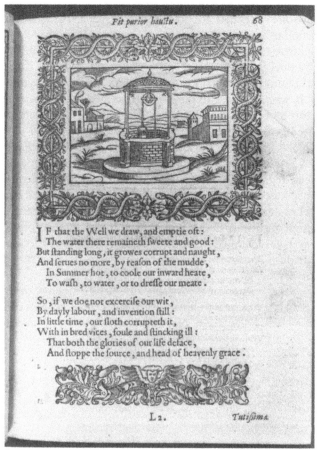

Figure 58. Well with bucket descending, "Descendendo adimpleor." Lady Drury's oratory. Photography by N. J. & L. Cotterell. Copyright Ipswich Museum Committee.

Figure 59. "Fit purior haustu," from Henry Peacham, *Minerva Britanna* (1612). Courtesy of Humanities Research Center, The University of Texas at Austin.

regeneration. Clearly intended to complement the preceding emblem, both image and mot urge persistence in the face of difficulty.

A hawk in mid-flight, clutching its prey in its talons and accompanied by the mot "Fruor nec quiesco" (I enjoy and do not rest) (fig. 61), is the first of a series of four which seem to be independent of a general sentence. Cullum identified the possible source of the picture in Camerarius (fig. 62), where the mot as well as the picture convey the idea of a task only partially completed. The next panel below this one (fig. 63) seems to be thematically consistent. It depicts a man rowing a boat evidently away from the town that is at the water's edge, and the mot reads "Et tamen aversor" (And yet I turn away). There appears to be no analogue to this panel in emblem literature, nor does the next picture (fig. 64) appear to have been taken from a book source. Here a creature that might be a seal, a large fowl, or perhaps even a beaver sits upon a stool reading a book on a reading stand. The mot is merely "CPQR." Almost as puz-

zling is the fourth panel in this row, which was either left incomplete or was subsequently altered. It is merely a landscape with no mot.

Beginning again at the top, the next panel (fig. 65) appears directly under the sentence expressing the importance of attaining security with one's own identity. It depicts an ape seated in an upper-story window throwing down coins. The mot reads "Ut parta labantur" (They flow away as they were born). Obviously a warning against profligacy, this picture seems to have been inspired by Geoffrey Whitney's emblem (fig. 66) whose similarity to the Hawstead panel even includes the mot. Like the symbolism of the bee, that of the ape is extensive.[11] But the meaning in this case seems fairly clear: "Woulde you learne to keepe, that you do winne?"

A fire raging upon a riverbank appears in the panel directly below (fig. 67), where the mot reads "Dum servi necessaria" (They are necessary so long as they are slaves). Cullum suggested that the picture refers to the adage "Fire and water are good servants but bad mas-

Figure 60. Well with bucket drawn up, "Haud facile emergit." Lady Drury's oratory. Photography by N. J. & L. Cotterell. Copyright Ipswich Museum Committee.

Figure 61. Flying hawk with prey, "Fruor nec quiesco." Lady Drury's oratory. Photography by N. J. & L. Cotterell. Copyright Ipswich Museum Committee.

ters." However, it is more likely that the Hawstead artist had a proverb by Bartholomew Young in mind: "As fier and water cannot agree . . . even so spiritual delights and corporal pleasures admit no Sympathye."[12] One must use discretion in the reliance upon nature's gifts, particularly since true baptism and ardent fire (suggested earlier by the well-and-bucket combination and by the burning wreath) can be antithetical if improperly regarded.

The picture that follows is one of the more curious (fig. 68). It depicts a winged tongue which has the scaly tail of a serpent and the mot "Quo tendis?" (Whither goest?). Claude Paradin's *Heroical Devises,* first published at Lyon in 1551 and republished several times subsequently, evidently inspired the design (fig. 69). The 1591 English translation by the anonymous "P. S." enables us to understand the web of ideas the picture then conveyed: "Besides other discommodities which the tongue bringeth with it, Saint James saith the same is tipped with poison, and bringeth death, comparing it to

the stearne of a ship, by which the whole vessell is ruled and governed. Which sentence agreeth with the opinion of Bias, to whom Amasis the king of Egypt sent a whole beast on this condition, that he shoulde sende him again the best and the worst piece thereof, who sent the tongue onely. Seeing then that that part of the body is of such great movement, it is no marvel if nature have compared it with double gates, which we must never use to open without the consent of reason and wisedome going before, else, where the tongue goeth before premeditation, the entrance into these gates is a feareful thing & the going out both dangerous and unfortunate." In one of the emblems from Georgette de Montenay's *Emblemes, ou Devises Chrestiennes* (1571) (fig. 70), the tongue runs ahead of the heart, lending further visual significance to the question, "Whither goest?"

A camel muddying water with its foot appears in the next panel (fig. 71) accompanied by the mot "Pura juvent alios" (Let pure things delight others). Again, as Cullum observed, Camerarius is the pictorial source (fig.

PARTA TENENS,
NON PARTA SE-
QVOR.

Multa licet fido sapiens in pectore condat,
Plura avido tamen usque appetit ingenio.

K   DE

Figure 62. "Parta tenens, non parta sequor," from Joachim Camerarius, *Symbolorum et Emblematum . . . Centuriae* (1590–1604). Courtesy of Humanities Research Center, The University of Texas at Austin.

Figure 63. Man rowing a boat, "Et tamen aversor." Lady Drury's oratory. Photography by N. J. & L. Cotterell. Copyright Ipswich Museum Committee.

Figure 64. Animal reading a book, "CPQR." Lady Drury's oratory. Photography by N. J. & L. Cotterell. Copyright Ipswich Museum Committee.

72) though the idea comes ultimately from Aristotle's *De historia animalum* (bk. 7), who declared that camels are wont to muddy their drinking water. The emblem, though, is hardly in favor of impurity. Rather, it contains a warning against the prideful sense of one's own purity and a corresponding ignorance of the impurities that must be brought to the surface. Agitation is thus necessary, an idea that is expressed in the sentence above the pictures on another wall of the room: "And yet there is no rest here."

Directly beneath the camel is the picture of an artist seated before an easel, upon which is the incomplete portrait of a woman (fig. 73). The mot reads "Dic mihi, qualis eris?" (Tell me, what will you be?). This question clearly follows from the sentence above, "Wish to be what you are, and wish to be nothing more." The goal of self-knowledge is thus modified for the person using the oratory by the need for patience. The unfolding of spiritual selfhood is slow and often difficult. The idea

Figure 65. Ape throwing coins from window, "Ut parta labantur." Lady Drury's oratory. Photography by N. J. & L. Cotterell. Copyright Ipswich Museum Committee.

Figure 67. Fire on a riverbank, "Dum servi necessaria." Lady Drury's oratory. Photography by N. J. & L. Cotterell. Copyright Ipswich Museum Committee.

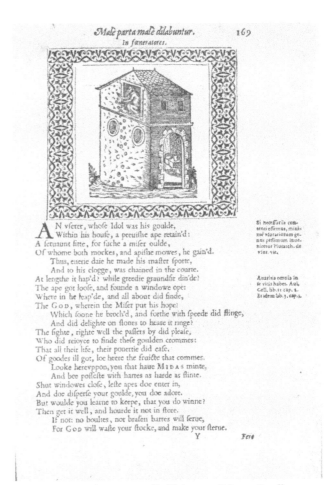

Figure 66. "Malè parta malè dilabuntur," from Geoffrey Whitney, *A Choice of Emblems* (1586). Courtesy of the Rare Book and Special Collections Division, Library of Congress.

behind this painting seems to have come from Whitney's *Choice of Emblems* (and ultimately from Alciati) (fig. 74). That the picture is of a woman suggests Lady Drury herself. However, it is curious that the mot associated with the Alciati and Whitney versions of the incomplete portrait—"Frontis nulla fides" (No trust in appearances)—is applied by the Hawstead artist to panel 18 where a man measures his own head with a pair of compasses. The symbolism of the incompleted portrait speaks largely for itself.

The last picture in the present sequence is of a tree in full leaf growing from a honeycomb beside a barren tree planted in the earth (fig. 75). The mot here is "Nocet empta dolore voluptas" (Pleasure bought with pain is harmful). Some preparation for this emblem occurs in the picture of the bee scap. It was Saint Ambrose who compared the church to a beehive and the Christian to the bee who worked ardently and was forever true to the hive. Honey came to represent the sweetness of religious

Figure 68. Tongue with wings and scaly tail, "Quo tendis?" Lady Drury's oratory. Photography by N. J. & L. Cotterell. Copyright Ipswich Museum Committee.

La langue aux mains & le cœur loing derriere.
D'Hipocrisie est la droite peinture,
Elle seduit par sa douce maniere,
Et rit mordant la simple creature.
Or Christ apprent en la saincte escriture
Que rien ne sert la langue sans le cœur,
Dont l'hipocrite a poure couuerture.
Dieu clair-voyant rend moqué le moqueur.
                                        i   Ce

Figure 70. "Frustra me colunt," from Georgette de Montenay, *Emblemes, ou Devises Chrestiennes* (1571). By permission of the Houghton Library, Harvard University.

Figure 69. "Quò tendis?" from Claude Paradin, *Heroical Devises* (1591). By permission of the Folger Shakespeare Library.

Figure 71. Camel muddying water with its foot, "Pura juvent alios." Lady Drury's oratory. Photography by N. J. & L. Cotterell. Copyright Ipswich Museum Committee.

eloquence. And in this picture the honeycomb is clearly a source of life-giving nourishment, something the earthbound tree lacks. It is also possible that the Hawstead painter is alluding to the legend of the green and dry trees and to the source of that legend in Luke 23:31: "If they do these things in the green tree, what shall be done in the dry?"[13]

The first picture beneath the next sentence—"Never less alone than when alone"—is of a man trying to light a candle at a glowworm (or perhaps vice versa) (fig. 76). The accompanying mot is "Nil tamen imperti" (He [or it] shares it not). The incompatibility between nature and the tools humanity employs for its own self-interest is expressed here. Fire and light are common enough allegorical figures for enlightenment, and the present emblem appears to be a warning against efforts to find enlightenment in the natural world. In this sense, the picture of the man and the glowworm is compatible with the foregoing image of the green tree growing out of the honeycomb and the barren tree rooted in earth.

Figure 72. "Turbata delectat," from Joachim Camerarius, *Symbolorum et Emblematum . . . Centuriae* (1590–1604). Courtesy of Humanities Research Center, The University of Texas at Austin.

A man measuring his own head with compasses with the mot "Fronti nulla fides" (No trust in appearances) appears next (fig. 77). Here, as in the pictures of the mermaid and of the artist with the incomplete portrait, the emblem invites consideration of futurity. The mermaid found hope in her forehead, the artist speculated on what the partial image before him would become, and now we view a picture expressing the idea that the brow reveals the man. The means of discovering identity here is the compass, whose symbolism is suggested by the emblem in Peacham's *Minerva Britanna* (fig. 78). And there, certainly not by coincidence, the second stanza of the accompanying poem contains the very idea stated in the sentence above the painting: "If that thou wouldst acquaint thee with the Muse, / Withdrew thy selfe, and be thou least alone, / Even when alone." The caution against excess, the goal of achieving a mean, the discovery of rest through labor—the ideas presented in the first stanza of that poem—are precisely the ideas in most of the foregoing paintings.

Being least alone when alone is the concept behind the next painting as well. It depicts a boar trampling on roses with the mot "Odi profanum vulgus" (I hate the common man) (fig. 79). Here the designer has chosen the opening words from Horace's *Third Ode*—"Odi profanum vulgus et arceo"—omitting only the second clause, "I keep them at a distance." The picture is one that appears in Camerarius (fig. 80), where the brief explanation of the emblem concludes that a mind drunk on luxury can never desire virtue. The Hawstead painting appears to caution against pleasure lest it become an excess; further, it warns against permitting the values of others to supplant the spiritual values carefully nurtured through meditation. In the moralized natural history of the late sixteenth and early seventeenth centuries, pigs were notorious for their hostility toward beauty. Lucretius wrote that "the pig flees from oil of marjoram and fears every kind of unguent; for that which sometimes seems to give us new life is rank poison to the bristly pig."[14] Erasmus, in his *Proverbes or Adages* (London, 1539), compares the foolish judgment of the people with this same "fonde beast" (fol. L1). And the pig trampling upon roses is for Valeriano in his *Hieroglyphica* (Lyon, 1615) a symbol of perverse, malevolent, and evil nature (p. 102).

The top painting in the middle of this sequence under the sentence proclaiming the superiority of aloneness shows a crab bearing the world on its back with the mot "Sic orbis iter" (So goes the world) (fig. 81). Camerarius is again the obvious source (fig. 82), and he provides practically the same mot. Where previous emblems seem to stress the future, this painting emphasizes the slow passage of time. "Why," asks Camerarius, "does the world go on the back of a crab? Because in one day is summed up the course of the world." Like the preceding panel, this one also has an analogue in Erasmus' *Adages*

Figure 73. Artist before easel with half-finished picture, "Dic mihi, qualis eris?" Lady Drury's oratory. Photography by N. J. & L. Cotterell. Copyright Ipswich Museum Committee.

Figure 75. Tree growing from a honeycomb, "Nocet empta dolore voluptas." Lady Drury's oratory. Photography by N. J. & L. Cotterell. Copyright Ipswich Museum Committee.

Figure 74. "Frontis nulla fides," from Geoffrey Whitney, *A Choice of Emblems* (1586). Courtesy of the Rare Book and Special Collections Division, Library of Congress.

as well as Valeriano's *Hieroglyphica*, which is not surprising given the variety of symbolism associated with the crab. Most commonly, it is a constellation associated with the summer solstice. When it shines in the highest part of the firmament, it is the home of the summer sun. It is also one of the tropics which quarter the heavens and fix the seasons and is mentioned thus by Pliny: "We have said that the summer solstice occurs at the 8th degree of Cancer, and the 8th of Calends of July (24 June). It is a great stage in the year, a great event in the world."[15] In view of the cosmic symbolism of the crab, it is significant that this emblem is at the top of a column midway through an entire succession of panels stressing the condition of aloneness.

The next painting depicts a man in fool's garb using a bellows on a flame (fig. 83). However, the pot containing the flame hangs from a balance, the other arm of which stretches into thin air. The mot is "Sat injussa calet" (It burns unbidden). The combination of fool, fire, bellows, and a balance makes this an iconographically complex picture, since each of these objects offers a number of meanings. Is it only a fool who would fan a

Figure 76. Man lighting candle at a glowworm, "Nil tamen imperti." Lady Drury's oratory. Photography by N. J. & L. Cotterell. Copyright Ipswich Museum Committee.

Figure 77. Man measuring his own head with compasses, "Fronti nulla fides." Lady Drury's oratory. Photography by N. J. & L. Cotterell. Copyright Ipswich Museum Committee.

flame balanced on the other end by air itself? Is this an emblem of futility, warning against foolish exertion of energies? A foolish person with bellows appears in Peacham's *Minerva Britanna* (fig. 84) beneath the mot "Levitas." There the accompanying poem identifies Cesare Ripa's *Iconologia* as a source of its ideas. The Hawstead panel may even contain a reference to the common emblematic significance of scales in which a feather weighs more than the hands of friendship or some other "weighty" object. In this connection Nicholas Hilliard once painted an unusual miniature where the world and a feather are shown in a balance suspended above the reclining figure of a young man.[16] The Hawstead painting and its mot evidently signify the importance of allowing one's love of the good to burn freely without excessive and thus artificial stimulation, for as in the panels depicting the burning wreath, the man attempting to ignite a candle at the tail of a glowworm, and the fire burning upon the riverbank this one stresses the foolishness of reliance upon mere nature. If the flame of one's devotion is tended foolishly, it amounts to little more than air.

Figure 78. "In Requie, Labor," from Henry Peacham, *Minerva Britanna* (1612). Courtesy of Humanities Research Center, The University of Texas at Austin.

Figure 79. Boar trampling on roses, "Odi profanum vulgus."
Lady Drury's oratory. Photography by N. J. & L. Cotterell.
Copyright Ipswich Museum Committee.

Figure 80. "Non bene conveniunt," from Joachim Camerarius, *Symbolorum et Emblematum . . . Centuriae* (1590–
1604). Courtesy of Humanities Research Center, The University of Texas at Austin.

Figure 81. Crab with the world on its back, "Sic orbis iter."
Lady Drury's oratory. Photography by N. J. & L. Cotterell.
Copyright Ipswich Museum Committee.

Directly below is the picture of a ship anchored on a
huge whale which seems to be in motion (fig. 85). The
mot, "Nusquam tuta fides" (Faith is nowhere safe), appears to follow from the picture of the fool above.
Cullum anachronistically associated this panel with the
passage in *Paradise Lost* where Milton writes of

> that sea beast
> Leviathan, which God of all his works
> Created hugest that swim the ocean stream:
> Him, haply slumb'ring on the Norway foam,
> The pilot of some small night-founder'd skiff,
> Dreaming some island, oft, as seamen tell,
> With fixed anchor in his scaly ring,
> Moors by his side, under the lee.
>
> [2.200–207]

But Milton, like the Hawstead painter, is probably
thinking of the passage from Ariosto's *Orlando Furioso*
(6.37) where Astolpho, Dudon, and Renaldo see a

Figure 82. "Orbis iter," from Joachim Camerarius, *Symbolorum et Emblematum . . . Centuriae* (1590–1604). Courtesy of Humanities Research Center, The University of Texas at Austin.

Figure 83. Fool blowing a flame with bellows, "Sat injussa calet." Lady Drury's oratory. Photography by N. J. & L. Cotterell. Copyright Ipswich Museum Committee.

Figure 84. "Levitas," from Henry Peacham, *Minerva Britanna* (1612). Courtesy of Humanities Research Center, The University of Texas at Austin.

whale so large that they take it for an island. The idea probably comes ultimately from Pliny, who writes of whales "covering three acres each" in the Indian sea (*Nat. Hist.*, 9.4). The Hawstead painter's visual source seems once again to be Camerarius (fig. 86), but if so more as an adaptation than as an imitation. Certainly the idea that faith is never wholly safe is compatible with the idea of discarding excess baggage in order to escape a whale.

That there is an order in the deployment of the paintings seems once again to be apparent in the next uppermost panel in which a dog, its collar lying on the ground, licks a hand extended from a tree (fig. 87). Here the mot reads "Non fugitiva fides" (Faith is steadfast). The dog is a common symbol of faithfulness.[17] Pliny gives it high marks (along with the horse) as one of the most faithful of all animals (*Nat. Hist.*, 8.40). And this view is picked up by Pierre L'Anglois in *Discours des Hieroglyphes AEgyptiens* (Paris, 1584) and by Ripa,

Figure 85. Ship anchored on a whale, "Nusquam tuta fides."
Lady Drury's oratory. Photography by N. J. & L. Cotterell.
Copyright Ipswich Museum Committee.

Figure 86. "His artibus," from Joachim Camerarius, *Symbolorum et Emblematum . . . Centuriae* (1590–1604). Courtesy of Humanities Research Center, The University of Texas at Austin.

Figure 87. Dog licking a hand extended from a tree, "Non
fugitiva fides." Lady Drury's oratory. Photography by N. J. &
L. Cotterell. Copyright Ipswich Museum Committee.

who identifies the dog as an attribute of "Fedelta." The Hawstead painter evidently wished to emphasize that faith is its own discipline, that no collar is needed in the exercise of faith. The hand emanating from the tree is, however, curious. Does it signify a relationship between nature and faith? Does it indicate that nature rewards faithfulness? There is no clear answer to such questions, but the panel below (fig. 88) seems to be thematically related.

It shows a death's head with branches bearing green leaves growing from the eye sockets. The mot reads "Ut moreris vives" (You will live as you will die). The green branches testify to the persistence of life—quite literally in the face of death. Camerarius offers a similar idea in his emblem of grain growing from a pile of bones. Similarly, Whitney shows a fruitful vine growing upon a dead elm in *A Choice of Emblems*. If the emblem directly above this panel affirms the rewards of faith in life, the skull and vegetation seem to affirm the continuity of those rewards after death.

Figure 88. Death's head with branches growing from the eye sockets, "Ut moreris vives." Lady Drury's oratory. Photography by N. J. & L. Cotterell. Copyright Ipswich Museum Committee.

Figure 89. Two rams fighting, "Nec habet victoria lauden." Lady Drury's oratory. Photography by N. J. & L. Cotterell. Copyright Ipswich Museum Committee.

Two rams fighting, with the mot "Nec habet victoria lauden" (And the victory has no praise), appear in the bottom panel of this column (fig. 98). The caution here seems directed at mindless competitiveness, a theme developed at some length by Valeriano, whose *Hieroglyphica* contains a woodcut showing practically the same image (fig. 90). Pierre L'Anglois, in his *Discours*, explains that a fiery and insolent temperament is comparable to the nature of rams who batter themselves mindlessly. The emblem thus cautions against compulsive and frantic behavior as well as against misguided impulses. It is apt as the final emblem beneath the sentence that reads "Never less alone than when alone."

Beneath the sentence "Small, but fit for me: and yet there is no rest here," the first panel appropriately depicts an old man with the ears of an ass, sleeping (fig. 91). Insects, possibly ants, carry objects to (or is it from?) his mouth. The mot is "Etiam asino dormienti" (Even to a sleeping ass). The emblem stresses the foolishness of inactivity. A man with an ass's ears immediately suggests King Midas, who figures in one of Whitney's emblems; and Midas is the symbol of those who want something for nothing, only to pay a price they never anticipated. The Hawstead designer, though, appears to have copied his picture from Valeriano's *Hieroglyphica* (fig. 92), where the sleeping figure has the ears of an ass because he merely dreams of future prosperity rather than working for it. More problematic are the insects which, according to the Hawstead mot, bring something to the sleeping man. If they are indeed ants, Ovid's

Figure 90. From Giovanni Pierio Valeriano Bolzani, *Hieroglyphica, sev de Sacris Egyptiorum . . . Commentarii* (1586). Courtesy of Humanities Research Center, The University of Texas at Austin.

Figure 92. From Giovanni Pierio Valeriano Bolzani, *Hieroglyphica, sev de Sacris Egyptiorum . . . Commentarii* (1586). Courtesy of Humanities Research Center, The University of Texas at Austin.

Figure 91. Old man with ass's ears, sleeping, "Etiam asino dormienti." Lady Drury's oratory. Photography by N. J. & L. Cotterell. Copyright Ipswich Museum Committee.

Figure 93. Ass on hind legs peering through a picture; below, horse and woodcock with lantern, "Et occulte, et aperte." Lady Drury's oratory. Photography by N. J. & L. Cotterell. Copyright Ipswich Museum Committee.

famous description in book 7 of *The Metamorphoses* is applicable. There he tells how the ants who labor unstintingly in the oak trees of Dodona's grove turn into the stout Myrmidons who retain the habits of their original condition after they have become human. According to the present mot the ants continue diligently to serve even a sleeping ass, the implication being that nature's and God's bounty is always available. A person meditating upon the Hawstead emblem, though, might also associate the ant with knowledge, for in the *Horapollo* it is written that "to represent knowledge, they [the Egyptians] draw an ant. For if a man should hide something safely, this animal would know it." Curiously, the *Horapollo* adds something to the definition of ears that could be pertinent to the Hawstead painting. The ear is "future work." As Artimidorus adds, "It is good for a workman to dream of ears, because it means he will hear of many orders for his work."[18] The emblem, then, warns against desultory conduct and commends diligence.

The image of the ass combines with that of the horse in the next emblem (fig. 93). The ass, standing on its hind legs, peers through a flat picture-plane beneath which grazes a horse; in the foreground a woodcock stands either with one foot holding a lantern or with the foot upon a lantern. The mot is "Et occulte, et aperte" (Both secretly and openly). The woodcock and the ass are obvious symbols of foolishness and stupidity. Secretly, and even openly, the ass wishes to become a horse, just as the woodcock desires enlightenment. It is

Figure 94. Bird with bill stuck in oyster, "Speravi et perii." Lady Drury's oratory. Photography by N. J. & L. Cotterell. Copyright Ipswich Museum Committee.

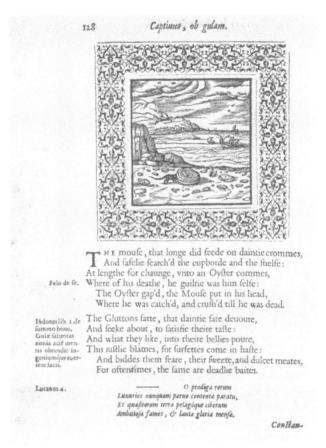

Figure 95. "Captiuus, ob gulam," from Geoffrey Whitney, *A Choice of Emblems* (1586). Courtesy of the Rare Book and Special Collections Division, Library of Congress.

just possible, though, that the animal on its hind legs is a mule that contemplates intercourse with the horse. The fact that mules are barren and sterile would, in this context, render the animal stupid, like a woodcock.

The emblem directly beneath this panel (fig. 94) shows a bird thrusting its bill into an oyster which holds it fast. The mot, "Speravi et perii" (I hoped and I died), is yet another warning that false hopes for the future are a detriment to genuine spiritual expectations. From the beginning emblem literature included a mouse in a similar predicament. Alciati, for example, used the mouse and the oyster to illustrate the mot "Captiuus ob gulam" (The captive of gluttony), and Whitney appropriated it for his *A Choice of Emblems* (fig. 95). The Hawstead version ignores the sin of gluttony and focuses attention instead upon misguided hopes.

The next upper panel shows the world with one man standing on top of it and another standing below; both appear to travel in the same direction (fig. 96). The mot, "Et hic vivatur" (There is life here too), seems to emphasize the principle of universality. Because this emblem appears directly beneath the sentence reading "Small,

but fit for me: and yet there is no rest here," there is particular emphasis on the present room. It is likely that the image owes a debt to one of the illustrations from Caxton's *Mirrour of the World*, the first work with illustrations printed in England. There, under the heading "How the erthe holdeth her right in the myddle of the world," is an illustration showing two men walking on the globe in opposite directions and meeting at the bottom.[19]

A bear sleeping in its den in the bottom emblem seems to complement the sleeping Midas that was first in the present grouping (fig. 97). The model appears to have come from Camerarius (fig. 98), an emblem that draws upon Pliny. There we read that bears after copulation retire apart to caves where, after thirty days, the female litters (*Nat. Hist.*, 8.127). Such retirement is accounted for in the Hawstead mot "Obscure, secure" (Security in obscurity), but Camerarius' emphasis on virtuous ease is especially applicable to this room.

The last panel in this series shows a bird, the trochilus, feeding at the mouth of a supine crocodile (fig. 99), a variation apparently on the theme of the oyster catcher

Figure 96. The world with a man standing on top and another upside down on the bottom, "Et hic vivatur." Lady Drury's oratory. Photography by N. J. & L. Cotterell. Copyright Ipswich Museum Committee.

XX.

MAIOR POST
OTIA VIRTVS.

Ceu luſtris latitant urſi & ſua membra relinquunt:
Sic meditatur opus doctus in arte novum.

F 2   PLY·

Figure 98. "Maior post otia virtus," from Joachim Camerarius, *Symbolorum et Emblematum . . . Centuriae* (1590–1604). Courtesy of Humanities Research Center, The University of Texas at Austin.

Figure 97. Bear sleeping in its den, "Obscure, secure." Lady Drury's oratory. Photography by N. J. & L. Cotterell. Copyright Ipswich Museum Committee.

discussed above. The mot here is "Pascor, at haud tuto" (I feed, but not safely). Given the Hawstead artist's previous dependence on Camerarius, it is not surprising to discover once again a parallel with *Symbolorum et Emblematum* (fig. 100). This was a popular emblem, owing no doubt to the curious bit of natural history it represented. The character of the bird and its relation to the crocodile is related by Pliny. "When sated with a meal of fish and sunk in sleep on the shore with its mouth always full of food, [the crocodile] is tempted by a small bird (called there the trochilus, but in Italy the kingbird) to open its mouth, and then the teeth and inner throat also, which yawns open as wide as possible for the pleasure of this scratching; and the ichneumon watches for it to be overcome with sleep in the middle of this gratification, and darts like a javelin through the throat so opened and gnaws out the belly" (*Nat. Hist.*, 8.90). This bizarre characterization led to interpretations of the crocodile as a symbol of gluttony. But unlike Camerarius' emblem, which emphasizes the danger of

Figure 99. Trochilus feeding at the mouth of a crocodile, "Pascor, at haud tuto." Lady Drury's oratory. Photography by N. J. & L. Cotterell. Copyright Ipswich Museum Committee.

Figure 100. "Acceptum redditur officium," from Joachim Camerarius, *Symbolorum et Emblematum . . . Centuriae* (1590–1604). Courtesy of Humanities Research Center, The University of Texas at Austin.

accepting a service in return, the Hawstead panel stresses the hazards to the bird. The significance is to beware of falling victim to a seemingly lethargic enemy.

In this visual journey we come next to the sentence "A larger home in heaven." Here the first emblem below presents a blackened sun which perhaps has been eclipsed by the moon, surmounted by golden stars (fig. 101). The mot is "Nec curo videri" (Nor do I care to be seen). There are numerous examples of eclipses in emblem literature,[20] but the relationship of this picture to the sentence above it suggests that the sun's indifference is of little terrestrial import after all. And as the light of the sun is sufficient unto itself, so the private enlightenment of the meditative person is its own gratification.

Directly beneath is the picture of a bat pursuing a large insect, possibly a firefly (fig. 102). The mot is "Trahit sua quemque" (Each led by his own desire). Once more the source appears to be Camerarius, though now there are two separate emblems, one for the bat (fig. 103) and the other for the firefly (fig. 104). This panel picks up the theme of predatory danger expressed above in the emblem of the trochilus and the crocodile, the firefly clearly being led by the desire to escape and the bat motivated by hunger. Here the meaning is possibly that darkness seeks to extinguish light (or enlightenment, as in the emblem where a man seeks to light a candle from the glowworm). Another possible signification is the common use of the bat to symbolize melancholy—the black humor would be set upon swallowing light.

The hedgehog with fruit impaled on its spines in the next emblem (fig. 105) is accompanied by the mot "Mihi plaudo ipse domi" (I applaud myself at home). It was Pliny who related how this creature prudently gathered fallen fruit on its spines by rolling about on the ground beneath trees (*Nat. Hist.*, 8.59). Paradin pictures it thus in his *Heroical Devises* (1557) (fig. 106), and this may well be the model used by the Hawstead artist. Such self-congratulation would not necessarily be an expression of pride, for by this point in the unfold-

Figure 101. Sun, in eclipse, surmounted with golden stars, "Nec curo videri." Lady Drury's oratory. Photography by N. J. & L. Cotterell. Copyright Ipswich Museum Committee.

Figure 102. Bat pursuing large insect, "Trahit sua quemque." Lady Drury's oratory. Photography by N. J. & L. Cotterell. Copyright Ipswich Museum Committee.

Figure 103. "Inter utrumque," from Joachim Camerarius, *Symbolorum et Emblematum . . . Centuriae* (1590–1604). Courtesy of Humanities Research Center, The University of Texas at Austin.

ment of the emblems (assuming our sequence is the same one the meditation followed), pride would have been quite purged away from thought.

The motif of blackness or darkness appears once more in the panel depicting a blackamoor smoking a pipe (fig. 107). The mot, "Intus idem" (The same inside) may have been inspired by the emblem of the Ethiopian in Whitney's *A Choice of Emblems* (fig. 108). The implication can be traced to early seventeenth-century objections to the "drinking" of tobacco (including King James', whose dislike of smoking was widely known). The emblem would thus be a warning that inner nature is quite like outer. The message would be to bring inner and outer into harmony, particularly in view of the goal: "A larger home in heaven."

The mot that accompanies the next picture, a rose and a poppy (fig. 109), is one of the most puzzling of all: "O puzzi, O ponga" (Either smells, or stinks?). The em-

Figure 104. "Meusignis abortu," from Joachim Camerarius, *Symbolorum et Emblematum . . . Centuriae* (1590–1604). Courtesy of Humanities Research Center, The University of Texas at Austin.

Figure 105. Hedgehog with fruit impaled on its spines, "Mihi plaudo ipse domi." Lady Drury's oratory. Photography by N. J. & L. Cotterell. Copyright Ipswich Museum Committee.

blem suggests that these two equally beautiful flowers offer quite different if not antithetical ideas. Pliny in his *Natural History* describes the rose as having medicinal properties (21.73) while the poppy has soporific properties (20.74). The poppy is commonly a symbol of sleep, ignorance, extravagance, and indifference; Donne in this connection associates it with death in the sonnet beginning "Death be not proud." The rose, on the other hand, symbolizes adoration and the splendors of paradise. Perhaps the Hawstead mot means that the scent of the rose is sweet while the poppy's is abhorrent, and that the flowers represent a choice in the conduct of one's inner life.

The astrologer peering through a quadrant at a star in the next emblem (fig. 110) is accompanied by the mot "Desipui sapiendo" (I am stultified with learning). In view of the recondite symbolism on the walls, this emblem has ironic overtones: it requires learning to puzzle

Figure 106. "Magnum victigal," from Claude Paradin, *Heroical Devises* (1591). By permission of the Folger Shakespeare Library.

Figure 107. Blackamoor smoking a pipe, "Intus idem." Lady Drury's oratory. Photography by N. J. & L. Cotterell. Copyright Ipswich Museum Committee.

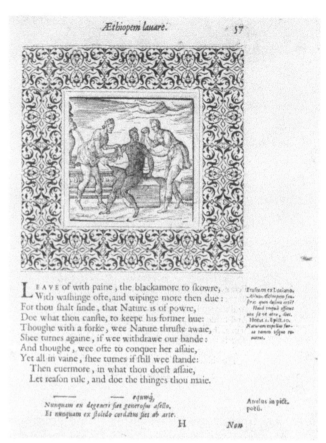

Figure 108. "Æthiopem lauare," from Geoffrey Whitney, *A Choice of Emblems* (1586). Courtesy of the Rare Book and Special Collections Division, Library of Congress.

Figure 109. Rose and poppy, "O puzzi, O ponga." Lady Drury's oratory. Photography by N. J. & L. Cotterell. Copyright Ipswich Museum Committee.

Figure 110. Astrologer peering through a quadrant, "Desipui sapiendo." Lady Drury's oratory. Photography by N. J. & L. Cotterell. Copyright Ipswich Museum Committee.

Figure 111. Eagle bearing an elephant in its talons, "Non vacat exiguis." Lady Drury's oratory. Photography by N. J. & L. Cotterell. Copyright Ipswich Museum Committee.

Figure 113. "Superest quod suprà est," from Geoffrey Whitney, A Choice of Emblems (1586). Courtesy of the Rare Book and Special Collections Division, Library of Congress.

Figure 112. Pilgrim with cockleshell badge, "Dum transis, time." Lady Drury's oratory. Photography by N. J. & L. Cotterell. Copyright Ipswich Museum Committee.

out the messages. But in this case the learning seems to be the occult, and the warning to be against efforts to read the stars and predict the future. The theme is thus consonant with that of the mermaid, the artist before an incompleted portrait, and the man measuring his head with compasses. The meditative practice induced by the room itself is antithetical to astrology, so it may also be correct to see a faint warning against alchemy in the picture of the fool.

We come at last to the final set of panels, those situated beneath the sentence that reads "I do not get what I desire." The first emblem below (fig. 111) shows an eagle bearing an elephant in its talons, with the mot "Non vacat exiguis" (No time for trifles). The elephant is associated emblematically with purity, intelligence, chastity, and strength—a harmonious blend with the eagle's generosity and sight (which can also mean insight). The physical impossibility of an eagle carrying an elephant may pertain to the need to assay large tasks in order to reap broad benefits. Certainly, the following emblem (fig. 112), which shows a pilgrim who wears the cockleshell badge of his occupation, expresses the frustration of worldly expectations. The accompanying mot

Figure 114. Eagle diving into flames, its young nearby, "Pie sed temere." Lady Drury's oratory. Photography by N. J. & L. Cotterell. Copyright Ipswich Museum Committee.

Figure 115. Sun and rainbow, "Iam satis." Lady Drury's oratory. Photography by N. J. & L. Cotterell. Copyright Ipswich Museum Committee.

is "Dum transis, time" (As long as you live, be on your guard). This emblem suggests a role model for one meditating in this room, particularly if it is viewed alongside the emblem from Whitney depicting a pilgrim and a globe (fig. 113). There the accompanying poem teaches resignation of this world and the need to store up one's treasures in heaven.

The panel below the pilgrim shows an eagle diving into flames; nearby is a nest of young (fig. 114). The mot reads "Pie sed temere" (Dutifully, but rashly). As with the eagle above, the bird suggests high-mindedness. However, high-mindedness does not necessarily include prudence, and the action of the eagle is a warning against self-destruction. As the wreath in flames indicated, too ardent a commitment may be counterproductive.

The final row of panels exhibits first a sun with a rainbow and what appears to be a storm-damaged landscape with the mot "Iam satis" (Enough now) (fig. 115). Just below is the picture of a hand holding a lighted fuse with the mot "Arsit, crepuit, evanuit" (It burned, it crackled, it disappeared) (fig. 116). The third panel shows a blackamoor pointing to a swan with one hand and to his own teeth with the other, the mot being "Jam sumus ergo pares" (So now we are alike) (fig. 117). There is a note of finality in each of these emblems. The sun with the rainbow symbolizes God's promise of calm

after the storm. The extinguished fuse in the next panel appears to be an expression of spiritual frustration, though it might mean that worldly desires have been consumed by the fire of spiritual meditation and prayer. The emblem of the blackamoor might affirm that despite appearances the inner self is at last pure.

It must now be clear that the person who designed the oratory spent many hours there and meditated upon these emblems in a variety of ways and combinations. The appeal to sight, though, is constant, as is the paucity of words—the use of words in this room is severely limited to inscription. Sir Francis Bacon's comments in his *Advancement to Learning* permit us insight into the nature of these inscriptions. As mentioned above, Bacon said that memory was grounded upon prenotion and emblem. Prenotion he identified as "the indefinite seeking of what we would remember," that is, the unfocused desire to remember. Emblem is that "narrow compass," a compact and visually "dense" construct which "reduceth conceits intellectual to images sensible" (bk. 2, xv, 3). Certainly, one would enter the room with a motive to meditate; that is the initial focus of intention. Secondly, the sentences focus prenotion more precisely. And then the individual emblems beneath take the thinker directly into the heart of meditation on such subjects as the relation of the individual to the world, the desirability of living within one's own center, the

Figure 116. Hand holding a lighted fuse, "Arsit, crepuit, evanuit." Lady Drury's oratory. Photography by N. J. & L. Cotterell. Copyright Ipswich Museum Committee.

Figure 117. Blackamoor pointing to a swan and his teeth, "Iam sumus ergo pares." Lady Drury's oratory. Photography by N. J. & L. Cotterell. Copyright Ipswich Museum Committee.

psychology of assertiveness, fear, anxiety, and the mysteries of the world itself. In this connection, the individual mots or inscriptions invite speculation on the visual messages. These verbal messages sharpen the prenotion of each emblem—they open the picture to interpretation by beginning a train of thought which develops the implications of each picture while inviting associations between the pictures.

Here in the Hawstead room the art of emblematics reaches a climax whose interest for us lies in its uniqueness. These visual images and their enigmatic verbal forms are deeply indebted to what was perhaps the most popular type of book after scripture and some specifically religious publications. That there are no other such rooms in England, and only a very few of them on the Continent, suggests that a very imaginative person conceived of this room quite literally as a book. Today, standing in the little room that houses these remarkable panels, one cannot help feeling the mystery of the world as it was thought to be before Sir Thomas Browne, and then the members of the Royal Society, chipped away at the mysteries embedded in lore inherited from the ancients and converted during the sixteenth and early seventeenth centuries into the hieroglyphics that appear in emblem books. Lady Drury's oratory is therefore very special, for it has become a window opened on a past that is increasingly difficult to imagine and recreate.

Notes

Preface

1. *Elizabethan Critical Essays*, ed. G. Gregory Smith (London: Oxford University Press, 1904), 1:342. Two articles by Wesley Trimpi discuss the passage in Horace: "The Meaning of Horace's *ut pictura poesis*," *JWCI* 36 (1973), 1–34 and "Horace's 'ut pictura poesis': The Argument for Stylistic Decorum," *Traditio* 34 (1978), 29–73. H. S. Thayer, "Plato's Quarrel with Poetry: Simonides," *JHI* 36 (1975), 3–26 offers reasons "why Plato should think of Simonides as occupying a central place in the philosopher's theorizing about and contention with poetry."

2. Forrest G. Robinson, *The Shape of Things Known: Sidney's "Apology" in its Philosophical Tradition* (Cambridge: Harvard University Press, 1972).

3. Rene Wellek, "The Parallelism between Literature and the Arts," *English Institute Annual for 1941* (New York: Columbia University Press, 1942), 29–63. Ulrich Weisstein, "Comparing Literature and Art: Current Trends and Prospects in Critical Theory and Methodology," *Literature and the Other Arts*, ed. Zoran Konstantinović, Steven P. Scher, and Ulrich Weisstein (Innsbruck: Inst. für Sprachwiss. d. Univ., 1981), 19–30. Jean Hagstrum, *The Sister Arts* (Chicago: University of Chicago Press, 1958) remains the most comprehensive survey of literary pictorialism though the emphasis is on English literature. A highly theoretical approach to seventeenth-century relations between the arts is H. James Jensen, *The Muses' Concord: Literature, Music and the Visual Arts in the Baroque Age* (Bloomington: Indiana University Press, 1976).

4. Wellek, "Parallelism," 41.

5. Jean Seznec, "Art and Literature: A Plea for Humility," *NLH* 3 (1972), 569–574. The quotation appears on page 574. Procedures designed to curb excess analogizing and to offer an antidote to the rage for *Geistesgeschichte* appear in G. Giovannini, "Method in the Study of Literature in its Relation to the Other Fine Arts," *JAAC* 8 (1950), 185–195 and James D. Merri-

man, "The Parallel of the Arts: Some Misgivings and a Faint Affirmation," *JAAC* 31 (1972–1973), 154–164, 309–321.

6. Weisstein, "Comparing Literature and Art," 23.

7. Any list here must be partial and suggestive. John Bender, *Spenser and Literary Pictorialism* (Princeton: Princeton University Press, 1972); John Doebler, *Shakespeare's Speaking Pictures: Studies in Iconic Imagery* (Albuquerque: New Mexico University Press, 1974); Ingold Dutz, *Shakespeare's 'Pericles' und 'Cymbeline' in der Bildkunst* (Bern: Lang, 1976); Roland M. Frye, *Milton's Imagery and the Visual Arts* (Princeton: Princeton University Press, 1978); Marcia R. Pointon, *Milton and English Art* (Toronto: University of Toronto Press, 1970). The following are also pertinent. Marianne Albrecht Bott, *Die bildende Kunst in der Italienischen Lyric der Renaissance und des Barock* (Wiesbaden: Steiner, 1976); Rosalie Colie, *"My Ecchoing Song": Andrew Marvell's Poetry of Criticism* (Princeton: Princeton University Press, 1970); Annabel M. Patterson, *Marvell and the Civic Crown* (Princeton: Princeton University Press, 1978); R. I. V. Hodge, *Foreshortened Time: Andrew Marvell and Seventeenth-Century Revolutions* (Cambridge: Cambridge University Press, 1978).

8. R. F. Hill, "Spenser's Allegorical Houses," *MLR* 65 (1970), 722–733. Bender, cited in note 7 above, discusses "Interior Space in the Cave of Mamon" in terms of what he calls scanning. He explains as well how focusing and framing are intrinsic to Spenser's poetic method. More recently Jonathan Z. Kamholtz, "Spenser and Perspective," *JAAC* 39 (1980), 59–66 proposed a perspective reading of *The Faerie Queene*, to which Judith Dundas, "Fairyland and the Vanishing Point," *JAAC* 40 (1981), 82–84 has replied that such interart associations are forced when they fail to account for the fundamental differences between the arts.

9. E. H. Gombrich, *Art and Illusion* (1960; reprint of 2d rev. ed., New York: Pantheon, 1965), 227–228, 230, 239. The quotations are from part 3 called "The Beholder's Share."

10. Norman K. Farmer, Jr., "Renaissance English Titlepages and Frontispieces: Visual Introductions to Verbal Texts," *Literature and the Other Arts*, ed. Zoran Konstantinović, Steven P. Scher, and Ulrich Weisstein (Innsbruck: Inst. für Sprachwiss. d. Univ., 1981) 61–65. At a time when new editions of Renaissance texts come frequently from our presses, we are in grave danger of losing touch with the ways those texts originally made their way into the imaginations and sensibilities of Renaissance readers. For an example of such appeals, see below, chapter 6, where the title page to Robert Herrick's *Hesperides* is discussed.

11. Gombrich, *Art and Illusion*, 5.

1. *Visual Art in the* New Arcadia

1. Changes made by Sidney on the *Old Arcadia* are discussed by Jon S. Lawry, *Sidney's Two Arcadias: Pattern and Proceeding* (Ithaca: Cornell University Press, 1972). Samual Lee Wolff, *The Greek Romances in Elizabethan Prose Fiction* (New York: Columbia University Press, 1912) and R. W. Zandvoort, *Sidney's Arcadia: A Comparison between the Two Versions* (Amsterdam: Swets & Zeitlinger, 1929) discuss Sidney's indebtedness to the romance tradition. A more recent study is A. C. Hamilton, "Sidney's Arcadia as Prose Fiction: Its Relation to Its Sources," *ELR* 2 (1972), 29–60.

2. *Miscellaneous Prose of Sir Philip Sidney*, ed. Katherine Duncan-Jones and Jan Van Dorsten (Oxford: Clarendon Press, 1973), 78. Subsequent quotations from the *Defence* will be followed by page references to this edition.

3. The letter is printed in Ronald Rebholz, *The Life of Fulke Greville, First Lord Brooke* (Oxford: Clarendon Press, 1971), 76.

4. *Sir Fulke Greville's Life of Sir Philip Sidney*, ed. Nowell Smith (Oxford: Clarendon Press, 1907), 14–16.

5. Among studies that discuss the Renaissance practice of using rhetorical terms interchangeably with literature and art are Rensselaer W. Lee, "Ut Pictura Poesis: The Humanistic Theory of Painting," *Art Bulletin* 22 (1940), 197–269; John Pope-Hennessey, "Nicholas Hilliard and Mannerist Art Theory," *JWCI* 6 (1943), 89–100; Creighton Gilbert, "Antique Frameworks for Renaissance Art Theory: Alberti and Pino," *Marsyas* 3 (1943–45), 87–106; Gerard LeCoat, *The Rhetoric of the Arts, 1550–1650* (Bern: Lang, 1975).

6. Paolo Lomazzo, "The Second Booke of the Actions, Gestures, Situation, Decorum, Motion . . . of Pictures," in *A Tract Containing the Artes of Curious Paintinge* (London, 1598), 4–5.

7. James M. Osborn, *Young Philip Sidney* (New Haven: Yale University Press, 1972), 153.

8. John Buxton, *Sir Philip Sidney and the English Renaissance* (London: Macmillan, 1954), 70.

9. "Well then (may Divine youth long encircle with soft down those cheeks wherein it resides,) who painted you, O Sidney, in such a unique manner, and who spread this rose charm lightly over your face? Who enlivened your forehead with expression, your eyes with radiant beame? Whose art has given your lips that keen expression? Has Zeuxis returned to this earth from the underworld? Have you derived that splendour from the finger of Apelles? But no, whoever it was that drew you with such art, he was greater than Zeuxis, he was a greater Apollo. For truly, the figure lives, and you, Sidney, live in it; who would have thought a human hand to be capable of it?

"When I look at that image, so like your own nature, it looks back at me with eloquent eyes. But oh, why is it muter than a silent fish, why does it not speak? It imitates your habits, for you are a follower of Pythagoras' praised silence, you seem to hear much and to speak little. The rest corresponds completely; the difference lies only in this, that you speak little, but that your picture is always mute."

The translation is by Jan A. Van Dorsten, *Poets, Painters and Professors* (Leiden, 1962), 62–67. Reprinted with permission of Leiden University Press.

10. Nicholas Hilliard, *A Treatise Concerning the Arte of Limning*, ed. Philip Norman, *Walpole Society*, vol. 1 (Oxford: Oxford University Press), 27–28.

11. Osborn, *Young Philip Sidney*, 86.

12. For inventories of Leicester's collection, see William J. Thoms, "Pictures of the Great Earl of Leicester," *N & Q*, 3d ser., no. 2 (September 11, 1862), 201–202, 225. An inventory of Kenilworth Castle is given in *H.M.C. DeLisle and Dudley* I (London, 1925), 290–291. There is an inventory of Archbishop Parker's "Pictures and Mappes" in *Archaeologia* 30 (1844), 10–12. For the Lumley inventory see Lionel Cust, "Notes on the Collections Formed by Thomas Howard, Earl of Arundel and Surrey," *Burlington Magazine* 19 (1911), 278–281, and Mary L. Cox, "Notes on the Collections Formed by Thomas Howard," *Burlington Magazine* 19 (1911), 282–286, 323–335.

13. M. Denkinger, "The *Impresa* Portrait of Sir Philip Sidney in the National Portrait Gallery," *PMLA* 47 (1932), 17–45. Alexander C. Judson, *Sidney's Appearance: A Study in Elizabethan Portraiture* (Bloomington: Indiana University Press, 1958). The identity of the sitter is now said by Roy Strong, *Tudor and Jacobean Portraits* (London: H.M.S.O., 1969), 197, to be Robert, not Philip, Sidney.

14. K. Duncan-Jones, "Sidney's Personal Imprese," *JWCI* 33 (1970), 321–324.

15. Moshe Barasch, "Character and Physiognomy: Bocchi on Donatello's St. George. A Renaissance Text on Expression in Art," *JHI* 36 (1975), 413–430.

16. The point is discussed by E. H. Gombrich, "Conditions of Illusion," in *Art and Illusion* (1960; reprint of

2d rev. ed., New York: Pantheon, 1965). Wesley Trimpi, "The Early Metaphorical Uses of ΣΚΙΑΓΡΑΦΙΑ and ΣΚΗΝΟΓΡΑΦΙΑ," *Traditio* 34 (1978), 403–413, discusses the way that optics offers an explanation of deceptive appearances. He also explains "Horace's 'Ut Pictura Poesis': The Argument for Stylistic Decorum," *Traditio* 34 (1978), 29–73, how the passage justifying literary pictorialism affirms a stylistic principle. Hilliard's account of the conversation with Sidney, if read in the light of these discussions, suggests that both were familiar with the theoretical problems and the texts that could be cited in discussions of those problems.

17. Sir Philip Sidney, *The Countess of Pembroke's Arcadia*, ed. Jean Robertson (Oxford: Clarendon Press, 1973), 328. Quotations from the *New Arcadia* will be drawn from *The Countess of Pembroke's Arcadia*, ed. Maurice Evans (New York: Penguin Books, 1977). References will follow quotations.

18. John Bender, *Spenser and Literary Pictorialism*, (Princeton: Princeton University Press, 1972), 112–122 discusses the application of such terms to *The Faerie Queene*. But where Spenser's scenes are "set into the narrative as if [they] were a subjectively observed picture," Sidney creates a sequence of scenes whose scope is progressively smaller.

19. Even in Montemayor's *Diana*, where there are numerous allusions to the arts of music and painting, there is nothing comparable to Sidney's sense of space. See F. Lopez Estrada, "Las Bellas Artes en la *Diana* de Jorge de Montemayor," *Actes du Cinquième Congrès International des Langues et Littératures Modernes* (Florence, 1955), 145–146.

20. *The Greek Romances of Heliodorus, Longus, and Achilles Tatius*, trans. Rev. Rowland Smith (London: Bell, 1901), 367. The fountain in Francesco Colonna's *Hynerotomachia: The Strife of Love in a Dreame*, trans. "R. D." (London, 1592), sig. N^v–N^3 differs in major respects. There is no mention of reflections and nothing comparable to the statue of Venus.

21. Max J. Friedländer, *Essays über die Landschaftsmalerie und andere Bildgattungen* (The Hague: A.A.M. Stols, 1947). Otto Pacht, "Early Italian Nature Studies and the Early Calendar Landscape," *JWCI* 13 (1950), 13–47. E. H. Gombrich, "The Renaissance Theory of Art and the Rise of Landscape," *Norm and Form: Studies in the Art of the Renaissance* (London: Phaidon, 1966). Norgate's comment appears in his *Miniatura; or, The Art of Limning*, ed. Martin Hardie (Oxford: Clarendon Press, 1919), 44.

22. British Museum, MS. Sloane 536. The *Treatise* is briefly discussed by Henry V. S. and Margaret Ogden, *English Taste in Landscape in the Seventeenth Century* (Ann Arbor: University of Michigan Press, 1955), 1–2.

23. The development from symbolic landscape to "the landscape of fact," "the landscape of fantasy," and to "ideal landscape" is discussed by Kenneth Clark, *Land-scape into Art* (1949; reprint, Boston: Beacon, 1969).

24. John Shearman, *Mannerism* (Harmondsworth: Penguin, 1969), 112–113.

25. It was many years after Sidney's death when Inigo Jones and William Webb designed the famous Cube and Double Cube rooms at Wilton House where Sidney had often visited his sister. The geometrical symbolism of these rooms, however, gives us reason to believe that the shape of Kalander's gallery was consciously distinguished from the conventional Elizabethan long gallery commonly used for the display of pictures. See Eric Mercer, *English Art, 1553–1625* (Oxford: Clarendon Press, 1962), 18–25.

26. Rudolf Arnheim, *Visual Thinking* (Berkeley: University of California Press, 1971), 231–232.

27. The "tradition of visual epistemology" is discussed by Forrest G. Robinson, *The Shape of Things Known: Sidney's Apology in its Philisophical Tradition* (Cambridge: Harvard University Press, 1972).

28. Geoffrey Shepherd, Introduction to *An Apology for Poetry* (London: T. Nelson, 1965), 64–66 discusses parallels between Lomazzo, Zuccaro, and Sidney.

29. Girolomo Fracastoro, *Naugerivs: sive, De poetica dialogvs*. . . . with English translation by Ruth Kelso and introduction by Muray W. Bundy (Urbana: University of Illinois Press, 1924).

30. Sidney was not alone in pondering this question. E. H. Gombrich, *Art and Illusion* writes of Albrecht Dürer's difficulty with the famous woodcut of a rhinoceros: "He had to rely on secondhand evidence which he filled in from his own imagination, colored, no doubt, by what he had learned of the most famous of exotic beasts, the dragon with its armored body. Yet it has been shown that this half-invented creature served as a model for all renderings of the rhinoceros, even in natural-history books, up to the eighteenth century" (p. 81).

31. In one of his sonnets, Michelangelo writes that

The greatest artist has no single concept
Which a rough marble block does not contain
Already in its core. . . .

The Complete Poems of Michaelangelo, trans. Joseph Tusiani (London: Peter Owen, 1969), 76. The process of liberating a figure from stone is a frequent metaphor in Renaissance literature for revealed truth. According to H. W. Janson, Marsilio Ficino writes in his commentary to Dionysos the Areopagite that "if God made man in his own image, God's statue is certainly in man." The notion that some force greater than that of the individual artist contributes to artistic form is discussed by H. W. Janson, "The 'Image Made by Chance' in Renaissance Thought," in *De Artibus Opuscula XL: Essays in Honor of Erwin Panofsky*, ed. Millard Meiss (Zurich: Buehler Buchdruck, 1960), 254–266. From Callistratus' *Descriptions* Sidney might have known the *ekphrasis* titled "On the Statue of an Indian." This statue was "of a marble verging on black and shifting of its own accord to the colour given by nature to his race." The eyes "were not of a colour to match the marble; for whiteness encircled the pupils of the eyes, since the marble changed to whiteness at that point where the natural colour of the Indian becomes white." Callistratus, *Descriptions*, trans. Arthur Fairbanks (London: William Heinemann, 1931), 389.

32. William S. Heckscher, "Recorded from Dark Recollection," in *De Artibus Opuscula XL*, ed. Meiss, 187–200.

33. A. Pigler, *Barockthemen. Eine Auswahl von verzeichnissen zur Ikonographie des 17. und 18. Jahrhunderts* (Budapest: Akademia Kaido, 1956), 2:244–247.

34. E. van der Berchen, *Die Gemalde des Jacopo Tintoretto* (Munich: R. Piper, 1942), plate 194.

2. Donne, Jonson, and the Priority of Picture

1. Wesley Trimpi, *Ben Jonson's Poems: A Study of the Plain Style* (Stanford: Stanford University Press, 1962).

2. Winfried Schleiner, *The Imagery of John Donne's Sermons* (Providence, R.I.: Brown University Press, 1970), 137–156.

3. *The Sermons of John Donne*, ed. Evelyn Simpson and George R. Potter (Berkeley: University of California Press, 1956), 8:221. Subsequent quotations will be followed by volume and page numbers.

4. Schleiner, *Imagery*, 145.

5. John Donne, *The Satires, Epigrams, and Verse Letters*, ed. Wesley Milgate (Oxford: Clarendon Press, 1967), 13.

6. See Reinhart Schleier, *Tabula Cebetis oder 'Spiegel des Menschlichten Lebens darin Tugent und untugent abgemalete ist'* (Berlin: Mann, 1973). The widespread popularity of the *Table* is evident in the facsimiles of vernacular texts, presented in *Cebes' Tablet: Facsimiles of the Greek Text. and of Selected Latin, French, English, Spanish, Italian, German, Dutch, and Polish Translations*, with introduction by Sandra Sider (New York: Renaissance Society of America, 1979).

7. *John Donne: The Anniversaries*, ed. with introduction and commentary by Frank Manley (Baltimore: Johns Hopkins University Press, 1963), 65–66.

8. William S. Heckscher, *Rembrandt's Anatomy of Dr. Nicholaas Tulp: An Iconological Study* (New York: New York University Press, 1958), 53.

9. *John Donne, Ignatius His Conclave*, ed. T. S. Healy, S.J. (Oxford: Clarendon Press, 1969), 5–7. In his introduction, the editor suggests that in this description "Donne seems to be following one of the contemporary popular sketches . . . by Thomas Digges, dated 1576. It shows the sun at the base with the orbiting planets set out in semicircles above it. Thus the sun is at the 'lowest

part' and the earth half-way up 'the Heavens.' Also from the earth only the rear of Venus' orbital track can be seen, which explains Ignatius' comment about our seeing her only 'aversly'" (p. xxix).

10. Wesley Milgate, "Dr. Donne's Art Gallery, *N & Q* (July 23, 1949), 318–319.

11. The rapidly increasing popularity of visual art is studied by J. W. Williamson, *The Myth of the Conqueror: Prince Henry Stuart, a Study of 17th Century Personation* (New York: AMS Press, 1977) and by Mary F. S. Hervey, *The Life, Correspondence and Collections of Thomas Howard, Earl of Arundel* (Cambridge: Cambridge University Press, 1921). W. Noel Sainsbury, *Original Unpublished Papers Illustrative of the Life of Sir Peter Paul Rubens* (London: Bradbury & Evans, 1859) and *The Letters of Peter Paul Rubens*, trans. and ed. Ruth Saunders Magurn (Cambridge: Harvard University Press, 1955) offer valuable documentation. Walter E. Houghton, "The English Virtuoso in the Seventeenth Century," *JHI* 3 (1942), 51–73, 190–219 is a useful survey of cultural developments that impinge on the priority of art. And Gervas Huxley, *Endymion Porter, the Life of a Courtier 1587–1649* (London: Chatto and Windus, 1959) is especially appropriate since Porter was a prominent collector and patron of artists as well as a friend of Jonson and Herrick. The activities of English connoisseurs abroad is documented in Francis C. Springell, *Connoisseur and Diplomat: The Earl of Arundel's Embassy to Germany* (London: Maggs Bros., 1963).

12. Louis L. Martz, *The Wit of Love: Donne, Carew, Crashaw, Marvell* (Notre Dame: University of Notre Dame Press, 1969), 29.

13. John Donne, *The Elegies, and the Songs and Sonnets*, ed. Helen Gardner (Oxford: Clarendon Press, 1965), 59. Subsequent quotations from poems in these genres are from this edition.

14. "To R. W." ("If, as mine is"), "Sapho to Philaenis" ("Where is that holy fire"), "Epithalamion" ("Thou art repriv'd old yeare"), and the Holy Sonnet that begins "What if this present."

15. Helen Gardner, "The Marshall Engraving and the Lothian Portrait," Appendix E in *The Elegies, and the Songs and Sonnets*, 266–270.

16. Athenaeus, *The Diepnosophists*, trans. C. B. Gulick (Cambridge, Mass.: Harvard University, 1937), 185–191.

17. Pliny, *Natural History*, trans. H. Rackham (Cambridge: Harvard University Press, 1952). Book 35 is devoted entirely to pigments and painting. In *The Book of the Courtier*, trans. Sir Thomas Hoby (London: J. M. Dent, 1928), Baldassare Castiglione writes: "And such a countenance as this is, will I have our Courtier to have, and not so soft and womanish as many procure to have, that doe not onely courle the haire, and picke the browes, but also pampre them selves in everie point like

the most wanton and dishonest women in the world" (p. 39).

18. *The Poems of Propertius*, trans. Constance Carrier (Bloomington: Indiana University Press, 1963), 27.

19. *Dolce's 'Aretino' and Venetian Art Theory of the Cinquecento*, trans. Mark W. Roskill (New York: New York University Press, 1968), 153, 155, 157. The rhetorical orientation of both art theory and music theory is discussed by Gerard LeCoat, *The Rhetoric of the Arts, 1550–1650* (Bern: Lang, 1975): "Through the intermediary of the spatial arts, music theory unexpectedly came to influence poets. Not only were the arts seen as interrelated in a harmonious whole, but also their techniques were thought of as convertible. In this intricate network of interinfluences, theoretical concepts merged to the point of becoming one all-embracing theory that we can rightly call *the* humanistic theory of the arts" (p. 62).

20. *The Literary Works of Leonardo da Vinci*, ed. Jean Paul Richter (London: Oxford University Press, 1939), 1:138.

21. Leon Battista Alberti, *On Painting*, trans. with introduction and notes by John R. Spencer (New Haven: Yale University Press, 1956), 63.

22. *Ben Jonson*, ed. C. H. Herford, Percy Simpson, and Evelyn Simpson (Oxford: Clarendon Press, 1947), 8:403. Subsequent quotations of Jonson's poems are from this edition.

23. See D. J. Gordon, "Poet and Architect: The Intellectual Setting of the Quarrel between Ben Jonson and Inigo Jones," *JWCI* 12 (1949), 152–178.

24. Herford, Simpson, and Simpson, *Ben Jonson*, 8:609–610, 635.

25. John Pope-Hennessey, "Nicholas Hilliard and Mannerist Art Theory," *JWCI* 6 (1943), 89–100.

26. Paulo Lomazzo, Proeme to "The Fifth Booke of the Perspectives," in *A Tract Containing the Artes of Curious Paintinge* (London, 1598), 181. It is revealing, further, to compare the principles of anamorphics as discussed, for example, by Jurgis Baltrušaitis, *Anamorphoses: ou, Magic artificielle des effects marveilleux* (Paris: O. Perrin, 1969), for it was only through an understanding of the rules of perspective that calculated visual tricks could be contrived.

27. Mary Tom Osborne, *Advice to a Painter Poems, 1633–1856: An Annotated Finding List* (Austin: University of Texas Press, 1949), 9–10.

28. The circumstances are described by R. T. Petersson, *Sir Kenelm Digby: The Ornament of England 1603–1665* (Cambridge: Harvard University Press, 1956), 102–103.

29. See Richter, *Leonardo da Vinci*, 1:3–101. See also Anthony Blunt, *Artistic Theory in Italy, 1450–1600* (Oxford: Clarendon Press, 1940) as well as "An Echo of the Paragone in Shakespeare," *JWCI* 2 (1938–39), 260–262.

30. The relation of poetic genre to rites of passage is discussed in Norman K. Farmer, Jr., "A Theory of Genre for Seventeenth-Century Poetry," *Genre* 3 (1970), 293–317.

3. Thomas Carew's "A Rapture" and Lord Herbert's "To his Mistress: for her true Picture": Poetic Invention on Pictorial Themes

1. George Chapman's letter to Matthew Roydon in *Ovid's Banquet of Sence* states the principle clearly: "That, *Enargia*, or cleerenes of representation, requird in absolute Poems is not the perspicuous deliuery of a lowe invention; but high, and harty inuention exprest in most significant, and vnaffected phrase; it serues not a skilfull Painters turne, to draw the figure of a face onely to make knowne who it represents; but hee must lymn, giue luster, shaddow, and heightening; which though ignorants will esteeme spic'd, and too curious, yet such as haue the iudicall perspectiue, will see it hath motion, spirit and life." *The Poems of George Chapman*, ed. Phyllis Bartlett (1941; reprint, New York: Russell and Russell, 1962), 49. See also Hagstrum, *The Sister Arts* (Chicago: University of Chicago Press, 1958), 11–12.

2. See John R. Spencer, "Ut Rhetorica Pictura: A Study in Quattrocento Theory of Painting," *JWCI* 20 (1957), 26–44, and articles by Lee, Pope-Hennessey, and Gilbert cited chapter 1, note 5.

3. *The Poems, English and Latin, of Edward, Lord Herbert of Cherbury*, ed. G. C. Moore Smith (Oxford: Clarendon Press, 1923), Citations are from this edition.

4. *The Poems of Thomas Carew*, ed. Rhodes Dunlap (Oxford: Clarendon Press, 1949). Citations are from this edition.

5. "Abraham Van Der Doort's Catalogue of the Collections of Charles I," ed. Oliver Millar, Walpole Society, vol. 37 (Oxford: Oxford University Press, 1958–1960), 44. The connection between the poem and this painting was suggested by Rhodes Dunlap.

6. Some idea of the very great number of such depictions may be had from A. Pigler, *Barockthemen. Eine Auswahl von verzeichnisses zur Ikonographie des 17. and 18. Jahrhunderts* (Budapest: Akademia Kaido, 1956).

7. The so-called Twenty Poses are discussed by Frederick Hartt, *Giulio Romano* (New Haven: Yale University Press, 1958), 1:280–283, and by Peter Webb, *The Erotic Arts* (London: Seker and Warburg, 1975), 345–354. They are discussed as follows by Aretino in *Dolce's 'Aretino' and Venetian Art Theory of the Cinquecento*, trans. Mark W. Roskill (New York: New York University Press, 1968), 163: "I could answer you by saying that it was not Raphael who invented them, but Giulio Romano, his pupil and successor. Even supposing, however, that Raphael had designed either the whole series

or a part of it, he did not put them on public display in the city squares or the churches. Rather, they came into the hands of Marcantonio, and he, for the profit it would bring him, engraved them for Baviera. This same Marcantonio, but for the action I took, would have been deservedly punished for his temerity by Pope Leo."

8. Webb, *The Erotic Arts*, Appendix 2, "The Restricted Collections of the British Museum and the Victoria and Albert Museum," 355–365 describes the difficulties of obtaining a view of these pictures. There has been of late an increased acceptance of art history studies devoted to erotic art. In addition to Webb, see Pierre Cabanne, *Psychologie de l'art erotique* (Paris: Somogy, 1971); Edward Lucie-Smith, *Eroticism in Western Art* (London: Thames and Hudson, 1972); and Robert Melville, *Erotic Art of the West* (London: Weidenfeld and Nicolson, 1973).

9. Spencer, "Ut Rhetorica Pictura."

10. Roskill, *Dolce's 'Aretino,'* 101, 119.

11. George Puttenham, *The Arte of English Poesie*, ed. Gladys P. Willcock and Alice Walker (Cambridge: Cambridge University Press, 1936), 243.

12. Nicholas Hilliard, *A Treatise Concerning the Arte of Limning*, ed. Philip Norman, Walpole Society, vol. 1 (Oxford: Oxford University Press, 1912), 27–28.

13. John Pope-Hennessey, "Nicholas Hilliard and Mannerist Art Theory," *JWCI* 6 (1943), 89–100.

14. Yee wormes my rivalls, whillst she was alive
   How many thousands were there that did strive
   To have your freedom? For their sakes forbeare
   Unseemly holes in her soft cheeks flesh to teare.
   If you needs must (as what worme can refraine
   To taste her tender body) yet remaine
   With your disordered eatings to deface her.
   Feed on her soe as that you most may grace her.
   First in her eare-tipps see you work apace
   Of holes, which as the moyst enclosed ayre
   Forms into water; may the cleare drop take
   And in her eares a paire of iewels make:
   Have you not yet enough of that white skin
   The touch wherof in times past might have bin
   Enough to have ransom'd many a thousand soule
   Captive to love? (If not) then upwards rowle
   Your little bodies; where I would you have
   This epitaph upon her forehead grave.

   Epitaph: Living she was fayre, young, and full of wit
   Dead: all her faults are in her forehead writt.

   [Folger Library, MS. V. a. 160, f. 10]

4. Richard Crashaw: The "Holy Strife" of Pencil and Pen

1. Ruth Wallerstein, *Richard Crashaw: A Study in Style and Poetic Development* (1935; reprint, Madison: University of Wisconsin Press, 1962), 134–135. The study does not take into account Crashaw's practice of visual art.

2. Austin Warren, *Richard Crashaw: A Study in Baroque Sensibility* (1939; reprint, Ann Arbor: University of Michigan Press, 1957), 63.

3. Louis L. Martz, *The Wit of Love: Donne, Carew, Crashaw, Marvell* (Notre Dame: University of Notre Dame Press, 1969), 113–147.

4. Austin Warren, "Crashaw's Painting at Cambridge," *MLN* 48 (1933), 365–366.

5. Henry V. S. Ogden and Margaret S. Ogden, "A Bibliography of Seventeenth-Century Writings on the Pictorial Arts in England," *Art Bulletin* 29 (1947), 196-201. Luigi Salerno, "Seventeenth-Century English Literature on Painting," *JWCI* 14 (1951), 234-258.

6. *Dolce's 'Aretino' and Venetian Art Theory of the Cinquecento*, ed. Mark W. Roskill (New York: New York University Press, 1968), 153, 155.

7. Nicholas Hilliard, *A Treatise Concerning the Art of Limning*, ed. Philip Norman, Walpole Society, vol. 1 (Oxford: Oxford University Press, 1912), 27–28.

8. *The Poems, English, Latin and Greek, of Richard Crashaw*, ed. L. C. Martin (Oxford: Clarendon Press, 1957), 156. Subsequent quotations are from this edition.

9. Ibid. Martin says, "Thomas Car's ambiguous words about 'the pictures in the following Poemes which the authour first made with his owne hand' can be taken to mean that Crashaw was the original artist of all the twelve engravings. That this was not the case seems clear both from the inequalities of style and technique which the engravings present, and from the fact that several of them are marked 'I. Messager excud.' or 'Messager excud.' Jean Messager was painter and publisher of engravings whose business . . . flourished between 1615 and 1631." "Nevertheless, it seems probable that at least the two engravings heading respectively the poem addressed to the Countess of Denbigh and 'The Weeper' represent Crashaw's own drawings" (p. xlviii).

10. Robert Martin Adams, "Taste and Bad Taste in Metaphysical Poetry: Richard Crashaw and Dylan Thomas," *Hudson Review* 8 (1955), 61–77.

11. Stephen Manning, "The Meaning of 'The Weeper,'" *ELH* 22 (1955), 34–47.

12. See Martin, *Poems*, 449, and Adams, "Taste and Bad Taste."

13. Walter J. Ong, S.J., "From Allegory to Diagram in the Renaissance Mind: A Study in the Significance of the Allegorical Tradition," *JAAC* 17 (1959), 423–440.

14. Adams, "Taste and Bad Taste," p. 65.

15. Quoted from Erwin Panofsky, *Idea: A Concept in Art Theory*, trans. Joseph J. S. Peake (Columbia: University of South Carolina Press, 1968), 155, 157.

16. Henry J. Chaytor, *From Script to Print* (Cambridge: Cambridge University Press, 1950). The topic is discussed as well by Walter J. Ong, S.J., *Ramus, Method,*

and the Decay of Dialogue (1958; reprint, Cambridge: Harvard University Press, 1974).

17. Elizabeth Eisenstein, *The Printing Press as an Agent of Change* (Cambridge: Cambridge University Press, 1979).

18. Marjorie Corbett and R. W. Lightbown, *The Comely Frontispiece* (London: Routledge and Kegan Paul, 1979).

19. Norman K. Farmer, Jr., "Renaissance English Title-pages and Frontispieces: Visual Introductions to Verbal Texts," *Literature and the Other Arts*, ed. Zoran Konstantinović, Steven P. Scher, and Ulrich Weisstein (Innsbruck: Inst. für Sprachwiss. d. Univ., 1981), 61–65.

20. Colin Cherry, *On Human Communication* (Cambridge: MIT Press, 1957).

21. See Gareth A. Davies, "'Pintura': Background and Sketch of a Seventeenth-Century Court Genre," *JWCI* 38 (1975), 288–313.

5. Richard Lovelace, Edmund Waller, and the Flowering of English Art

1. The portrait is reproduced in Mary F. S. Hervey, *The Life, Correspondence and Collections of Thomas Howard, Earl of Arundel* (Cambridge: Cambridge University Press, 1921), plate 13.

2. Gervas Huxley, *Endymion Porter: The Life of a Courtier, 1587–1649* (London: Chatto and Windus, 1959), 158.

3. Ellis Waterhouse, *Painting in Britain, 1530 to 1790* (London: Penguin, 1953), 46–51. Margaret Whinney and Oliver Millar, *English Art, 1625–1714* (Oxford: Clarendon Press, 1957), 60, 68–74. The catalogue of a recent exhibition at the Tate Gallery, Oliver Millar, *The Age of Charles I: Painting in England, 1620–1649* (London, 1972), shows the range of the visual record, while Roy Strong, *Van Dyck: Charles I on Horseback* (London: Viking, 1972) examines the pictorial and conceptual backgrounds of one of the most famous pictures of the age.

4. Paul Oppé, "Sir Anthony Van Dyck in England," *Burlington Magazine* 79 (1941), 186–190.

5. *The Poems of Richard Lovelace*, ed. C. H. Wilkinson (Oxford: Clarendon Press, 1930), 211. Subsequent quotations are from this edition.

6. Edmund Waller, *Poems*, ed. G. Thorn Drury (1893; reprint, New York: Greenwood Press, 1968), 44–45. Subsequent quotations are from this edition.

7. Waterhouse, *Painting in Britain*: "It is not for nothing that Waller speaks of Van Dyck's studio as a 'shop of beauty.' The beauty specialist is concerned with studying the temperament of the individual and advising how that can best be exploited along the lines of prevailing taste. Van Dyck had precisely this sensibility which

he directed not only towards individuals but towards nations and classes of society" (p. 49).

8. Wilkinson, *Richard Lovelace*, 321, n.

9. *To his much honoured Friend Mr. Richard Lovelace, on his Poems.*

He that doth paint the beauties of your verse
Must use your pensil, be polite, soft, terse;
Forgive that man whose best of Art is love,
If he no equall Master to you prove;
My heart is all my Eloquence, and that
Speaks sharp affection, when my words fall flat.
I reade you like my Mistresse, and discry
In every line the quicknesse of her eye,
Her smoothnesse in each syllable, her grace
To marshall ev'ry word in the right place:
It is the excellence, and soule of wit
When ev'ry thing is free, as well as fit,
For Metaphors packt up and crowded close,
Swath ý minds sweetnes, & display the throws,
And like those chickens hatcht in furnaces,
Produce or one limbe more, or one limbe lesse
Then nature bids: survey such when they write,
No clause but's justl'd with an Epithite;
So powerfully you draw when you perswade,
Passions in you, in us are Vertues made;
Such is the Magick of that lawfull shell
That where it doth but talke, it doth compell:
  For no Apelles 'till this Time e're drew
  A Venus to the waste so well as you.
                                                    W. RUDYERD.

To the Honorable, Valiant, and Ingenious Colonel RICHARD LOVELACE, on his Exquisite POEMS.

Poets, and Painters have some near relation,
Compar'd with Fancy and Imagination;
The one paints shadowed persons (in pure kind,)
The other points the Pictures of the Mind
In purer Verse. And as rare Zeuxes fame
Shin'd till Apelles Art eclips'd the same
By a more exquisite, and curious line
Than Zeuxeses (with pensill far more fine,)
So have our modern Poets, late done well
Till thine appear'd (which scarce have paralel.)
  They like to Zeuxes Grapes beguile the sense,
But thine do ravish the Intelligence;
Like the rare banquet of Apelles, drawn,
And covered over with most curious Lawn.
  Thus if thy careles draughts are cal'd the best,
What would thy lines have beene, had'st thou profest
That faculty (infus'd) of Poetry,
Which adds such honour unto thy Chivalry?
Doubtles thy verse had all as far transcended
As Sydneyes Prose, who Poets once defended.
  For when I read thy much renowned Pen,
My Fancy there finds out another Ben

In thy brave language, judgment, wit & art,
Of every piece of thine, in every part:
Where thy seraphique Sydneyan fire is raised high,
In Valour, Vertue, Love, and Loyalty:
   Virgil was styl'd the loftiest of All,
Ovid the smoothest, and most naturall,
Martiall concise, and witty, quaint, and pure,
Iuvenall grave and learned, (though obscure:)
   But all these rare ones, which I heere reherse,
Do live againe in Thee, and in thy Verse:
Although not in the language of their time,
Yet in a speech as copious and sublime:
   The rare Apelles, in thy picture wee
Perceive, and in thy soule Apollo see.

   Wel may each grace, & muse then crown thy
praise
With Mars his Banner, and Minerva's Bayes.
                FRA. LENTON.

10. Honthorst's English reputation began with Sir Dudley Carleton's purchase of his *Aeneas Flying from the Sack of Troy* and subsequent gift of the painting to Lord Arundel in 1621. Arundel's letter acknowledging receipt of the painting also praises it "for the postures & ye colouringe," and he says he has "seene fewe Duch men arrive unto it, for it hath more of ye Italian then the Flemish & much of ye Manor of Coravaggioes Colouringe." See W. Noel Sainsbury, *Original Unpublished Papers Illustrative of the Life of Sir Peter Paul Rubens* (London: Bradbury & Evans, 1859), 291–292. C. H. Collins Baker, *Lely and the Stuart Portrait Painters* (London: P. L. Warner, 1912), says Honthorst's "position as a drawing master to the royal ladies is well known. The Princess Louise seems to have been one of the most successful of his pupils" (1:60–61).

11. Huxley, *Porter*, 224.

12. See Svetlana Leontief Alpers, "Ekphrasis and Aesthetic Attitudes in Vasari's Lives," *JWCI* 23 (1960), 190–215.

13. Junius' fourth chapter is devoted almost entirely to relations between poetry and painting. While both have "a hidden force to move and compell our minds to severall Passions," it is "Picture for all that seemeth to doe it more effectually." Junius' reason, comparable to what Lovelace suggests, is that (according to Quintilian) "picture . . . is a silent worke and constantly keeping the same forme." It therefore "doth so insinuate itselfe into our most inward affections, that it seemth now and then to be of greater force then Eloquence it selfe." Another point of similarity between Junius and Lovelace occurs in the former's remark that both arts "doe shew their strength in great and eminent men, deifying or at least eternising all them whose names and shapes they doe vouchsafe to bequeathe unto posteritie." In addition to assuring fame, both arts "are most of all advanced by the ready help of a strong and well-exercised Imagination." "So doth . . . the Art of Painting as well as Poesie relie upon a generous and bold strength of Imagination, so that they will no more creepe and crawle to feele and to follow the steppes of them that are gone before, but they take upon themselves to trie it somewhat further, if by chance they might be esteemed worthy to lead others the way. The Poets impelled by the sudden heate of a thoroughly stirred Phantasie . . . doe cleerely behold the round rings of prettily dancing Nymphs, together with the ambushes of lurking lecherous Satyrs." And "painters in like manner doe fall to their worke invited and drawne on by the tackling pleasure of their nimble Imaginations."

14. Waterhouse, *Painting in Britain*, 84, n. 4. See also R. B. Beckett, *Lely* (Boston: Boston Book and Art Shop, 1955), 5–6, and plates 3 (*Cimon and Iphigenia*), 4 (*Europa and the Bull*), and 52 (*Nymphs at a Fountain*). Lely also introduced into English portraiture the convention of placing swans, urns, and statuary within the settings chosen for his subject.

15. Baker, *Lely*, 1:144–149.

16. Ibid., 2:234–235. Baker quotes extracts from MS. Harleian 2337.

17. Mary Tom Osborne, "'Advice to a Painter' Poems, 1665–1688: With Some Account of Earlier and Later Poems of This Type," Ph.D. diss., University of Texas, 1947.

18. Waterhouse, *Painting in Britain*, 46, 50, 64. Beckett, *Lely*, 11. The document was signed by Lely, Gerbier, and Geldorp. It is titled a "Humble Proposal to the Parliament." The scheme was to include pictures of battles and sieges as well as portraits of the commanders who had captured the towns. Lely's full-length of Sir Edward Massey (Beckett, plate 28) may have been included for a sample of what was proposed.

19. Osborne presents these facts in her dissertation, but she ignores Higgons' dedication to Lord Peterbourgh.

20. Gio. Francesco Busenello, *A Prospective of the Naval Triumph* (London, 1658), sig. A2^r.

21. Etienne Gilson, "Physical Existence," in *Painting and Reality* (1959; reprint, New York: Meridian Books, 1967).

22. Gerard LeCoat, *The Rhetoric of the Arts, 1550–1650* (Bern: Lang, 1975).

23. Sigs. A6^v–A7^r.

24. Paulo Lomazzo, "The Second Booke of the Actions, Gestures . . . and Grace of Pictures," in *A Tract Containing the Artes of Curious Paintinge* (London, 1598), p. 1. It is this book that contains Lomazzo's most detailed comments on relations between poetry and painting.

25. Henry Peacham, "To the Reader," *Drawing with the Pen* (London, 1606), sigs. A3^v–A4^r.

26. Ibid., 29–30, 33. The italics are imposed for emphasis.

27. Quoted from the facsimile included in Osborne, "'Advice to a Painter' Poems." Italics are added for comparative emphasis.

28. Edward Norgate, *Miniatura; or, The Art of Limning*, ed. Martin Hardie (Oxford: Clarendon Press, 1919), 55. He also declares that "this kind of painting . . . differs from picture by the Life as much as a Poet from an Historian, or . . . Ariosto from Phillip de Comines. The one doth plainly and truly *narrare rem gestam*, tells very honestly what he saw and did, the other describes such a Ruggiero or Orlando as hee could wish it to be" (p. 56). Norgate is here applying to art some commonplaces of literary criticism presented by Sidney in his *Defence of Poetry*.

29. See, for example, Leone Battista Alberti, *On Painting*, trans. with introduction and notes by John Spencer (Westport, Conn.: Greenwood Press, 1976), 72–85 and the introduction, which discusses concepts underlying the idea of *istoria*.

30. Ibid., 96.

31. Earl Miner, "The 'Poetic Picture, Painted Poetry' of *The Last Instructions to a Painter*," MP 63 (1966), 288–294. Patterson, "'The Painter and the Poet Dare': Experiments in Satire," in *Marvell and the Civic Crown*, discusses Marvell's *Instructions*.

32. Werner Hofmann, "Comic Art and Modern Caricature in the Western World," in *Encyclopedia of World Art*, vol. 3, (New York: McGraw-Hill, 1960), cols. 760-768.

33. See Conrad Hilberry, Introduction to *The Poems of John Collop* (Madison: University of Wisconsin Press, 1962), 19–26.

6. Herrick's Hesperidean Garden: Ut pictura poesis Applied

1. Robert Burton, *The Anatomy of Melancholy*, ed. Holbrook Jackson (London: J. M. Dent, 1961), 2: 74–75.

2. Henry Hawkins, *Partheneia Sacra* (London, 1633), 2.

3. G. C. Moore Smith, "Herrick's 'Hesperides,'" MLR 9 (1914), 373–374.

4. Roger B. Rollin, *Robert Herrick* (New York: Twayne Publishers, 1966), 29.

5. Edward Phillips, *Theatrum Poetarum; or, A Compleat Collection of the Poets* (London, 1675), 162.

6. Quoted in H. V. S. Ogden and M. S. Ogden, *English Taste in Landscape in the Seventeenth Century* (Ann Arbor: University of Michigan Press, 1955), 5–7.

7. J. Max Patrick, "A Note on the Title-page and the Text," *The Complete Poetry of Robert Herrick*, ed.

J. Max Patrick (New York: Anchor Books, 1968), 7–8. The poems discussed in this chapter are quoted from this edition.

8. Alfred Johnson, *A Catalogue of Engraved and Etched Title-Pages* (London: Oxford University Press, 1934), vii–viii.

9. A number of examples appear in Giulia Bologna, *Miniature italiane della Biblioteca Trivulziana* (Milan: Comune Ripartizione cultura, 1974) and J. J. G. Alexander, *Italian Renaissance Illuminations* (New York: Braziller, 1977).

10. Other title pages engraved by William Marshall are reproduced in Margary Corbett and Michael Norton, *Engraving in England in the Sixteenth and Seventeenth Centuries* (Cambridge: Cambridge University Press, 1964), 102–192.

11. See Walter J. Ong, S.J., "From Allegory to Diagram in the Renaissance Mind: A Study in the Significance of the Allegorical Tradition," *JAAC* 17 (1959), 423–440.

12. Corbett and Norton, *Engraving in England*, plates 54, 57, 58, 60, and 68. See also Thomas Clayton, "An Historical Study of the Portraits of Sir John Suckling," *JWCI* 23 (1960), 105–125. Marshall's engraving of John Milton for the 1645 edition of the *Poems*, however, bears the following verse (translated from the Greek by W. R. Parker, *Milton: A Biography* [Oxford: Clarendon Press, 1968], 289):

> You, who really know my face,
> Fail to find me in this place,
> Portraiture the fool pretends,
> Laugh at the result my friends.

Does this mean that the portrait is not of John Milton? Surely not, for while Milton objects to the engraver's interpretation of his features and, perhaps, his draftsmanship, he does not deny that he was the object of the artist's endeavors.

13. See in this connection John Sparrow, *Visible Words: A Study of Inscriptions in and as Books and Works of Art* (Cambridge: Cambridge University Press, 1969).

14. The concept of such "occurrence" and a definition of its enabling conditions are uncommon in the vocabulary of literary criticism. It may best be approached through the concept of "liminality" offered by Arnold van Gennep, *The Rites of Passage*, trans. Monika B. Vizedom and Gabrielle L. Chaffe (Chicago: University of Chicago Press, 1960) and the extensive discussion of that term by Victor Turner, *The Ritual Process: Structure and Anti-Structure* (Chicago: Aldine, 1969), *Dramas, Fields, and Metaphors: Symbolic Action in Human Society* (Ithaca: Cornell University Press, 1974), and the essay "Myth and Symbol," in *The International Encyclopedia of the Social Sciences* (New York: Collier and

Macmillan, 1968), 576–582. "Myths," he says in the latter, "are liminal phenomena: they are frequently told at a time or in a site that is 'betwixt and between.'" "Liminality is a period of structural [social] impoverishment and symbolic enrichment." "Liminality is pure potency." Herrick, it appears, is inviting his reader into an imagined situation which lies in the particularly fruitful region for recreativity "betwixt and between" the visual and the verbal, a situation corresponding to the region between words on the page and words from the mouth discussed above.

15. Ellis Waterhouse, *Painting in Britain, 1530 to 1790* (London: Penguin), 55-56.

16. Huxley, p. 149.

17. Fritz Saxl and Rudolf Wittkower, *British Art and the Mediterranean* (London: Oxford University Press, 1948), sec. 42.

18. D. E. L. Haynes, *The Arundel Marbles* (Oxford: Ashmolean Museum, 1975), 9–10.

19. See Mary Tom Osborne, "'Advice to a Painter' Poems, 1665–1688: With Some Account of Earlier and Later Poems of This Type," Ph.D. diss., University of Texas, 1947.

20. See Jean Hagstrum, *The Sister Arts* (Chicago: University of Chicago Press, 1958) and Trimpi, cited in the preface above, note 1. Additionally, the most complete discussion of the Horatian maxim is by Rensselaer W. Lee, "Ut Pictura Poesis: The Humanistic Theory of Painting," *Art Bulletin* 22 (1940), 197–269.

21. Achille Bertarelli, *L'Imagerie populaire italienne* (Paris: Editions Ducharte & Van Buggenhoudt, 1929); Carlo Angeleri, *Bibliografia delle stampe popolari a carattere profano dei secoli XVI–XVII, conservate nella Biblioteca Nazionale di Firenze* (Firenze: Sansoni, 1953); Jean Adhemar, Michele Herbert, J. P. Seguin, Elise J. P. Seguin, and Philippe Siguret, *Imagerie populaire francaise* (Milan: Electa, 1968); Samuel Chew, *The Pilgrimage of Life* (New Haven: Yale University Press, 1962).

22. Such vicarious performance requires an awareness of the signals the poet includes in his poem. They are cues that suggest not only literary expectations but an implicit social context. See, for example, the discussion of "Corinna's going a Maying" in Roger D. Abrahams, "Folklore and Literature as Performance," *Journal of the Folklore Institute* 9 (1972), 75–94 and Arnold Berleant, "The Verbal Presence: An Aesthetics of Literary Performance," *JAAC* 31 (1972–1973), 339–346.

23. Rosalie L. Colie, *"My Ecchoing song": Andrew Marvell's Poetry of Criticism* (Princeton: Princeton University Press, 1970), 205.

24. Norman K. Farmer, Jr., "Robert Herrick and 'King Oberon's Clothing': New Evidence for Attribution," *The Yearbook of English Studies* 1 (1971), 68–77.

25. See Ogden and Ogden, note 6 above, and Wolf-gang Stechow, *Dutch Landscape Painting of the Seventeenth Century* (London, 1968). John Hayes, "British Patrons and Landscape Painting," *Apollo* 82, (1965), 38–44 discusses the popularity of the genre among collectors at the time.

26. "A Country Life: To his Brother," "To Springs and Fountains," "To Dean-bourn," "To Meddowes," and "Faire dayes: or, Dawnes deceitful."

27. "The Lilly in a Cristal," "Divination by a Daffadill," "To Daffadills," and "To the Willow-tree."

28. "The Hock-cart, or Harvest home," "Corinna's going a Maying," "Twelfe-night, or King and Queene," "Ceremonies for Candlemasse Eve," "Ceremonies for Christmass," "The Wake," "The Wassaile," "A New Years gift sent to Sir Simeon Steward," and "An Epithalamie to Sir Thomas Southwell."

29. "A Beucolick, or discourse of Neatherds," "Charon and Phylomel, a Dialogue sung," "An Eclogue, or Pastorall between Endimion Porter and Lycidas Herrick," and "A Pastorall sung to the King."

7. Lady Drury's Oratory: The Painted Closet from Hawstead Hall

1. A Continental example of emblematic decoration is given in *Ausserliterarische Wirkungen barocker Emblembücher*, ed. Wolfgang Harms and Harmut Freytag (Munich: A. Fink, 1975). Emblems were apparently affixed to furniture as well. A note in *The Gentleman's Magazine* for November 1811 describes an oak bedstead "with various pannelled compartments." According to the description, the twenty-nine emblems (each accompanied by a mot) are all different from those at Hawstead. The curator of the Leicester Museum and Art Gallery informed me that the bedstead appears to be lost and that no record of it presently exists beyond this note. There is a series of articles on Tudor wall paintings of various kinds by Francis W. Reader in *Archaeological Journal* (vols. 89–92), but they mention no rooms that compare to Hawstead's painted chamber.

2. E. N. S. Thompson, *Literary Bypaths of the Renaissance* (New Haven: Yale University Press, 1924). Rosemary Freeman, *English Emblem Books* (London: Chatto and Windus, 1948). Mario Praz, *Studies in Seventeenth-Century Imagery*, rev. ed. (Rome: Edizione di Storia e Letteratura, 1964). Albrecht Schöne, *Emblematik und Drama im Zeitalter des Barock* (Munich: Beck, 1964). Peter Daly, *Literature in the Light of the Emblem* (Toronto: University of Toronto Press, 1978).

3. Frances A. Yates, "Renaissance Memory: The Memory Theatre of Giulio Camillo," in *The Art of Memory* (Chicago: University of Chicago Press, 1966).

4. *The Complete Works of John Davies of Hereford*, vol. 1, ed. Rev. Alexander Grosart (1878; reprint, New York: AMS Press, 1967).

5. R. C. Bald, *Donne and the Drurys* (Cambridge: Cambridge University Press, 1959), 80–84 explains that Anne Donne, sister of the poet, was the wife of William Lyly, a member of Sir Robert Drury's household at Hawstead. But the poet himself never visited there and was probably speaking the truth when he said of Elizabeth Drury following her death, "I never saw the Gentlewoman."

6. Sir John Cullum, *The Histories and Antiquities of Hawstead*, London: J. Nichols, 1784), 159.

7. I am indebted to my colleague Douglass Parker for supplying translations of the Latin mots.

8. W. Deonna, "L'Abielle et le roi," *Revue belge d'archeologie et d'historie de l'art*, 25 (1956), 105–131.

9. *The Hieroglyphics of Horapollo*, trans. George Boas (New York: Pantheon Books, 1950), 84, 117.

10. Arthur Henkel and Albrecht Schöne, *Emblemata: Handbuch zur Sinnbildkunst des XVI. und XVII. Jahrhunderts* (Stuttgart: J. B. Metzler, 1967) provides no examples of the burning wreath, though this should not be construed as definitive evidence that the Hawstead artist had no particular model in mind.

11. H. W. Janson, *Apes and Ape Lore in the Middle Ages and the Renaissance* (London: University of London Press, 1952).

12. M. P. Tilley, *A Dictionary of the Proverbs in England in the Sixteenth and Seventeenth Centuries* (Ann Arbor: University of Michigan Press, 1950).

13. See M. R. Bennett, "The Legend of the Green Tree and the Dry," *Archaeological Journal* 83 (2d ser., 33; 1929), 21–32.

14. Lucretius, *De rerum natura*, trans. W. H. D. Rouse (1937; 3d ed., rev., Cambridge: Harvard University Press, 1947).

15. W. Deona, "The Crab and the Butterfly," *JWCI* 17 (1954), 47–86.

16. Erna Auerbach, *Nicholas Hilliard* (Boston: Boston Book and Art Shop, 1964), 119. Henkel and Schöne, *Emblemata*, col. 1430 gives examples of emblematic scales.

17. Guy de Terverant, *Attributs et symboles dans l'art profane*, 1450–1600 (Geneva: Librarie E. Droz, 1958), col. 94.

18. Boas, *Hieroglyphics*, 80, 90.

19. William Caxton, *Mirrour of the World*, ed. Oliver H. Prior (London: Oxford University Press, 1913), 53–55.

20. Henkel and Schöne, *Emblemata*, cols. 30–38.

Index